Taste of Home's
CASSEROLE COOKBOOK

PAGE 47

Editor: Heidi Reuter Lloyd
Food Editor: Janaan Cunningham
Art Director: Bonnie Ziolecki
Associate Editors: Kristine Krueger, Julie Schnittka, Jean Steiner
Senior Recipe Editor: Sue A. Jurack
Recipe Editor: Janet Briggs
Test Kitchen Director: Karen Johnson
Test Kitchen Home Economists: Karen Wright, Sue Draheim,
Peggy Fleming, Julie Herzfeldt, Joylyn Jans, Kristin Koepnick
Test Kitchen Assistants: Rita Krajcir, Megan Taylor
Food Photography: Rob Hagen, Dan Roberts
Food Photography Artists: Stephanie Marchese, Vicky Marie Moseley
Photo Studio Manager: Anne Schimmel
Production: Ellen Lloyd, Catherine Fletcher
Publisher: Roy Reiman

Taste of Home Books
© 2001 Reiman Publications, LLC
5400 S. 60th St., Greendale WI 53129
International Standard Book Number:
0-89821-324-X
Library of Congress Catalog Card Number:
2001135766

PICTURED ON FRONT COVER: Chicken Potpie (p. 197).

PICTURED ON BACK COVER: Biscuit-Topped Italian Casserole (p. 54).

To order additional copies of this book or any other Reiman Publications book,
write *Taste of Home* Books, P.O. Box 908, Greendale WI 53129, call toll-free 1-800/344-2560
to order with a credit card or visit our Web site at **www.reimanpub.com**.

TABLE OF CONTENTS

PAGE 10   PAGE 152   PAGE 284

Taste of Home's
CASSEROLE COOKBOOK

One Big Collection Filled with 442 of the Best Casseroles Ever

IT PROBABLY won't surprise you to learn that casseroles are among the most popular comfort foods.

While a casserole bakes, its aroma wafts out of the oven, filling the house with a tantalizing promise of flavors yet to come. And when it's time to dig in, everyone seated around the table will add at least an "Mmm-mmm" to the mealtime conversation.

This collection of great recipes started with a single thought: Wouldn't it be *wonderful* to have a big cookbook completely filled with family-pleasing casseroles?

We put that question to the readers of *Taste of Home*, *Quick Cooking* and *Country Woman* magazines. They thought so, too, and started mailing in casserole recipes that their families liked so much, they'd asked for them again and again.

We sorted through those, tested some in our *Taste of Home* Test Kitchen, then searched our files for tried-and-true favorites that readers loved the first time we shared them. This collection wouldn't be complete without those "keepers" from days past.

The result is *Taste of Home's Casserole Cookbook*, packed with recipes for 442 of the best casseroles ever.

How the Book Is Organized

To get you started, we created a chapter called Casserole Basics (page 6). Here you'll find information on choosing baking dishes, freezing casseroles and stocking your pantry. There aren't any hard-to-find ingredients in these recipes, so they're easy to make.

We grouped the recipes in chapters based on how you'd use the book. There are chapters for poultry, beef, pork, seafood, meatless dishes, side dishes, meat pies and pastries, along with breakfast and brunch casseroles.

In addition, there's a Quick & Easy chapter, for when

you need to have dinner on the table in a hurry...a Potluck Pleasers section, for when you're serving a group...and a World Favorites chapter, for when you feel like trying something new and different with an international flair.

How to Find a Recipe

Let's say you have chicken on hand and want to make it for dinner. You can start by browsing through the poultry chapter, or, to make sure you see *all* the chicken dishes—including those in the Potluck Pleasers and World Favorites chapters—simply turn to the general index (page 310) and look under "Chicken".

If you look under any major ingredient, from apples to zucchini, you'll find a list of the main- and side-dish casseroles featuring that ingredient.

The general index highlights non-oven casseroles, too, so if you'd rather use your microwave or a stovetop skillet, just look under those categories. There's also a heading for "Cooking for One or Two", pointing out the small-quantity recipes in this book.

The alphabetical index starts on page 317, so once you've discovered a few favorites, you can easily find them by name the next time you want to make them.

On page 320, you'll find the handy Reference Index. Turn here when you're looking for such things as quick dessert or salad ideas, tips on buying and storing vegetables or options for toppings that will add crunch to your casseroles.

So, now it's time to turn the pages, choose a recipe and start cooking. Enjoy!

CASSEROLE BASICS

Whether you're a new cook
or a veteran who practically lives in
the kitchen, you'll find useful
information in this chapter
...about types and sizes
of bakeware...stocking your
pantry...freezing casseroles
...and much more.

PAGE 108

CHOOSING BAKEWARE

Casseroles are best made in baking dishes made of oven-safe glass or ceramic. Metal pans may discolor, if the ingredients are acidic, or may give off a metallic flavor.

For even cooking, try to bake the casserole in the dish size called for in the recipe. Round and oval baking dishes are identified by quart capacity. Square and oblong dishes are measured in inches across the top, from inside edge to inside edge.

If you are unsure of the size of a baking dish, fill a measuring cup with water and pour into the dish. Continue until the dish is full, counting the number of cups. Refer to the table below, which is also helpful if you need to substitute a similar size pan.

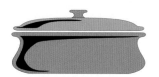

BAKING DISH SUBSTITUTION GUIDE

Casserole Capacity	Baking Dish Size	Cups
1-1/2 quarts	8-inch square	6-8
2 quarts	11- x 7- x 2-inch or 8-inch square	8
2-1/2 quarts	9-inch square	10
3 quarts	13- x 9- x 2-inch	12 to 14

HELPFUL HINTS

To save prep time later, chop several onions and green peppers in advance. Store separately in resealable freezer bags. When you need chopped vegetables for a casserole, just measure the amount called for, reseal the bag and return it to the freezer.

Commercially cut and frozen onions, green peppers and mixed peppers also are available in the frozen foods section of most grocery stores.

Many casseroles taste better when made in advance because time allows the flavors to mingle.

Dried herbs will hold up better than fresh if a casserole bakes longer than 1 hour.

Casseroles are a good way to use up leftovers by giving them a different look and flavor.

EAT ONE, FREEZE ONE

Plan ahead by doubling a casserole recipe. Make one now and freeze one for later.

Line the casserole dish that will be frozen with heavy-duty aluminum foil. Spritz with nonstick cooking spray. Add the casserole ingredients. Wrap tightly in foil and freeze until solid. Then remove the foil packet from the dish and return to the freezer. Use it within 2 months.

When you're ready to bake the frozen one, place the foil-encased casserole back in the original container. Thaw completely in the refrigerator overnight. Bake as directed in the original recipe.

STOCKING UP

Your pantry becomes your best friend when you're hungry for a comforting, creamy casserole. Below are lists of common casserole ingredients to stock in your pantry, freezer and refrigerator. We recommend keeping at least two cans or packages of each of the following items on hand, so you'll be ready to make just about any casserole that catches your eye or appetite!

IN THE PANTRY

- Canned soups, including tomato, cream of mushroom, cream of celery and other cream soups
- Chili and kidney beans
- Chunk white chicken
- Corn bread/muffin mix
- Cream-style corn
- Croutons or bread cubes
- Diced tomatoes
- Dried bread crumbs
- French-fried onions
- Green chilies
- Instant rice
- Long grain and wild rice mix
- Mushrooms in cans or jars
- Pasta, including egg noodles, spaghetti, lasagna noodles and elbow macaroni
- Pimientos
- Seasoned bread crumbs
- Sliced ripe olives
- Slivered almonds
- Spaghetti sauce
- Stewed tomatoes
- Stuffing mix
- Tomato paste
- Tomato sauce
- Tuna
- Water chestnuts

IN THE FREEZER

- Beef stew meat
- Cubed cooked chicken
- Cubed fully cooked ham
- Frozen broccoli, corn, spinach and mixed vegetables
- Ground beef
- Ground turkey
- Shredded or cubed hash browns
- Whitefish fillets

IN THE FRIDGE

- Bulk or shredded cheeses
- Cottage cheese
- Flour tortillas
- Parmesan cheese
- Refrigerated crescent rolls and biscuits
- Sour cream
- Various fresh vegetables, such as carrots, celery and onions

POULTRY CLASSICS

If poultry is a staple on your dinner table, you'll love the variety offered in this chapter. You'll find 48 mouth-watering dishes that pair chicken or turkey with stuffing, vegetables, pasta and more. Plan on serving second helpings!

CHICKEN AMANDINE (P. 21)

Lattice Chicken Potpie (p. 12)
Tomato Garlic Chicken (p. 12)

LATTICE CHICKEN POTPIE

(Pictured on page 11)

*My sister shared this great recipe with me. Because it features all four food groups,
it's the only dish you have to prepare for dinner.*
—Angie Cottrell, Sun Prairie, Wisconsin

1 package (16 ounces) frozen
  California-blend vegetables
2 cups cubed cooked chicken
1 can (10-3/4 ounces) condensed
  cream of potato soup, undiluted
1 cup milk
1 cup (4 ounces) shredded cheddar
  cheese
1 can (2.8 ounces) french-fried onions
1/2 teaspoon seasoned salt
1 tube (8 ounces) refrigerated
  crescent rolls

In a large bowl, combine the vegetables, chicken, soup, milk, cheese, onions and seasoned salt. Transfer to a greased 13-in. x 9-in. x 2-in. baking dish.

Unroll the crescent roll dough and separate into two rectangles. Seal the perforations; cut each rectangle lengthwise into 1/2-in. strips. Form a lattice crust over the chicken mixture. Bake, uncovered, at 375° for 35-40 minutes or until golden brown. **Yield:** 4-6 servings.

SIMPLE SUBSTITUTION

*If you don't have a bag of frozen California-blend vegetables on hand, use
another mixed-vegetable medley, such as winter blend or peas and carrots.*

TOMATO GARLIC CHICKEN

(Pictured on page 11)

*I came up with this recipe many years ago as a way to warm up my family during cooler weather.
The appealing aroma of garlic and fresh basil wafts through the house as it bakes.*
—Barbara Hasanat, Tucson, Arizona

3 to 4 garlic cloves, minced
1 teaspoon salt
5 medium red potatoes, cut into
  1/4-inch slices
5 tablespoons olive *or* vegetable oil,
  divided
1 large onion, thinly sliced
1 broiler/fryer chicken
  (3 to 4 pounds), cut up
2 medium tomatoes, chopped
1 tablespoon minced fresh basil

In a large bowl, combine garlic and salt; let stand for 15-20 minutes. Add potatoes and 2 tablespoons oil. In a greased 13-in. x 9-in. x 2-in. baking dish, layer potato mixture, onion, chicken and tomatoes. Sprinkle with basil. Drizzle with remaining oil.

Cover and bake at 350° for 1 hour. Uncover; bake 15-20 minutes longer or until chicken juices run clear and potatoes are tender. **Yield:** 4 servings.

MONEY-SAVING TIP

*When you're shopping for poultry, choose meaty, full-breasted birds.
A skinny bird costs too much, proportionally, for the bone.*

CORDON BLEU CASSEROLE

(Pictured below)

I often roast a turkey just to have leftovers for this creamy casserole.
It makes for a pretty presentation at potluck dinners.
—Joyce Paul, Qu'Appelle, Saskatchewan

2 cups cubed fully cooked ham
4 cups cubed cooked turkey
1 cup (4 ounces) shredded Swiss
   cheese
1 large onion, chopped
1/3 cup butter *or* margarine
1/3 cup all-purpose flour
1/8 teaspoon ground mustard
1/8 teaspoon ground nutmeg
1-3/4 cups milk
TOPPING:
1-1/2 cups soft bread crumbs
1/2 cup shredded Swiss cheese
1/4 cup butter *or* margarine, melted

In a nonstick skillet, saute ham for 4-5 minutes or until browned; drain and pat dry. In a greased 2-qt. baking dish, layer the turkey, cheese and ham; set aside.

In a saucepan, saute the onion in butter until tender. Stir in the flour, mustard and nutmeg until blended. Gradually stir in milk. Bring to a boil; cook and stir for 2 minutes or until thickened. Pour over ham. Combine topping ingredients; sprinkle over the top. Bake, uncovered, at 350° for 25-30 minutes or until golden brown and bubbly. **Yield:** 6 servings.

CURRIED CHICKEN WITH ASPARAGUS

(Pictured above)

*A mild curry sauce nicely coats tender chicken and asparagus in this
"must-have" recipe. It's a classic dish I've used for years.*
—Miriam Christophel, Battle Creek, Michigan

1 can (10-3/4 ounces) condensed
  cream of chicken soup, undiluted
1/3 cup mayonnaise*
1 teaspoon lemon juice
1/2 teaspoon curry powder
1/8 teaspoon pepper
1 package (10 ounces) frozen
  asparagus spears, thawed
1 pound boneless skinless chicken
  breasts, cut into 1/2-inch pieces
2 tablespoons vegetable oil
1/4 cup shredded cheddar cheese

In a bowl, combine the soup, mayonnaise, lemon juice, curry and pepper; set aside. Place half of the asparagus in a greased 8-in. square baking dish. Spread with half of the soup mixture.

In a skillet, saute chicken in oil until no longer pink. Place chicken over soup mixture. Top with remaining asparagus and soup mixture. Cover and bake at 375° for 20 minutes. Uncover; sprinkle with cheese. Bake 5-8 minutes longer or until cheese is melted. **Yield:** 4 servings.

*Editor's Note: Reduced-fat or fat-free mayonnaise may not be substituted for regular mayonnaise.

TURKEY NOODLE CASSEROLE

Celery, water chestnuts and mushrooms add texture and crunch to this hearty casserole that is full of ground turkey. I'll fix two and serve one with a salad to make a complete meal. I keep the second one in the freezer to bake when company's coming.
—Georgia Hennings, Alliance, Nebraska

2 pounds ground turkey
4 celery ribs, chopped
1/4 cup chopped green pepper
1/4 cup chopped onion
1 can (10-3/4 ounces) condensed cream of mushroom soup, undiluted
1 can (8 ounces) sliced water chestnuts, drained
1 jar (4-1/2 ounces) sliced mushrooms, drained
1 jar (4 ounces) diced pimientos, drained
1/4 cup soy sauce
1/2 teaspoon salt
1/2 teaspoon lemon-pepper seasoning
1 cup (8 ounces) sour cream
8 ounces wide egg noodles, cooked and drained

In a large skillet over medium heat, cook the turkey until no longer pink. Add the celery, green pepper and onion; cook until vegetables are tender. Stir in the soup, water chestnuts, mushrooms, pimientos, soy sauce, salt and lemon-pepper. Bring to a boil. Reduce heat; simmer, uncovered, for 20 minutes.

Remove from the heat; add sour cream and noodles. Spoon half into a freezer container; cover and freeze for up to 3 months. Place the remaining mixture in a greased 2-qt. baking dish. Cover and bake at 350° for 30-35 minutes or until heated through.

To use the frozen casserole: Thaw in the refrigerator. Transfer to a greased 2-qt. baking dish and bake as directed. **Yield:** 2 casseroles (6 servings each).

BROCCOLI CHICKEN DELIGHT

I often take this dish to new moms in our church. It's great topped off with a salad and fresh bread.
—Connie Schmidt, Plano, Illinois

1 package (16 ounces) frozen broccoli cuts, thawed
3-1/2 cups cubed cooked chicken
2 cans (10-3/4 ounces *each*) condensed cream of chicken soup, undiluted
1 cup mayonnaise*
1 tablespoon lemon juice
1/4 teaspoon curry powder
2 cups (8 ounces) shredded cheddar cheese
1 cup crushed butter-flavored crackers (about 25 crackers)

In a greased 13-in. x 9-in. x 2-in. baking dish, layer broccoli and chicken. In a bowl, combine the soup, mayonnaise, lemon juice and curry; pour over chicken. Sprinkle with cheese and cracker crumbs. Cover and bake at 350° for 1 hour or until heated through. **Yield:** 8-10 servings.

*Editor's Note: Reduced-fat or fat-free mayonnaise may not be substituted for regular mayonnaise.

FARMHOUSE CHICKEN

This dish gets its great flavor from dressed-up canned soup and its ease of preparation from stuffing mix. In less than an hour, I can assemble this casserole, bake it and put it on the table.
—Alice Faye Ellis, Elkton, Oregon

2 packages (6 ounces *each*) stuffing
   mix
4 cups cubed cooked chicken
2 cans (10-3/4 ounces *each*)
   condensed cream of celery soup,
   undiluted
1 cup milk
2 celery ribs, chopped
1 teaspoon dried minced onion
1/4 teaspoon salt
1/4 teaspoon pepper

Prepare stuffing mix according to package directions; set aside. Place the chicken in a greased 13-in. x 9-in. x 2-in. baking dish. Combine the soup, milk, celery, onion, salt and pepper until blended; pour over chicken. Top with stuffing. Bake, uncovered, at 350° for 30-35 minutes or until bubbly. **Yield:** 8 servings.

TIMELY TIP

Keep a package of frozen cubed cooked chicken from the freezer section of your supermarket handy for those days when you're in a hurry to put Farmhouse Chicken or Chicken Lasagna Rolls on the table.

CHICKEN LASAGNA ROLLS

Whether for an everyday meal or a special occasion, this is a fun and creative way to serve lasagna. Chicken and almonds add a tasty new twist.
—Virginia Shaw, Modesto, California

1 medium onion, chopped
1/2 cup chopped sweet red pepper
1/2 cup chopped almonds
1/3 cup butter *or* margarine
1/2 cup cornstarch
1-1/2 teaspoons salt
2 cans (10-1/2 ounces *each*)
   condensed chicken broth, undiluted
2 cups cubed cooked chicken
1 package (10 ounces) frozen
   chopped spinach, thawed and
   squeezed dry
1/4 teaspoon pepper
1/4 teaspoon ground nutmeg
10 lasagna noodles, cooked and
   drained
2 cups milk
1 cup (4 ounces) shredded Swiss
   cheese, *divided*
1/4 cup dry white wine *or* water

In a large saucepan, saute onion, red pepper and almonds in butter until onion is tender and almonds are toasted. Stir in cornstarch and salt until blended. Stir in broth. Bring to a boil; cook and stir for 2 minutes or until thickened.

Transfer half of sauce to a bowl; stir in the chicken, spinach, pepper and nutmeg. Spread about 3 tablespoons over each lasagna noodle. Roll up and place seam side down in a greased 11-in. x 7-in. x 2-in. baking dish.

Add milk, 1/2 cup Swiss cheese and wine or water to remaining sauce. Cook and stir over medium heat until thickened and bubbly. Pour over roll-ups. Bake, uncovered, at 350° for 20-25 minutes. Sprinkle with remaining cheese; bake 5 minutes longer or until cheese is melted. **Yield:** 5 servings.

TURKEY SAUSAGE AND NOODLES

(Pictured above)

During the winter months when our appetites are in full gear, my family practically licks this pan clean. I sometimes toss in a can of white kidney beans to make it even heartier.
—Helen Wanamaker Vail, Glenside, Pennsylvania

2 cups uncooked egg noodles
2 pounds Italian turkey sausage, cut into 1-inch slices
1 large onion, chopped
2 medium carrots, sliced
1/2 cup chopped green pepper
1/2 cup all-purpose flour
2-1/2 cups milk
1/4 cup Worcestershire sauce
1/4 teaspoon rubbed sage

Cook noodles according to package directions; drain. In a large skillet, cook sausage, onion, carrots and green pepper over medium heat until meat is no longer pink and carrots are crisp-tender. Stir in flour until blended. Gradually add milk. Bring to a boil; cook and stir for 2 minutes or until thickened. Stir in the noodles, Worcestershire sauce and sage.

Transfer to a greased 2-1/2-qt. baking dish. Cover and bake at 350° for 20 minutes. Uncover; bake 10-15 minutes longer or until bubbly. **Yield:** 8 servings.

CHICKEN 'N' STUFFING

(Pictured at right)

*This recipe provides all the fabulous flavor of a stuffed whole chicken
with little fuss. It's a big hit with our son as well as other family and friends.*
—Pamela Key, Sandy Lake, Pennsylvania

2 celery ribs, chopped
1 large onion, chopped
1/2 cup butter *or* margarine
1 package (14 ounces) seasoned
stuffing croutons
2 tablespoons minced fresh parsley
1/4 teaspoon salt
1/8 teaspoon pepper
2 eggs, beaten
2 cans (14-1/2 ounces *each*) chicken
broth
4 cups cubed cooked chicken

In a small skillet, saute celery and onion in butter until tender. In a bowl, combine the croutons, parsley, salt, pepper and celery mixture. Combine eggs and broth; pour over bread mixture and toss to combine. Add chicken; toss gently.

Transfer to a greased 13-in. x 9-in. x 2-in. baking dish. Cover and bake at 350° for 40-50 minutes or until a meat thermometer reads 160°. **Yield:** 6-8 servings.

CHICKEN LASAGNA

(Pictured at right)

*When my nephews were younger, I would make their favorite meal for their birthdays...
this is what they usually requested. The cheese makes it easier for kids to eat their vegetables.*
—Janet Lorton, Effingham, Illinois

9 uncooked lasagna noodles
2 cans (10-3/4 ounces *each*)
condensed cream of chicken soup,
undiluted
2/3 cup milk
2-1/2 cups frozen mixed vegetables
2 cups cubed cooked chicken
18 slices process American cheese

Cook noodles according to package directions; drain. In a large saucepan, combine soup and milk. Cook and stir over low heat until blended. Remove from the heat; stir in vegetables and chicken. In a greased 13-in. x 9-in. x 2-in. baking dish, layer three noodles, a third of the soup mixture and six cheese slices. Repeat layers twice.

Cover and bake at 350° for 30 minutes. Uncover; bake 5-10 minutes longer or until bubbly. Let stand for 15 minutes before cutting. **Yield:** 9-12 servings.

PERFECT PARTNERS

*To complement Chicken Lasagna, serve seasoned sliced tomatoes
over a bed of lettuce with a crusty whole-grain roll.*

CHICKEN 'N' STUFFING
CHICKEN LASAGNA

COLORFUL CHICKEN CASSEROLE

*This all-in-one entree is a nice change of pace from traditional chicken dishes.
I make one for dinner and keep the other in the freezer for unexpected company.
—Bernice Morris, Marshfield, Missouri*

1 medium green pepper, chopped
2 celery ribs, chopped
3/4 cup chopped onion
2 tablespoons butter *or* margarine
1 cup chicken broth
1 cup frozen peas
1 cup frozen corn
1 teaspoon salt
1/4 teaspoon pepper
3 cups cubed cooked chicken
1 package (7 ounces) ready-cut
   spaghetti *or* elbow macaroni,
   cooked and drained
1 jar (4-1/2 ounces) sliced mushrooms,
   drained
1 cup (4 ounces) shredded cheddar
   cheese

In a large skillet, saute the green pepper, celery and onion in butter until tender. Add the broth, peas, corn, salt and pepper; heat through. Stir in the chicken and spaghetti. Transfer to two greased 8-in. square baking pans. Top with mushrooms and cheese.

Cover and freeze one casserole for up to 3 months. Cover and bake the second casserole at 350° for 20 minutes; uncover and bake 10 minutes longer.

To use frozen casserole: Cover and bake at 350° for 35 minutes. Uncover; bake 15 minutes longer or until heated through. **Yield:** 2 casseroles (4 servings each).

MUSHROOM CHICKEN DELUXE

*My family could eat noodles at every meal. We all go for seconds of
this creamy casserole, which is packed with chicken and mushrooms.
—Jean Voermans, Whitefish, Montana*

1-1/2 cups sliced fresh mushrooms
1 medium onion, chopped
1/2 cup chopped green pepper
2 tablespoons butter *or* margarine
1 can (10-3/4 ounces) condensed
   cream of chicken soup, undiluted
1/2 cup milk
1/4 cup chopped pimientos
3/4 teaspoon dried basil
8 ounces spiral pasta, cooked and
   drained
2 cups (16 ounces) small-curd cottage
   cheese
1-1/2 cups (6 ounces) shredded cheddar
   cheese
1/2 cup grated Parmesan cheese,
   divided
3 cups cubed cooked chicken

In a skillet, saute the mushrooms, onion and green pepper in butter until tender. Add the soup, milk, pimientos and basil; mix well and heat through.

Place pasta in a greased 13-in. x 9-in. x 2-in. baking dish. Combine the cottage cheese, cheddar cheese and 1/4 cup Parmesan cheese; spread over pasta. Top with chicken. Pour mushroom sauce over chicken. Sprinkle with remaining Parmesan. Cover and bake at 350° for 50-55 minutes or until bubbly. **Yield:** 6-8 servings.

CHICKEN AMANDINE

(Pictured below and on page 10)

*With colorful green beans and pimientos, this attractive casserole is
terrific for the holidays. This is true comfort food at its finest.*
—Kate Woolbright, Wichita Falls, Texas

1/4 cup chopped onion
1 tablespoon butter *or* margarine
1 package (6 ounces) long grain and
  wild rice
2-1/4 cups chicken broth
3 cups cubed cooked chicken
2 cups frozen French-style green
  beans, thawed
1 can (10-3/4 ounces) condensed
  cream of chicken soup, undiluted
3/4 cup sliced almonds, *divided*
1 jar (4 ounces) diced pimientos,
  drained
1 teaspoon pepper
1/2 teaspoon garlic powder
1 bacon strip, cooked and crumbled

In a saucepan, saute onion in butter until tender. Add rice with contents of seasoning packet and broth. Bring to a boil. Reduce heat; cover and simmer for 25 minutes or until liquid is absorbed. Uncover; set aside to cool.

In a large bowl, combine the chicken, green beans, soup, 1/2 cup of almonds, pimientos, pepper and garlic powder; mix well. Stir in rice. Transfer to a greased 2-1/2-qt. baking dish. Sprinkle with bacon and remaining almonds. Cover and bake at 350° for 30-35 minutes or until heated through.
Yield: 8 servings.

HARVEST CHICKEN AND VEGETABLES

This delicious dish is packed with a large assortment of vegetables.
Served with a green salad, it makes an excellent entree.
—Janet Weisser, Seattle, Washington

2-1/2 to 3 pounds chicken thighs, skin
    removed
   2 bay leaves
   4 small red potatoes, cut into 1-inch
    pieces
   4 small onions, quartered
   4 small carrots, cut into 2-inch pieces
   2 celery ribs, cut into 2-inch pieces
   2 small turnips, peeled and cut into
    1-inch pieces
   1 medium green pepper, cut into
    1-inch pieces
  12 small fresh mushrooms
   2 teaspoons salt
   1 teaspoon dried rosemary, crushed
1/2 teaspoon pepper
   1 can (14-1/2 ounces) diced tomatoes,
    undrained

Place chicken in a greased 13-in. x 9-in. x 2-in. baking dish; add bay leaves. Top with potatoes, onions, carrots, celery, turnips, green pepper and mushrooms. Sprinkle with salt, rosemary and pepper. Pour tomatoes over all. Cover and bake at 375° for 1-1/2 hours or until chicken juices run clear and vegetables are tender. Discard bay leaves. **Yield:** 6-8 servings.

TIMELY TIP

Thaw frozen poultry in the refrigerator, not on the countertop or in the kitchen sink. Allow about 5 hours per pound.

GOLDEN CHICKEN 'N' TATERS

My sister and I developed this colorful, creamy casserole from a few others we had tried.
The whole family likes the hearty layers of chicken, Tater Tots, vegetables and cheese.
—Ione Senn, Salt Lake City, Utah

   1 can (10-3/4 ounces) condensed
    cream of chicken soup, undiluted
   1 can (10-3/4 ounces) condensed
    cream of celery soup, undiluted
1/2 cup water
1/4 to 1/2 teaspoon salt
   1 package (32 ounces) frozen Tater
    Tots
   1 package (16 ounces) frozen mixed
    vegetables
   2 cups cubed cooked chicken
   1 cup (4 ounces) shredded cheddar
    cheese

Combine the soups, water and salt; mix well. In a greased 13-in. x 9-in. x 2-in. baking dish, layer a third of the soup mixture, half of the Tater Tots, half of the vegetables and half of the chicken. Repeat layers. Top with the remaining soup mixture. Sprinkle with cheese.

   Cover and bake at 350° for 60-70 minutes or until bubbly. Uncover; bake 5-10 minutes longer or until golden brown and heated through. **Yield:** 6-8 servings.

TURKEY POTATO SUPPER

*Lightly seasoned turkey and broccoli are nestled in a tender
mashed potato shell. I like to share this dish with our bachelor neighbors.*
—Mrs. John Dziedzic, Holland, Michigan

2 cups water
1/4 cup butter *or* margarine
1 teaspoon salt
2-2/3 cups mashed potato flakes
2 eggs, lightly beaten
1 can (10-3/4 ounces) condensed
   cream of chicken soup, undiluted
1/4 cup mayonnaise*
1 teaspoon lemon juice
1/2 teaspoon curry powder
2 cups cubed cooked turkey
1 package (10 ounces) frozen
   chopped broccoli, thawed
1/4 cup slivered almonds, toasted,
   optional

In a large saucepan, bring the water, butter and salt to a boil. Remove from the heat; stir in potato flakes. Let stand for 30 seconds. Whip with a fork. Stir in eggs. Spoon the potatoes onto the bottom and up the sides of a greased 8-in. square baking dish, forming a shell.

In a bowl, combine soup, mayonnaise, lemon juice and curry. Stir in turkey and broccoli. Bake, uncovered, at 350° for 20 minutes. Sprinkle with almonds if desired. Bake 15-20 minutes longer or until potato edges are golden brown and filling is heated through. Let stand for 10 minutes before serving. **Yield:** 4-6 servings.

*Editor's Note: Reduced-fat or fat-free mayonnaise may not be substituted for regular mayonnaise.

CHICKEN TETRAZZINI

*In winter, we see lots of snow here in the northwest mountains of North Carolina.
Hearty casseroles like this are filling, warming and welcome.*
—Athel Wilcox, West Jefferson, North Carolina

8 ounces uncooked egg noodles
1/2 pound fresh mushrooms, sliced
1 small onion, chopped
1/4 cup butter *or* margarine
2 cups chicken broth
3 tablespoons cornstarch
1/2 teaspoon salt
Dash pepper
1 cup half-and-half cream
1/2 cup shredded mozzarella cheese
2 cups cubed cooked chicken
1/4 cup grated Parmesan cheese

Cook noodles according to package directions; drain. In a large saucepan, saute mushrooms and onion in butter until tender. Stir in broth.

Combine the cornstarch, salt, pepper and cream until smooth. Stir into the mushroom mixture. Bring to a boil; cook and stir for 2 minutes or until thickened. Reduce heat; stir in mozzarella cheese until melted. Stir in chicken and noodles.

Transfer to a greased 2-qt. baking dish. Sprinkle with Parmesan cheese. Bake, uncovered, at 350° for 25-30 minutes or until lightly browned. **Yield:** 4-6 servings.

SIMPLE SUBSTITUTION

*Out of cubed cooked chicken? Substitute three 5-ounce cans of
boned chicken for the 2 cups of cooked chicken in Chicken Tetrazzini.*

CREAMY CHICKEN 'N' GREEN BEANS

My husband is a real "meat and potatoes" man, but he'll always try whatever I prepare. He especially enjoys this creamy casserole served over hot homemade biscuits.
—Sandra Wanamaker, Germansville, Pennsylvania

1 can (10-3/4 ounces) condensed cream of chicken soup, undiluted
1 can (10-3/4 ounces) condensed cheddar cheese soup, undiluted
1 can (5 ounces) evaporated milk
3 cups frozen cut green beans, thawed and drained
3 cups cubed cooked chicken
2 celery ribs, chopped
2 tablespoons chopped onion
1 jar (2 ounces) diced pimientos, drained
1/2 cup chow mein noodles
1/2 cup slivered almonds, toasted
1/2 teaspoon salt
1/4 teaspoon pepper
1/2 cup french-fried onions
Hot biscuits

In a large bowl, stir soups and milk until smooth. Add the next nine ingredients. Transfer to a greased 2-1/2-qt. baking dish. Bake, uncovered, at 350° for 40 minutes or until bubbly. Sprinkle with onions; bake 10 minutes longer. Serve over biscuits. **Yield:** 4-6 servings.

WILD WILD RICE

Wild rice really shines in this pretty and tasty chicken dish, which has such a fun name. Hearty helpings always satisfy hunger in a hurry.
—Lisa Neu, Fond du Lac, Wisconsin

1/4 cup chopped green pepper
1/4 cup chopped onion
2 tablespoons butter *or* margarine, *divided*
2-1/3 cups water
1 package (6 ounces) long grain and wild rice mix
4 cups cubed cooked chicken
1 can (10-3/4 ounces) condensed cream of chicken soup, undiluted
1 can (8 ounces) French-style green beans, drained
1 can (8 ounces) sliced water chestnuts, drained
1 medium carrot, grated
1/4 cup mayonnaise*
1 cup (4 ounces) shredded cheddar cheese, optional

In a small skillet, saute green pepper and onion in 1 tablespoon butter until crisp-tender; set aside.

In a large saucepan, bring the water, rice and remaining butter to a boil. Reduce heat; cover and simmer for 25 minutes or until rice is tender. Stir in the chicken, soup, green beans, water chestnuts, carrot, mayonnaise and green pepper mixture.

Transfer to a greased 2-1/2-qt. baking dish. Sprinkle with cheese if desired. Cover and bake at 350° for 35-40 minutes or until heated through. **Yield:** 6-8 servings.

*Editor's Note: Reduced-fat or fat-free mayonnaise may not be substituted for regular mayonnaise.

ALMOND TURKEY CASSEROLE

(Pictured above)

My husband and I have enjoyed cooking together since we were married some 40 years ago.
This recipe is a favorite. We make it whenever we have leftover turkey or chicken.
—Lucille Rowland, Stillwater, Minnesota

2 cups uncooked egg noodles
1 package (10 ounces) frozen broccoli
  cuts
2 tablespoons butter *or* margarine
2 tablespoons all-purpose flour
1 teaspoon salt
1/2 teaspoon ground mustard
1/4 teaspoon pepper
1-1/2 cups milk
1 cup (4 ounces) shredded Swiss
  cheese
2 cups cubed cooked turkey
1/2 cup slivered almonds, toasted

Cook noodles according to package directions; drain. Cook broccoli according to package directions; drain. Place noodles and broccoli in a large bowl; set aside.

In a saucepan, melt the butter. Stir in the flour, salt, mustard and pepper until smooth. Gradually stir in milk. Bring to a boil; cook and stir for 2 minutes or until thickened. Remove from the heat; stir in cheese until melted. Add the turkey; pour over noodle mixture.

Transfer to a greased 1-1/2-qt. baking dish. Sprinkle with almonds. Bake, uncovered, at 350° for 20-25 minutes or until heated through. **Yield:** 4 servings.

THREE-CHEESE CHICKEN

I try to keep the ingredients for this creamy casserole on hand for last-minute meals.
Whenever I serve this at family dinners and potlucks, it's well-received.
—Doris Cohn, Denville, New Jersey

1 package (7 ounces) thin spaghetti, cooked and drained
1 package (10 ounces) frozen chopped spinach, thawed and squeezed dry
1/2 cup half-and-half cream
1/3 cup grated Parmesan cheese, *divided*
1/2 teaspoon salt
1/4 teaspoon pepper
1/8 to 1/4 teaspoon ground nutmeg
2 cups cubed cooked chicken
1 cup (4 ounces) shredded Swiss cheese
1/2 cup sliced fresh mushrooms
2 bacon strips, cooked and crumbled
4 eggs, lightly beaten
1 cup ricotta cheese
1/4 cup chopped onion
1 garlic clove, minced

In a bowl, combine the spaghetti, spinach, cream, 4 tablespoons Parmesan cheese, salt, pepper and nutmeg. Transfer to a greased 9-in. square baking dish. Top with chicken, Swiss cheese, mushrooms and bacon.

In a bowl, combine the eggs, ricotta, onion and garlic; spread over the chicken mixture. Sprinkle with remaining Parmesan. Bake, uncovered, at 350° for 30-35 minutes or until bubbly. **Yield:** 4-6 servings.

HUNGARIAN CABBAGE AND CHICKEN

When we had a bumper crop of cabbage a few years back, I searched for new cabbage entrees.
I was delighted to find this one...and happy when my family said they loved it.
—Ruth Kannenberg, Luverne, Minnesota

1/4 cup butter *or* margarine
1 broiler/fryer chicken (3 to 4 pounds), cut up
2 teaspoons paprika
1 medium cabbage, cut into 1/2-inch slices
3/4 teaspoon salt
1/4 teaspoon pepper
2 medium tart apples, sliced
1 medium onion, chopped
1 tablespoon caraway seeds
2 teaspoons grated lemon peel
1 teaspoon sugar
1 cup (4 ounces) shredded Swiss cheese, optional

In a large skillet, heat butter over medium heat. Sprinkle chicken with paprika; brown in butter on all sides. Reduce heat; cover and simmer for 20 minutes.

Meanwhile, place cabbage in a greased 13-in. x 9-in. x 2-in. baking dish. Sprinkle with salt and pepper. Cover and bake at 375° for 20 minutes. Arrange apples and onion over cabbage. Sprinkle with caraway, lemon peel and sugar. Top with chicken.

Cover and bake for 30 minutes or until chicken juices run clear and cabbage is tender. Uncover; sprinkle with cheese if desired. Bake 5 minutes longer or until cheese is melted. **Yield:** 4 servings.

TURKEY MANICOTTI

My teenage daughter enjoys making this main course. It's one of my favorites because it blends turkey and garlic, two flavors I love.
—Connie Nelson-Smith, Sugar Land, Texas

2 slices bread
1-1/2 pounds ground turkey
1/4 cup chopped onion
2 garlic cloves, minced
1/2 teaspoon salt
1/4 teaspoon pepper
1 cup (4 ounces) shredded mozzarella cheese
1/2 cup grated Parmesan cheese
14 manicotti shells (8 ounces), cooked and drained
1 jar (30 ounces) meatless spaghetti sauce

Soak bread in water; squeeze to remove excess water. Tear into small pieces; set aside. In a skillet, cook the turkey, onion, garlic, salt and pepper over medium heat until meat is no longer pink; drain. Stir in the bread and cheeses; mix well. Spoon into manicotti shells.

Pour half of the spaghetti sauce into a greased 13-in. x 9-in. x 2-in. baking dish. Arrange shells over sauce; top with the remaining sauce. Cover and bake at 350° for 25-30 minutes or until heated through. **Yield:** 7 servings.

SERVING SUGGESTION

For a simple dessert, try this quick version of a banana split. Top a scoop of vanilla ice cream with strawberry preserves and sliced bananas. Drizzle with chocolate syrup.

CREAMY CHICKEN CURRY

A delicate curry sauce pairs well with tender chicken, colorful vegetables and crunchy almonds. Try serving spoonfuls of this tasty blend over rice.
—Janis Vandervort, Portland, Oregon

3/4 pound boneless skinless chicken breasts, cut into 1/4-inch strips
1-1/2 cups broccoli florets
1-1/2 cups cauliflowerets
1 can (10-3/4 ounces) condensed cream of chicken soup, undiluted
1/2 cup mayonnaise*
1/2 cup shredded cheddar cheese
1 teaspoon lemon juice
1/2 to 1 teaspoon curry powder
1/8 to 1/4 teaspoon cayenne pepper
1/2 cup slivered almonds

Place the chicken in a greased 8-in. square baking dish. Top with broccoli and cauliflower. Combine the soup, mayonnaise, cheese, lemon juice, curry and cayenne; spoon over vegetables. Sprinkle with almonds. Bake, uncovered, at 375° for 25-30 minutes or until chicken juices run clear and vegetables are tender. Stir before serving. **Yield:** 4 servings.

*Editor's Note: Reduced-fat or fat-free mayonnaise may not be substituted for regular mayonnaise.

CHICKEN AND SHELLS DINNER

(Pictured above)

Like most kids, mine love macaroni and cheese. The addition of chicken and peas makes this a meal-in-one they never refuse.
—*LeeAnn McCue, Charlotte, North Carolina*

1 package (12 ounces) shells and cheese dinner mix
1/4 cup chopped onion
4 tablespoons butter *or* margarine, *divided*
2 cups cubed cooked chicken
1 package (10 ounces) frozen peas, thawed
2/3 cup mayonnaise*
1/3 cup seasoned bread crumbs

Prepare dinner mix according to package directions. Meanwhile, in a small skillet, saute onion in 2 tablespoons butter until tender. Stir the chicken, peas, mayonnaise and sauteed onion into dinner mix.

Transfer to a greased 1-1/2-qt. baking dish. Melt remaining butter; toss with bread crumbs. Sprinkle over top. Bake, uncovered, at 350° for 20-25 minutes or until bubbly. **Yield:** 4-6 servings.

*Editor's Note: Reduced-fat or fat-free mayonnaise may not be substituted for regular mayonnaise.

COMFORTING CHICKEN 'N' NOODLES

A friend in Arizona gave me this recipe more than 25 years ago. It quickly became a family-favorite dish. One bite of this creamy casserole and you'll see why!
—Diane Tindall, Baltimore, Maryland

   6 ounces uncooked wide egg noodles
1/2 cup butter *or* margarine, *divided*
1/3 cup all-purpose flour
   3 teaspoons salt, *divided*
1-1/2 cups milk
   1 cup chicken broth
   2 tablespoons white wine *or*
      additional chicken broth, optional
   4 tablespoons grated Parmesan
      cheese, *divided*
1/2 pound fresh mushrooms, sliced
   1 garlic clove, minced
1/8 teaspoon pepper
   4 cups cubed cooked chicken
Paprika

Cook noodles according to package directions; drain. In a saucepan, melt 1/4 cup butter. Stir in flour and 1-1/2 teaspoons salt until smooth. Gradually add milk and broth. Bring to a boil; cook and stir for 2 minutes or until thickened. Remove from the heat; stir in wine or additional broth if desired.

In a bowl, combine the noodles, 1 cup white sauce, 2 tablespoons Parmesan cheese, 2 tablespoons butter and 1 teaspoon salt. Transfer to a greased 3-qt. baking dish; set aside.

In a skillet, saute mushrooms and garlic in remaining butter until tender. Stir in pepper and remaining salt. Spoon over noodle mixture. Top with chicken. Pour the remaining white sauce over chicken. Sprinkle with remaining Parmesan. Garnish with paprika. Cover and bake at 350° for 30-35 minutes or until bubbly. **Yield:** 6 servings.

FRYER CHICKEN WITH VEGGIES

I adapted a recipe for an all-vegetable dish by adding chicken. Now it's a mouth-watering main meal.
—Dorothy McGrew Hood, Northbrook, Illinois

   1 broiler/fryer chicken (3 to 4
      pounds), cut up and skin removed
   4 celery ribs, sliced
   2 cups fresh *or* frozen cut green
      beans
   3 medium carrots, sliced
   1 large onion, sliced
   1 small zucchini, diced
   1 can (14-1/2 ounces) diced tomatoes,
      undrained
   3 tablespoons quick-cooking tapioca
   1 tablespoon sugar
   2 teaspoons salt
1/2 teaspoon pepper

In an ungreased 13-in. x 9-in. x 2-in. baking dish, place the chicken, celery, green beans, carrots and onion. In a small bowl, combine the zucchini, tomatoes, tapioca, sugar, salt and pepper. Pour over chicken and vegetables.

Cover and bake at 350° for 1-1/2 hours or until chicken juices run clear and vegetable mixture is thickened, stirring occasionally. **Yield:** 4 servings.

OVERNIGHT SCALLOPED CHICKEN

This has to be one of the greatest casseroles ever! It serves the family or company equally well but really draws raves every time I take it to a potluck.
—Arlyss Gray, Lafayette, Indiana

2 cans (10-3/4 ounces *each*) condensed cream of mushroom soup, undiluted
2-1/2 cups milk
1/2 pound process cheese (Velveeta), cubed
4 cups cubed cooked chicken *or* turkey
1 package (7 ounces) elbow macaroni
3 hard-cooked eggs, chopped
1/2 cup butter *or* margarine, melted, *divided*
1-1/2 cups soft bread crumbs

In a large bowl, combine the soup, milk, and cheese. Add the chicken, uncooked macaroni and eggs. Stir in 1/4 cup butter. Transfer to a greased 13-in. x 9-in. x 2-in. baking dish. Cover and refrigerate for 8 hours or overnight.

Remove from the refrigerator 30 minutes before baking. Toss the bread crumbs with remaining butter; sprinkle over the top. Bake, uncovered, at 350° for 60-65 minutes or until bubbly and golden brown. **Yield:** 8-10 servings.

TIMELY TIP

Use leftover cooked poultry as the start of another meal. Simply cube it and saute with diced potatoes, onions and green pepper until the potatoes are tender. The flavorful hash is great for breakfast or dinner.

APRICOT ALMOND CHICKEN

This tender chicken topped with sweet apricot preserves and crunchy almonds is special enough for guests, yet requires no complicated cooking. The hearty brown rice, with colorful flecks of red and green pepper, makes a pretty accompaniment.
—Betty Due, Mendota, Illinois

2-1/4 cups chicken broth
1 cup uncooked long grain brown rice
1 small onion, chopped
1/4 cup chopped green pepper
1/4 cup chopped sweet red pepper
1 teaspoon salt
1/4 teaspoon dried thyme
1/4 teaspoon dried marjoram
4 boneless skinless chicken breast halves
1/4 cup apricot preserves
1/3 cup sliced almonds, toasted

In a bowl, combine the first eight ingredients; mix well. Transfer to a greased 13-in. x 9-in. x 2-in. baking dish; top with chicken. Cover and bake at 350° for 55-60 minutes or until rice is tender.

Uncover. Place a tablespoon of preserves on each chicken breast; sprinkle with almonds. Bake 10 minutes longer or until chicken juices run clear. Let stand for 5 minutes before serving. **Yield:** 4 servings.

CHICKEN SPAGHETTI

My family prefers this creamy chicken spaghetti to the more traditional tomato-based variety. The smoky flavor of bacon adds interest.
—Dave Portman, Cincinnati, Ohio

   8 ounces uncooked spaghetti
   1 medium onion, chopped
1/2 cup chopped green pepper
   2 celery ribs, chopped
   4 tablespoons butter *or* margarine, *divided*
   2 cans (10-3/4 ounces *each*) condensed cream of mushroom soup, undiluted
   1 can (4 ounces) mushroom stems and pieces, drained
2-1/2 cups cubed cooked chicken
   2 cups (8 ounces) shredded cheddar cheese
1/2 cup dry bread crumbs
   5 bacon strips, cooked and crumbled

Cook spaghetti according to package directions; drain. In a small skillet, saute the onion, green pepper and celery in 2 tablespoons butter until tender. Transfer to a large bowl. Add the soup, mushrooms, spaghetti, chicken and cheese; toss to coat.

Transfer to a greased 13-in. x 9-in. x 2-in. baking dish. Sprinkle with bread crumbs and bacon; dot with remaining butter. Bake, uncovered, at 350° for 30-35 minutes or until heated through. **Yield:** 8-10 servings.

SERVING SUGGESTION

Complete a casserole dinner with slices of crusty Italian bread topped with cheese, then browned in the oven.

CHICKEN RICE CASSEROLE

Mushrooms, celery and water chestnuts add texture and crunch in this comforting casserole. Chicken and rice are perfect partners that always satisfy.
—Linda Durnil, Decatur, Illinois

   2 cups cubed cooked chicken
   2 cups cooked rice
   1 can (10-3/4 ounces) condensed cream of chicken soup, undiluted
   1 can (8 ounces) sliced water chestnuts, drained
   1 jar (4-1/2 ounces) sliced mushrooms, drained
   2 celery ribs, thinly sliced
3/4 cup mayonnaise*
   1 tablespoon chopped onion
   1 tablespoon lemon juice
1/2 teaspoon salt
1/3 cup crushed saltines (about 10 crackers)
   1 tablespoon butter *or* margarine, melted

In a bowl, combine the first 10 ingredients. Transfer to a greased 2-1/2-qt. baking dish. Combine the cracker crumbs and butter; sprinkle over the top. Bake, uncovered, at 350° for 30-35 minutes or until bubbly. **Yield:** 4-6 servings.

*Editor's Note: Reduced-fat or fat-free mayonnaise may not be substituted for regular mayonnaise.

STUFFING-TOPPED CHICKEN AND BROCCOLI

(Pictured at right)

People tell me hot and hearty foods like this remind them of their mom's cooking.
—Dar Jackson, Greenville, South Carolina

1 package (6 ounces) stuffing mix
2 cans (10-3/4 ounces *each*) condensed cream of chicken soup, undiluted
1 cup water
3 tablespoons sour cream
3-1/2 cups cubed cooked chicken
2 cups instant rice, cooked
2 packages (10 ounces *each*) frozen broccoli cuts, thawed

Prepare stuffing mix according to package directions; set aside. In a bowl, combine the soup, water and sour cream until blended. Stir in the chicken, rice and broccoli. Transfer to a greased 3-qt. baking dish. Top with stuffing.

Cover and bake at 350° for 30 minutes. Uncover; bake 15-20 minutes longer or until bubbly. **Yield:** 8-10 servings.

SAUSAGE 'N' CHICKEN CASSEROLE

(Pictured at right)

Meat-and-potato fans will fall for this recipe because simple seasonings bring out the flavors.
—Alice Ceresa, Rochester, New York

5 medium potatoes (about 3 pounds), peeled and quartered
1 teaspoon salt
1 teaspoon dried oregano
1 teaspoon paprika
1/2 teaspoon garlic salt
1/2 pound Italian sausage links, cooked and cut into 1-inch pieces
4 bone-in chicken breast halves, skin removed
2 tablespoons vegetable oil

Place potatoes in a greased 13-in. x 9-in. x 2-in. baking dish. Combine the salt, oregano, paprika and garlic salt; sprinkle half over potatoes. Arrange the sausage and chicken over potatoes. Drizzle with oil; sprinkle with remaining seasonings.

Cover and bake at 400° for 55-60 minutes or until chicken juices run clear and potatoes are tender. **Yield:** 4 servings.

SOUTHWESTERN CHICKEN

Prepared salsa and canned corn and beans add fun color, texture and flavor to this tender dish.
—Karen Waters, Laurel, Maryland

2 cans (15-1/4 ounces *each*) whole kernel corn, drained
1 can (15 ounces) black beans, rinsed and drained
1 jar (16 ounces) chunky salsa, *divided*
6 boneless skinless chicken breast halves
1 cup (4 ounces) shredded cheddar cheese

In a slow cooker, combine the corn, black beans and 1/2 cup salsa. Top with chicken; pour the remaining salsa over chicken. Cover and cook on high for 3-4 hours, or on low for 7-8 hours, or until meat juices run clear. Sprinkle with cheese; cover until cheese is melted, about 5 minutes. **Yield:** 6 servings.

STUFFING-TOPPED CHICKEN AND BROCCOLI
SAUSAGE 'N' CHICKEN CASSEROLE

ARTICHOKE CHICKEN

This recipe has evolved through generations to satisfy my family's fondness for artichokes.
I enjoy preparing this for casual suppers as well as special-occasion dinners.
—Roberta Green, Hemet, California

2 cans (14 ounces *each*) water-packed
   artichoke hearts, drained and
   quartered
2 tablespoons olive *or* vegetable oil
3 garlic cloves, minced
2-2/3 cups cubed cooked chicken
2 cans (10-3/4 ounces *each*)
   condensed cream of chicken soup,
   undiluted
1 cup mayonnaise*
1 teaspoon lemon juice
1/2 teaspoon curry powder
1-1/2 cups (6 ounces) shredded cheddar
   cheese
1 cup seasoned bread crumbs
1/4 cup grated Parmesan cheese
2 tablespoons butter *or* margarine,
   melted

In a bowl, combine the artichokes, oil and garlic. Place in a greased 2-1/2-qt. baking dish. Top with chicken. Combine the soup, mayonnaise, lemon juice and curry; pour over the chicken. Sprinkle with cheddar cheese. Combine the bread crumbs, Parmesan cheese and butter; sprinkle over top. Bake, uncovered, at 350° for 30-35 minutes or until bubbly. **Yield:** 6-8 servings.

   *Editor's Note: Reduced-fat or fat-free mayonnaise may not be substituted for regular mayonnaise.

TIMELY TIP

When you don't have enough time to finely chop three garlic cloves for the
Artichoke Chicken, use 1 tablespoon of ready-to-use minced garlic.
It's available in jars in the produce section of most grocery stores.

CHICKEN STUFFING BAKE

At my bridal shower a few years ago, each guest brought a recipe card with
her best dish. We've tried everyone's recipe, but this is a favorite.
—Nicole Vogl Harding, Spokane, Washington

6 boneless skinless chicken breast
   halves
6 slices Swiss cheese
1 can (10-3/4 ounces) condensed
   cream of chicken soup,
   undiluted
1/3 cup white wine *or* chicken broth
3 cups seasoned stuffing croutons
1/2 cup butter *or* margarine, melted

Place chicken in a greased 13-in. x 9-in. x 2-in. baking dish; top with cheese. Combine soup and wine or broth; spoon over the cheese. Combine the croutons and butter; sprinkle over soup. Bake, uncovered, at 350° for 45-55 minutes or until chicken juices run clear. **Yield:** 6 servings.

SAUCY CHICKEN SQUARES

(Pictured below)

When I serve a meal that's considered good by all eight members of my family, I call that recipe a winner. These chicken squares with mushroom sauce passed the test.
—Irene Burkholder, Leola, Pennsylvania

2 cups soft bread crumbs
2 cups chicken broth
4 eggs, lightly beaten
1 celery rib, chopped
1 jar (4 ounces) diced pimientos, drained
2 tablespoons finely chopped onion
1/2 teaspoon salt
1/4 teaspoon poultry seasoning
3 cups cubed cooked chicken
1 cup cooked rice
1 cup sliced fresh mushrooms
1/3 cup butter *or* margarine
3 tablespoons all-purpose flour
1/2 teaspoon salt
1/4 teaspoon pepper
1-1/2 cups milk

In a bowl, combine bread crumbs, broth, eggs, celery, pimientos, onion, salt and poultry seasoning. Add the chicken and rice; mix well. Transfer to a greased 8-in. square baking dish. Bake, uncovered, at 350° for 55-65 minutes or until bubbly and golden brown.

Meanwhile, in a saucepan, saute mushrooms in butter. Stir in the flour, salt and pepper until blended. Gradually add the milk. Bring to a boil; cook and stir for 2 minutes or until thickened. Cut chicken casserole into squares and serve with mushroom sauce. **Yield:** 6-8 servings.

WILD RICE TURKEY DISH

(Pictured below)

My aunt, Dorothy Riethman, brought this casserole to my house when I returned to work after maternity leave. It was a delicious and appreciated gift.
—Jane Pleiman, Fort Loramie, Ohio

1 package (6 ounces) long grain and wild rice mix
3 cups cubed cooked turkey
1 can (10-3/4 ounces) condensed cream of chicken soup, undiluted
1 can (8 ounces) sliced water chestnuts, drained and halved
3/4 cup water
1/4 cup chopped onion
3 tablespoons soy sauce
1 cup soft bread crumbs
1 tablespoon butter *or* margarine, melted

Prepare rice according to package directions. Stir in the turkey, soup, water chestnuts, water, onion and soy sauce. Transfer to a greased 2-qt. baking dish. Cover and bake at 350° for 30 minutes.

Uncover. Toss bread crumbs and butter; sprinkle over the top. Bake 15-20 minutes longer or until bubbly and golden brown. Let stand for 15 minutes before serving. **Yield:** 6 servings.

CHICKEN CRESCENT CASSEROLE

With a family of five, I've found that casseroles are a quick and filling meal.
The crescent roll topping bakes up to a beautiful golden brown.
—Laurie Bus, Reno, Nevada

1 celery rib, sliced
3 tablespoons butter *or* margarine, *divided*
1 can (10-3/4 ounces) condensed cream of mushroom soup, undiluted
2/3 cup mayonnaise*
1/2 cup sour cream
2 tablespoons dried minced onion
3 cups cubed cooked chicken
1 can (8 ounces) sliced water chestnuts, drained
1 jar (4-1/2 ounces) sliced mushrooms, drained
2/3 cup shredded Swiss cheese
1 tube (8 ounces) refrigerated crescent rolls
1/2 cup sliced almonds

In a large saucepan, saute celery in 1 tablespoon butter until tender. Stir in the soup, mayonnaise, sour cream, onion, chicken, water chestnuts and mushrooms. Cook and stir over medium heat just until mixture begins to boil. Transfer to an ungreased 13-in. x 9-in. x 2-in. baking dish. Sprinkle with cheese.

Unroll crescent roll dough into a rectangle; seal seams and perforations. Place over cheese. Melt the remaining butter; toss with nuts and sprinkle over top. Bake, uncovered, at 375° for 20-25 minutes or until golden brown. **Yield:** 8-10 servings.

*Editor's Note: Reduced-fat or fat-free mayonnaise may not be substituted for regular mayonnaise.

PERFECT PARTNERS

A colorful salad makes a perfect side dish to Chicken Crescent Casserole.
Simply add mandarin orange segments and shredded carrots to mixed greens.

CHICKEN BROCCOLI BAKE

My husband claims to not like broccoli but has second helpings whenever I serve
this casserole. Lemon bars are a great dessert to finish the meal.
—Kristin Zanetti, Milwaukee, Wisconsin

2 packages (6.2 ounces *each*) broccoli au gratin rice mix
2-1/4 cups water
1 can (10-3/4 ounces) condensed cream of chicken soup, undiluted
1 to 2 tablespoons Dijon mustard
1-1/2 pounds boneless skinless chicken breasts, cut into 1-inch cubes
1 package (10 ounces) frozen broccoli florets, thawed
1 cup (4 ounces) shredded cheddar cheese

In a greased 13-in. x 9-in. x 2-in. baking dish, evenly spread rice from rice packages. In a bowl, combine the water, soup, mustard and contents of sauce packets from the rice; pour half over rice. Layer with chicken and broccoli. Pour remaining sauce over top.

Bake, uncovered, at 375° for 30-40 minutes or until chicken juices run clear and rice is tender. Sprinkle with cheese. Bake 10 minutes longer or until cheese is melted. **Yield:** 8 servings.

Turkey Squash Casserole

I combined two recipes to come up with this casserole, and it suits
my family's tastes perfectly. Using ground turkey adds to the convenience.
—Mildred Sherrer, Bay City, Texas

1 pound ground turkey
1 tablespoon vegetable oil
2 cups sliced yellow summer squash
1 medium onion, chopped
2 eggs
1 cup evaporated milk
1 cup (4 ounces) shredded mozzarella cheese
6 tablespoons butter *or* margarine, melted
1/2 teaspoon salt
1/4 teaspoon pepper
1 cup crushed saltines (about 30 crackers)

In a large skillet, cook turkey in oil over medium heat until no longer pink. Add the squash and onion. Cook until vegetables are crisp-tender; drain.

In a bowl, combine eggs, milk, cheese, butter, salt and pepper. Stir into the turkey mixture. Transfer to a greased 8-in. square baking dish. Sprinkle with the cracker crumbs. Bake, uncovered, at 375° for 35-40 minutes or until heated through. **Yield:** 6 servings.

Serving Suggestion

For a quick dessert, sprinkle toasted coconut over fresh or canned pineapple chunks. To toast coconut, spread on a cookie sheet and bake at 350° for about 7 minutes or until light golden brown, stirring occasionally.

Potato Chicken Delight

French-fried onions, potato chips and cheddar cheese provide a
pleasant golden color to this dish. It's a meat-and-potato lover's dream come true!
—Nicki Ussery, Mt. Sterling, Illinois

1 can (10-3/4 ounces) condensed cream of chicken soup, undiluted
3/4 cup sour cream
3/4 cup milk
1/2 teaspoon salt
2 cups cubed cooked chicken
2 cups (8 ounces) shredded cheddar cheese, *divided*
1 package (30 ounces) frozen shredded hash brown potatoes, thawed
1/2 cup crushed sour cream and onion potato chips
1/2 cup crushed french-fried onions

In a large bowl, combine the soup, sour cream, milk and salt. Stir in chicken and 1-1/2 cups cheese. Stir in potatoes. Transfer to a greased 2-1/2-qt. baking dish. Cover and bake at 350° for 50 minutes.

Uncover; sprinkle with remaining cheese. Top with potato chips and onions. Bake 10-15 minutes longer or until edges are bubbly and cheese is melted. Let stand for 5 minutes before serving. **Yield:** 8 servings.

TURKEY BEAN BAKE

*Baked beans, brown sugar and molasses give a slightly sweet flavor to this
bean bake. People at potluck dinners often ask me for this recipe.
—Lisa Sjursen Darling, Rochester, New York*

1 pound ground turkey
1 large onion, chopped
2 garlic cloves, minced
1 can (16 ounces) baked beans
1 can (16 ounces) kidney beans,
    rinsed and drained
1 can (15 ounces) black beans, rinsed
    and drained
1/2 cup ketchup
2 tablespoons brown sugar
2 tablespoons molasses
1 tablespoon red wine vinegar *or*
    cider vinegar
1 teaspoon prepared mustard
1/4 teaspoon pepper

In a large skillet, cook the turkey, onion and garlic over medium heat until meat is no longer pink; drain. Stir in the remaining ingredients. Transfer to a greased 1-1/2-qt. baking dish. Bake, uncovered, at 350° for 25-30 minutes or until bubbly. **Yield:** 4-6 servings.

CHICKEN 'N' CORN BREAD DRESSING

*My nursing career keeps me busy, so easy recipes that taste great are
important to me. I came up with this one by combining items I had on hand.
—Pam West, Ernul, North Carolina*

2 celery ribs, chopped
1 large onion, chopped
1/4 cup butter *or* margarine
2 eggs
2 cups buttermilk
1 can (10-1/2 ounces) condensed
    chicken broth, undiluted
2 packages (8-3/4 ounces *each*) corn
    bread/muffin mix
1 can (8-3/4 ounces) cream-style corn
2 teaspoons poultry seasoning
1/2 teaspoon salt
1/2 teaspoon pepper
5 cups seasoned stuffing croutons
3 cans (5 ounces *each*) white chicken,
    drained
1 medium potato, peeled and diced

In a small saucepan, saute celery and onion in butter until tender; set aside. In a bowl, beat the eggs, buttermilk and broth. Stir in the muffin mixes, corn, poultry seasoning, salt and pepper; mix well. Add croutons, chicken, potato and celery mixture.

Transfer to a greased 13-in. x 9-in. x 2-in. baking dish. Bake, uncovered, at 375° for 30-35 minutes or until golden brown. **Yield:** 10-12 servings.

PERFECT PARTNERS

*For a simple side dish that goes well with casseroles, steam fresh green beans.
Drizzle with melted butter, then sprinkle with lemon-pepper seasoning.*

SPICY CHICKEN CORN SKILLET

We think this supper tastes even better the next day, so any leftovers
quickly disappear around here. You can adjust the cayenne pepper to suit your taste.
—Kelly Patterson, Lafayette, Louisiana

1 pound boneless skinless chicken breasts, cut into thin strips
1 tablespoon vegetable oil
1 medium onion, chopped
1 medium green pepper, chopped
1 tablespoon butter *or* margarine
1 can (14-1/2 ounces) stewed tomatoes, cut up
1 cup frozen corn, thawed
1/2 teaspoon salt
1/2 teaspoon dried oregano
1/2 teaspoon paprika
1/4 teaspoon pepper
1/8 to 1/4 teaspoon cayenne pepper
1 cup cooked rice

In a large skillet, stir-fry chicken in oil until no longer pink; remove and set aside. In the same skillet, saute onion and green pepper in butter until tender. Stir in the tomatoes, corn and seasonings. Bring to a boil. Stir in chicken and rice. Reduce heat; cover and cook until heated through. **Yield:** 4 servings.

SERVING SUGGESTION

Need an idea for a quick salad? Chopped hard-cooked eggs,
red onions and ripe olives will add interest to a mixed green salad,
especially in winter, when fresh vegetables are harder to find.

RITZY CHICKEN

When your family is hungry and the clock is ticking closer to dinnertime,
you can't go wrong with this chicken and noodle casserole.
—Millie Poe, Corning, Arkansas

2-1/2 cups uncooked egg noodles
1 can (10-3/4 ounces) condensed cream of chicken soup, undiluted
3/4 cup milk
1/2 cup sour cream
1/2 teaspoon poultry seasoning
1/4 teaspoon salt
Dash pepper
2 cups cubed cooked chicken
1/2 cup crushed butter-flavored crackers (about 12 crackers)
2 tablespoons butter *or* margarine, melted

Cook noodles according to package directions; drain. In a bowl, combine the soup, milk, sour cream, poultry seasoning, salt and pepper until blended. Stir in the noodles and chicken. Transfer to a greased 1-1/2-qt. baking dish. Combine cracker crumbs and butter; sprinkle over the top. Bake, uncovered, at 350° for 30-35 minutes or until bubbly and golden brown. **Yield:** 4 servings.

ZESTY CHICKEN CASSEROLE

(Pictured above)

Broccoli, chicken and rice get a little "zip" from Italian salad dressing.
Anyone who favors food with lots of flavor will enjoy this dish.
—Dianne Spurlock, Dayton, Ohio

2 cups uncooked instant rice
1 package (16 ounces) frozen broccoli cuts, thawed
1 medium onion, chopped
1 celery rib, chopped
2 tablespoons minced fresh parsley
1 teaspoon salt
6 boneless skinless chicken breast halves
1 can (10-3/4 ounces) condensed cream of celery soup, undiluted
1-1/4 cups water
3/4 cup process cheese sauce
1/2 cup Italian salad dressing
1/2 cup milk
Fresh red currants, optional

Place rice in a greased 13-in. x 9-in. x 2-in. baking dish. Top with the broccoli, onion, celery, parsley and salt. Arrange chicken over vegetables. In a saucepan, combine the soup, water, cheese sauce, salad dressing and milk. Cook and stir until cheese sauce is melted and mixture is smooth. Pour over chicken.

Cover and bake at 375° for 45 minutes. Uncover; bake 10-15 minutes longer or until chicken juices run clear and rice and vegetables are tender. Garnish with red currants if desired. **Yield:** 6 servings.

BEEF CLASSICS

Your family is sure to find
new favorites in this chapter
filled with hearty dishes
featuring pasta, rice, biscuits,
vegetables and more.
There are plenty of ways to
save money, too, because
many of these 44 casseroles
are made with ground beef.

FOUR-CHEESE LASAGNA (P. 57)

Sloppy Joe Pasta (p. 44)
Beef Potpie with Biscuits (p. 44)

SLOPPY JOE PASTA

(Pictured on page 43)

Since I found this recipe a few years ago, it's become a regular part of my menu plans.
My husband and our four kids love this quick-to-fix dish.
—Lynne Leih, Idyllwild, California

1 pound ground beef
1 envelope sloppy joe mix
1 cup water
1 can (8 ounces) tomato sauce
1 can (6 ounces) tomato paste
1 package (7 ounces) small shell
** pasta, cooked and drained**
1 cup small-curd cottage cheese
1/2 cup shredded cheddar cheese

In a large saucepan, cook beef over medium heat until no longer pink; drain. Stir in the sloppy joe mix, water, tomato sauce and tomato paste. Bring to a boil. Reduce heat; simmer, uncovered, for 5-10 minutes. Remove from the heat; stir in pasta.

Spoon half into a greased 2-1/2-qt. baking dish. Top with cottage cheese and remaining pasta mixture. Sprinkle with cheddar cheese. Bake, uncovered, at 350° for 30-35 minutes or until bubbly and cheese is melted. **Yield:** 4-6 servings.

PERFECT PARTNERS

To complete a casserole dinner, serve hot herbed rolls
and a simple fruit salad made of melon cubes,
sliced strawberries and green grapes.

BEEF POTPIE WITH BISCUITS

(Pictured on page 43)

I'm a stay-at-home mom who home-schools our three daughters, so my days are very busy.
I often rely on meal-in-one casseroles like this.
—Dolores Jensen, Arnold, Missouri

1-1/2 pounds boneless beef top round
** steak, cut into 1/2-inch cubes**
2 cups frozen peas and carrots,
** thawed**
1 large potato, peeled, cooked and
** diced**
1 medium onion, chopped
1 jar (18 ounces) beef gravy
1/2 teaspoon dried thyme
1/4 teaspoon pepper
1 tube (12 ounces) refrigerated
** buttermilk biscuits**

In a large skillet, cook beef over medium heat until no longer pink; drain. Stir in the vegetables, gravy, thyme and pepper. Transfer to a greased deep-dish pie plate or 11-in. x 7-in. x 2-in. baking dish. Bake, uncovered, at 400° for 25 minutes.

Place the biscuits in a single layer over meat mixture. Bake 10-15 minutes longer or until biscuits are golden brown. **Yield:** 6-8 servings.

BEEFY EGGPLANT PARMIGIANA

(Pictured below)

I developed this recipe one summer when my husband planted eggplant and tomatoes. I was thrilled when this special casserole won high honors at a national beef contest.
—Celeste Cooper, Baton Rouge, Louisiana

1/3 cup chopped onion
1/4 cup finely chopped celery
1 teaspoon dried parsley flakes
1/8 teaspoon garlic powder
2 tablespoons vegetable oil
1 can (14-1/2 ounces) Italian stewed
tomatoes
1/4 cup tomato paste
1/2 teaspoon dried oregano
1-1/4 teaspoons salt, *divided*
1/2 teaspoon pepper, *divided*
1 bay leaf
3/4 cup all-purpose flour
1 cup buttermilk
1 medium eggplant, peeled and cut
into 3/8-inch slices
Additional vegetable oil
1/2 cup grated Parmesan cheese
1 pound ground beef, cooked and
drained
2 cups (8 ounces) shredded
mozzarella cheese, *divided*
1-1/2 teaspoons minced fresh parsley

In a large saucepan, saute onion, celery, parsley and garlic powder in oil until tender. Stir in the tomatoes, tomato paste, oregano, 1/2 teaspoon salt, 1/4 teaspoon pepper and bay leaf. Bring to a boil. Reduce heat; cover and simmer for 1 hour. Discard bay leaf.

In a shallow dish, combine flour and remaining salt and pepper. Place buttermilk in another shallow dish. Dip eggplant in buttermilk, then in flour mixture.

In a large skillet, cook eggplant in batches in 1 in. of hot oil until golden brown on each side; drain. Place half of eggplant in a greased 13-in. x 9-in. x 2-in. baking dish. Top with half of Parmesan cheese, beef, tomato mixture and mozzarella cheese. Top with remaining eggplant, Parmesan cheese, beef and tomato mixture.

Bake, uncovered, at 350° for 30 minutes or until heated through. Sprinkle with the remaining mozzarella cheese. Bake 5-10 minutes longer or until cheese is melted. Let stand for 10 minutes before serving. Garnish with parsley. **Yield:** 8 servings.

HAMBURGER HOT DISH

Working full-time and attending school part-time leaves me little time for fancy meals.
My family enjoys hearty helpings of this casserole, alongside a salad, bread and dessert.
—Dawn Farris, Pekin, Illinois

    8 ounces uncooked elbow macaroni
    1 pound ground beef
    12 ounces process cheese (Velveeta),
       cubed
1-1/2 cups milk
    1 cup sliced fresh mushrooms
    1 cup diced seeded tomatoes
  1/3 cup sliced green onions
  1/8 teaspoon cayenne pepper
    2 tablespoons grated Parmesan
       cheese

Cook macaroni according to package directions. Meanwhile, in a skillet, cook beef over medium heat until no longer pink; drain. In a large saucepan, combine cheese and milk. Cook and stir over medium-low heat until cheese is melted and mixture is smooth. Stir in the beef, mushrooms, tomatoes, onions and cayenne; remove from the heat.

Drain macaroni and stir into beef mixture. Transfer to a greased 2-qt. baking dish. Cover and bake at 350° for 20 minutes. Uncover and stir mixture; sprinkle with Parmesan cheese. Bake 5-10 minutes longer or until bubbly. **Yield:** 6-8 servings.

PERFECT PARTNERS

For a quick dessert, top slices of purchased pound cake with
canned peaches and a scoop of vanilla ice cream.

MEAT AND POTATO CASSEROLE

For variety, you can use another kind of cream soup (cream of mushroom, for instance).
But try it this way first. I think you'll like it.
—Marna Heitz, Farley, Iowa

    3 to 4 cups thinly sliced peeled
       potatoes
    2 tablespoons butter *or* margarine,
       melted
  1/2 teaspoon salt
    1 pound ground beef
    1 package (10 ounces) frozen corn,
       thawed
    1 can (10-3/4 ounces) condensed
       cream of celery soup, undiluted
    1 cup (4 ounces) shredded cheddar
       cheese, *divided*
  1/3 cup milk
    1 tablespoon chopped onion
  1/4 teaspoon garlic powder
  1/8 teaspoon pepper
Minced fresh parsley, optional

Toss potatoes with butter and salt; arrange on the bottom and up the sides of a greased 11-in. x 7-in. x 2-in. baking dish. Bake, uncovered, at 400° for 25-30 minutes or until potatoes are almost tender.

Meanwhile, in a skillet, cook beef over medium heat until no longer pink; drain. Spoon beef and corn over potatoes. Combine the soup, 1/2 cup of cheese, milk, onion, garlic powder and pepper; pour over beef mixture.

Bake, uncovered, at 400° for 20 minutes or until vegetables are tender. Sprinkle with remaining cheese; bake 2-3 minutes longer or until cheese is melted. Sprinkle with parsley if desired. **Yield:** 6 servings.

BAKED BEEF STEW

(Pictured above)

*We get plenty of cold winter days here in the Midwest. Nothing
warms us up like this chunky oven-baked stew.*
—Joanne Wright, Niles, Michigan

1 can (14-1/2 ounces) diced tomatoes,
  undrained
3/4 cup water
1/4 cup red wine *or* beef broth
3 tablespoons quick-cooking tapioca
2 teaspoons sugar
1-1/2 teaspoons seasoned salt
1 teaspoon browning sauce, optional
1/2 teaspoon dried marjoram
1/2 teaspoon pepper
2 pounds lean beef stew meat, cut
  into 1-inch cubes
5 small red potatoes, quartered
4 medium carrots, cut into 1-inch
  chunks
2 celery ribs, cut into 3/4-inch chunks
1 medium onion, cut into chunks
1/2 cup soft bread crumbs
1 cup frozen peas, thawed

In a large bowl, combine the tomatoes, water, wine or broth, tapioca, sugar, seasoned salt, browning sauce if desired, marjoram and pepper. Let stand for 15 minutes. Add the meat, potatoes, carrots, celery, onion and bread crumbs.

Pour into a greased 13-in. x 9-in. x 2-in. baking dish. Cover and bake at 375° for 1-1/4 hours. Uncover; stir in peas. Bake 15-20 minutes longer or until meat and vegetables are tender. **Yield:** 6-8 servings.

FRIES 'N' BEEF BAKE

(Pictured below)

My family never turns down this casserole loaded with ground beef,
fries and flavor. The day after I make it, I reheat the leftovers for a quick meal.
—Doris Pfohl, St. Jacobs, Ontario

1 pound ground beef
1 medium onion, chopped
1 pound frozen crinkle-cut French
   fries, thawed
2 cups frozen peas, thawed
1 can (10-3/4 ounces) condensed
   cream of mushroom *or* cream of
   chicken soup, undiluted
3/4 cup water
2 tablespoons ketchup
1 teaspoon dried parsley flakes
1 teaspoon Worcestershire sauce
1/2 teaspoon dried marjoram
1/4 teaspoon ground mustard
Salt and pepper to taste

In a skillet, cook beef and onion over medium heat until meat is no longer pink; drain. In a greased 13-in. x 9-in. x 2-in. baking dish, layer half of the French fries, peas and meat mixture. Repeat layers.

In a bowl, combine the soup, water, ketchup, parsley, Worcestershire sauce, marjoram, mustard, salt and pepper. Pour over top. Bake, uncovered, at 350° for 45-50 minutes or until heated through. **Yield:** 6-8 servings.

BEEF PASTITSIO

My children love this dish, and it reheats beautifully...
when we do have any left over, that is!
—Sharon Drys, Shelburne, Ontario

1 pound ground beef
1 large onion, chopped
1 can (15 ounces) tomato sauce
1/2 teaspoon dried oregano
1/2 teaspoon salt
1/4 teaspoon pepper
1 garlic clove, minced
2 cups uncooked elbow macaroni
1 cup (4 ounces) shredded cheddar
  cheese
1 egg, beaten
CHEESE SAUCE:
3 tablespoons butter *or* margarine,
  melted
3 tablespoons all-purpose flour
1-1/2 cups milk
1 cup (4 ounces) shredded cheddar
  cheese
1/2 teaspoon salt

In a skillet, cook beef and onion over medium heat until meat is no longer pink; drain. Stir in the tomato sauce, oregano, salt, pepper and garlic. Bring to a boil. Reduce heat; cover and simmer for 15 minutes.

Meanwhile, cook macaroni according to package directions; drain. Combine the macaroni, cheese and egg; set aside.

For cheese sauce, melt the butter in a saucepan. Stir in flour until smooth. Gradually add milk. Bring to a boil; cook and stir for 2 minutes or until thickened. Remove from the heat; stir in cheese and salt.

Spoon half of macaroni mixture into a greased 13-in. x 9-in. x 2-in. baking dish. Top with meat mixture and remaining macaroni. Spoon cheese sauce over macaroni. Bake, uncovered, at 350° for 30 minutes or until heated through. Let stand for 5-10 minutes before serving. **Yield:** 6-8 servings.

ORANGE-FLAVORED BEEF AND POTATOES

This stick-to-your-ribs dish has never failed me. While it's baking,
I can prepare a simple vegetable side dish or salad to complete the meal.
—Paula Pelis Marchesi, Rocky Point, New York

2 green onions, sliced
3 tablespoons soy sauce
2 tablespoons water
2 tablespoons white wine *or*
  additional water
1 tablespoon sugar
4 teaspoons vegetable oil, *divided*
1 tablespoon orange juice
1 teaspoon grated orange peel
1 teaspoon white wine vinegar *or*
  cider vinegar
3/4 teaspoon ground ginger *or* 1
  tablespoon minced fresh gingerroot
1 tablespoon quick-cooking tapioca
1-1/2 pounds beef stew meat, cut into
  1-inch cubes
1 pound small red potatoes,
  quartered

In a bowl, combine the green onions, soy sauce, water, wine or additional water, sugar, 3 teaspoons oil, orange juice, peel, vinegar and ginger. Stir in tapioca and let stand for 15 minutes.

Place the beef and potatoes in a greased 11-in. x 7-in. x 2-in. baking dish. Pour tapioca mixture over the top. Cover and bake at 350° for 2 hours or until meat is tender. **Yield:** 6 servings.

SPAGHETTI HOT DISH

*My grandmother, mom and aunt inspired me to start cooking when I was a young girl.
It's still a favorite pastime. This creamy, chow-mein-like casserole is sure to please.*
—Barb Miller, Concord, Michigan

1 pound lean ground beef
2 medium onions, diced
3 celery ribs with leaves, diced
1/4 cup butter *or* margarine
5 tablespoons all-purpose flour
Salt and pepper to taste
3-1/2 cups milk
2 tablespoons chopped pimientos
1 to 2 teaspoons soy sauce
1-1/4 cups broken spaghetti, cooked and
    drained
1 cup finely crushed butter-flavored
    crackers (about 25 crackers)

In a large skillet, cook beef, onions and celery in butter over medium heat until meat is no longer pink and vegetables are tender. Stir in the flour, salt and pepper until blended. Gradually add the milk, pimientos and soy sauce. Bring to a boil; cook and stir for 2 minutes or until thickened. Stir in spaghetti; mix well.

Transfer to a greased 11-in. x 7-in. x 2-in. baking dish. Sprinkle with cracker crumbs. Bake, uncovered, at 350° for 30-35 minutes or until heated through. **Yield:** 4 servings.

PERFECT PARTNERS

*For a pretty but easy dessert, layer instant tapioca pudding in
parfait glasses with fresh strawberries, raspberries or blueberries.
Dollop with whipped cream, then garnish with whole berries.*

SPICY CABBAGE CASSEROLE

*This is a deliciously different main course and so easy to prepare.
Best of all, you can put it in the oven and forget about it.*
—Georgia Kelly, Houma, Louisiana

1 small head cabbage, finely chopped
1 pound lean ground beef
1 can (14-1/2 ounces) Mexican diced
    tomatoes, undrained
1 can (10-1/2 ounces) condensed
    French onion soup, undiluted
1 cup uncooked long grain rice
1 large onion, chopped
1 medium green pepper, chopped
1/2 cup vegetable oil
1 egg, lightly beaten
3 teaspoons salt
3 teaspoons garlic salt
3 teaspoons chili powder
Dash cayenne pepper

In a large bowl, combine all ingredients; mix well. Pour into a greased 3-qt. baking dish. Cover and bake at 350° for 1-1/2 hours or until meat is no longer pink and rice is tender. **Yield:** 6 servings.

PARTY BEEF CASSEROLE

(Pictured above)

Round steak is economical and delicious. That's why I was thrilled to find the recipe for this comforting meal-in-one casserole. With a salad and rolls, it's a hearty dinner.
—Kelly Hardgrave, Hartman, Arkansas

3 tablespoons all-purpose flour
1 teaspoon salt
1/2 teaspoon pepper
2 pounds boneless beef round steak, cut into 1/2-inch cubes
2 tablespoons vegetable oil
1 cup water
1/2 cup beef broth
1 garlic clove, minced
1 tablespoon dried minced onion
1/2 teaspoon dried thyme
1/4 teaspoon dried rosemary, crushed
2 cups sliced fresh mushrooms
2 cups frozen peas, thawed
3 cups mashed potatoes (prepared with milk and butter)
1 tablespoon butter *or* margarine, melted
Paprika

In a large resealable plastic bag, combine flour, salt and pepper; add beef in batches and shake to coat. In a skillet, brown beef in oil over medium heat. Transfer to a greased shallow 2-1/2-qt. baking dish.

To skillet, add the water, broth, garlic, onion, thyme and rosemary; bring to a boil. Reduce heat; simmer, uncovered, for 5 minutes. Stir in mushrooms. Pour over meat and mix well.

Cover and bake at 350° for 1-1/2 to 1-3/4 hours or until meat is tender. Sprinkle with peas. Spread potatoes evenly over the top. Brush with butter; sprinkle with paprika. Bake 15-20 minutes longer or until potatoes are heated through. **Yield:** 6-8 servings.

CRESCENT-TOPPED CASSEROLE

(Pictured at right)

My husband is a fairly picky eater but he requests this dish for dinner at least once a month.
I keep the ingredients on hand for last-minute preparation.
—Tranna Foley, Columbia, Missouri

2 pounds ground beef
1/4 cup chopped onion
2 cans (8 ounces *each*) tomato sauce
1 envelope spaghetti sauce mix
3/4 cup sour cream
2 cups (8 ounces) shredded
  mozzarella cheese
1 tube (8 ounces) refrigerated
  crescent rolls
2 tablespoons butter *or* margarine,
  melted
1/3 cup grated Parmesan cheese

In a large skillet, cook beef and onion over medium heat until meat is no longer pink; drain. Stir in tomato sauce and spaghetti sauce mix. Reduce heat; simmer, uncovered, for 5 minutes. Remove from the heat; stir in sour cream. Spoon into a greased 13-in. x 9-in. x 2-in. baking dish. Sprinkle with mozzarella cheese.

Unroll crescent dough into one rectangle; seal seams and perforations. Place over cheese. Brush with butter and sprinkle with Parmesan cheese. Bake, uncovered, at 375° for 25-30 minutes or until golden brown. **Yield:** 6-8 servings.

ZUCCHINI BEEF BAKE

(Pictured at right)

Zucchini is a favorite vegetable for cooks because it can be used in countless ways.
Here it teams up with ground beef, rice and cheese for a pretty, palate-pleasing meal.
—Christy Saniga, Tacoma, Washington

6 cups water
4 cups sliced zucchini
1 pound ground beef
1 large onion, chopped
1 garlic clove, minced
2 cups cooked rice
1 can (8 ounces) tomato sauce
1 cup small-curd cottage cheese
1 egg, lightly beaten
1-1/2 teaspoons minced fresh oregano
  or 1/2 teaspoon dried oregano
1 teaspoon minced fresh basil *or* 1/4
  teaspoon dried basil
1/2 teaspoon salt
1 cup (4 ounces) shredded cheddar
  cheese

In a large saucepan, bring water to a boil. Add the zucchini. Return to a boil. Reduce heat; cover and simmer for 3 minutes or just until tender. Drain and immediately place zucchini in ice water. Drain and pat dry.

In a skillet, cook the beef, onion and garlic over medium heat until meat is no longer pink; drain. Stir in the rice, tomato sauce, cottage cheese, egg, oregano, basil and salt.

Arrange half of the zucchini in a greased 13-in. x 9-in. x 2-in. baking dish. Top with meat mixture. Arrange remaining zucchini over top; sprinkle with cheddar cheese. Bake, uncovered, at 350° for 25-30 minutes or until bubbly and cheese is melted. **Yield:** 6-8 servings.

CRESCENT-TOPPED CASSEROLE
ZUCCHINI BEEF BAKE

BISCUIT-TOPPED ITALIAN CASSEROLE

(Pictured above and on back cover)

*A saucy beef and vegetable mixture is topped with herb biscuits
to create a mouth-watering one-dish dinner.
—Kathy Ravis, Vermilion, Ohio*

1 pound ground beef
1 can (8 ounces) tomato sauce
3/4 cup water
1/4 teaspoon pepper
1 package (10 ounces) frozen mixed
  vegetables
2 cups (8 ounces) shredded cheddar
  cheese, *divided*
1 tube (12 ounces) refrigerated
  buttermilk biscuits
1 tablespoon butter *or* margarine,
  melted
1/2 teaspoon dried oregano

In a large skillet, cook beef over medium heat until no longer pink; drain. Stir in the tomato sauce, water and pepper. Bring to a boil. Reduce heat; cover and simmer for 15 minutes. Remove from the heat. Stir in vegetables and 1-1/2 cups cheese. Transfer to a greased 13-in. x 9-in. x 2-in. baking dish.

Split each biscuit in half. Arrange biscuits around edge of dish, overlapping slightly; brush with butter and sprinkle with oregano. Sprinkle remaining cheese over the meat mixture. Bake, uncovered, at 375° for 25-30 minutes or until the biscuits are golden brown. **Yield:** 6-8 servings.

BEEFY SPINACH NOODLE BAKE

I enjoy trying new, uncomplicated dishes, and when I find a winner like this, I'm eager to share the recipe. I round out the meal with steamed buttered carrots and oven-fresh rolls.
—Priscilla Gilber, Indian Harbour Beach, Florida

1 pound ground beef
1 small onion, chopped
4-3/4 cups uncooked wide egg noodles
1 can (10-3/4 ounces) condensed
    cream of mushroom soup, undiluted
3/4 cup milk
SPINACH LAYER:
    3 tablespoons butter *or* margarine
    2 tablespoons all-purpose flour
    1/2 teaspoon paprika
    1/2 teaspoon salt
    1/4 teaspoon pepper
    1/8 teaspoon ground nutmeg
    1 cup milk
    2 packages (10 ounces *each*) frozen
        chopped spinach, thawed and
        squeezed dry
    1/4 cup thinly sliced green onions
    2 cups (8 ounces) shredded Swiss
        cheese, *divided*
2/3 cup crushed french-fried onions

In a skillet, cook beef and onion over medium heat until meat is no longer pink; drain. Cook noodles according to package directions; drain. In a large bowl, combine soup and milk until blended. Stir in beef mixture and noodles; set aside.

For spinach layer, in a large saucepan, melt butter. Whisk in flour, paprika, salt, pepper and nutmeg until smooth. Gradually whisk in milk. Bring to a boil; cook and stir for 1-2 minutes or until thickened. Stir in spinach and green onions.

In a greased shallow 2-1/2-qt. baking dish, layer half of beef mixture and half of cheese. Top with spinach mixture and remaining beef mixture. Cover and bake at 375° for 35 minutes. Uncover; sprinkle with remaining cheese. Top with french-fried onions. Bake 5-10 minutes longer or until cheese is melted. **Yield:** 6-8 servings.

DINNER IN A DISH

I haven't found anyone yet who can resist this saucy casserole topped with mashed potatoes. The frozen peas and canned tomatoes add color and make a helping or two a complete meal.
—Betty Sitzman, Wray, Colorado

2 pounds ground beef
1 medium onion, chopped
2 tablespoons all-purpose flour
2 cans (14-1/2 ounces *each*) diced
    tomatoes, undrained
3 cups frozen peas
2/3 cup ketchup
1/4 cup minced fresh parsley
2 teaspoons dried marjoram
2 teaspoons beef bouillon granules
1 teaspoon salt
1/2 teaspoon pepper
6 cups hot mashed potatoes
    (prepared with milk and butter)
2 eggs, beaten

In a large skillet, cook beef and onion over medium heat until meat is no longer pink; drain. Sprinkle with flour. Stir in the next eight ingredients. Bring to a boil; cook and stir for 2 minutes or until thickened.

Pour into an ungreased shallow 3-qt. baking dish. Combine potatoes and eggs; mix well. Drop by 1/2 cupfuls over beef mixture. Bake, uncovered, at 350° for 35-40 minutes or until bubbly and potatoes are golden brown. **Yield:** 10-12 servings.

BEEF AND RICE FOR TWO

*Many casseroles make enough to feed a crowd, but this easy recipe
is perfectly portioned for two people. It's a great find.*
—Emma Magielda, Amsterdam, New York

2/3 cup uncooked long grain rice
1 tablespoon vegetable oil
2 cups water
2 teaspoons beef bouillon granules
2 celery ribs, thinly sliced
1 small green pepper, chopped
1 small onion, chopped
2 teaspoons soy sauce
1-1/2 cups cubed cooked beef

In a large saucepan over medium heat, saute rice in oil until golden brown. Add the water, bouillon, celery, green pepper, onion and soy sauce. Bring to a boil. Reduce heat; cover and simmer for 15 minutes.

Stir in the beef. Cover and simmer for 5-10 minutes or until rice and vegetables are tender. **Yield:** 2 servings.

ROUND STEAK 'N' DUMPLINGS

*My husband and I both grew up on farms and enjoyed lots of down-home dumplings and gravy.
This is my own meaty version of the dishes our moms made.*
—Fancheon Resler, Goshen, Indiana

1/3 cup all-purpose flour
1 teaspoon paprika
2 pounds boneless beef round steak,
   cut into 1/2-inch cubes
2 cups frozen pearl onions, thawed
1/4 cup vegetable oil
2-1/2 cups water
1/2 teaspoon salt
1/4 teaspoon pepper
1 can (10-3/4 ounces) condensed
   cream of mushroom soup, undiluted
2 jars (4-1/2 ounces *each*) whole
   mushrooms, drained
DUMPLINGS:
2 cups all-purpose flour
4 teaspoons baking powder
1 teaspoon dried minced onion
1 teaspoon celery seed
1 teaspoon poultry seasoning
1/2 teaspoon salt
1/2 teaspoon rubbed sage
1 cup milk
1/4 cup vegetable oil
1-1/2 cups soft bread crumbs
1/4 cup butter *or* margarine, melted

In a large resealable plastic bag, combine the flour and paprika; add beef in batches and shake to coat. In a Dutch oven, cook beef and onions in oil over medium heat until meat is no longer pink. Add the water, salt and pepper; bring to a boil. Reduce heat; cover and simmer for 35-45 minutes. Stir in soup and mushrooms.

For dumplings, combine the first seven ingredients in a bowl. Stir in milk and oil just until moistened. In a shallow dish, combine bread crumbs and butter. Drop heaping tablespoonfuls of dumpling batter into crumb mixture; turn to coat. Transfer hot beef mixture to a greased 2-1/2-qt. baking dish. Top with dumplings.

Bake, uncovered, at 425° for 25-30 minutes or until bubbly and golden brown and a toothpick inserted in dumplings comes out clean. **Yield:** 8 servings.

FOUR-CHEESE LASAGNA

(Pictured below and on page 42)

This cheese-packed lasagna can be prepared ahead of time and baked later. I sometimes make up a couple batches and freeze them in case company drops by.
—Janet Myers, Napanee, Ontario

1 pound ground beef
1 medium onion, chopped
2 garlic cloves, minced
1 can (28 ounces) diced tomatoes, undrained
1 jar (6 ounces) sliced mushrooms, drained
1 can (6 ounces) tomato paste
1 teaspoon salt
1 teaspoon dried oregano
1 teaspoon dried basil
1/2 teaspoon pepper
1/2 teaspoon fennel seed
2 eggs
2 cups (16 ounces) small-curd cottage cheese
2/3 cup grated Parmesan cheese
1/4 cup shredded cheddar cheese
1-1/2 cups (6 ounces) shredded mozzarella cheese, *divided*
1 package (16 ounces) lasagna noodles, cooked and drained

In a skillet, cook beef, onion and garlic over medium heat until meat is no longer pink; drain. Place tomatoes in a blender; cover and process until smooth. Add to beef mixture; stir in the mushrooms, tomato paste and seasonings. Bring to a boil. Reduce heat; cover and simmer for 15 minutes.

In a bowl, combine the eggs, cottage cheese, Parmesan, cheddar cheese and 1/2 cup mozzarella. Spread 2 cups meat sauce in an ungreased 13-in. x 9-in. x 2-in. baking dish. Arrange half of the noodles over sauce. Spread with cottage cheese mixture; top with remaining noodles and meat sauce.

Cover and bake at 350° for 45 minutes. Uncover; sprinkle with the remaining mozzarella. Bake 15 minutes longer or until cheese is melted. **Yield:** 12 servings.

POTATO-TOPPED CASSEROLE

My family enjoys this basic, comforting casserole because it always satisfies.
I sometimes stir in sliced black olives.
—Cheryl Buker, Eagle, Colorado

2 pounds ground beef
2 cans (8 ounces *each*) tomato sauce
1 cup sliced fresh mushrooms,
   optional
2 garlic cloves, minced
Salt and pepper to taste
4 cups hot mashed potatoes
   (prepared with milk and butter)
2 cups (8 ounces) shredded cheddar
   cheese

In a large skillet, cook beef over medium heat until no longer pink; drain. Stir in the tomato sauce, mushrooms if desired, garlic, salt and pepper.

Transfer to a greased 13-in. x 9-in. x 2-in. baking dish. Top with potatoes; sprinkle with cheese. Bake, uncovered, at 350° for 35-40 minutes or until heated through and cheese is melted. **Yield:** 8-10 servings.

CABBAGE HAMBURGER BAKE

You'll need only five ingredients to make this economical casserole. White rice,
potatoes or bread would make a nice accompaniment.
—Mildred Klein, Richfield, Minnesota

1 pound ground beef
1 medium onion, chopped
1 to 1-1/2 teaspoons salt
1 medium head cabbage, chopped
1 can (10-3/4 ounces) condensed
   tomato soup, undiluted

In a skillet, cook beef and onion over medium heat until meat is no longer pink; drain. Stir in salt. In a greased 2-1/2-qt. baking dish, layer half of the beef mixture, cabbage and soup. Repeat layers (dish will be full). Cover and bake at 350° for 50-60 minutes or until cabbage is tender. Serve with a slotted spoon. **Yield:** 4 servings.

GROUND BEEF DRESSING

As is true with most families, food is an important part of all our celebrations.
That's why I know everyone at your table will savor this delicious dressing.
—Lynn Ireland, Lebanon, Wisconsin

1 pound ground beef
1 medium onion, chopped
1 medium tart apple, chopped
2 celery ribs, chopped
8 cups bread cubes
1 tablespoon poultry seasoning
1 teaspoon salt
1/2 teaspoon pepper
2 cups chicken broth

In a Dutch oven, cook beef over medium heat until no longer pink; drain. Stir in the remaining ingredients.

Transfer to a greased 3-qt. baking dish. Cover and bake at 325° for 1-1/2 hours. Uncover; bake 10 minutes longer or until lightly browned. **Yield:** 16 servings.

DOUBLE-CHEESE BEEF PASTA

Provolone and mozzarella cheeses star in this comforting pasta dish. My mother shared the recipe with me when I was married more than 50 years ago.
—Marilyn Pearson, Billings, Montana

2-1/2 cups uncooked medium shell pasta
2 pounds ground beef
2 medium onions, chopped
1 jar (14 ounces) spaghetti sauce
1 can (14-1/2 ounces) stewed tomatoes, undrained and finely chopped
1 jar (4-1/2 ounces) sliced mushrooms, drained
1 garlic clove, minced
1 teaspoon salt
1/2 teaspoon pepper
2 cups (16 ounces) sour cream
1 package (6 ounces) sliced provolone cheese
1 cup (4 ounces) shredded mozzarella cheese

Cook pasta according to package directions. Meanwhile, in a large skillet, cook beef and onions over medium heat until meat is no longer pink; drain. Add the spaghetti sauce, tomatoes, mushrooms, garlic, salt and pepper. Bring to a boil. Reduce heat; simmer, uncovered, for 20 minutes, stirring occasionally.

Drain pasta; place half in a greased 3-qt. baking dish. Top with half of the beef mixture. Layer with sour cream and provolone cheese. Top with remaining pasta and beef mixture. Sprinkle with mozzarella cheese. Cover and bake at 350° for 40 minutes. Uncover; bake 5-10 minutes longer or until cheese is melted. **Yield:** 6-8 servings.

TIMELY TIP

To save time, buy packages of cheese that's already sliced or shredded. If you'd rather save money, buy blocks of cheese and slice or shred your own.

SKILLET CASSEROLE

If my family and friends gave out blue ribbons for their favorite casserole dish, this one would win a fistful!
—Joan Govier, Victoria Harbour, Ontario

1 pound ground beef
2 medium onions, diced
1 medium green pepper, diced
4 medium potatoes, peeled, cubed and cooked
2 medium tomatoes, seeded and chopped
1 can (10-3/4 ounces) condensed cream of chicken soup, undiluted
1/4 cup chili sauce
3/4 teaspoon salt
1/4 teaspoon pepper
1/4 cup grated Parmesan cheese

In a large skillet, cook beef, onions and green pepper over medium heat until meat is no longer pink; drain. Stir in the potatoes, tomatoes, soup, chili sauce, salt and pepper.

Transfer to a greased 13-in. x 9-in. x 2-in. baking dish. Sprinkle with Parmesan. Bake, uncovered, at 350° for 15 minutes or until bubbly. **Yield:** 4 servings.

ZIPPY BEEF BAKE

With its south-of-the-border flavor, this filling meal is a much-requested recipe in our home. In fact, we like it so much, we have it about once a week!
—Gay Kelley, Tucson, Arizona

3/4 pound ground beef
2 medium zucchini, thinly sliced
1/4 pound fresh mushrooms, sliced
2 tablespoons sliced green onions
1 tablespoon butter *or* margarine
1-1/2 cups cooked rice
1 can (4 ounces) chopped green chilies
1/2 cup sour cream
1 cup (4 ounces) shredded Monterey Jack cheese, *divided*
1-1/2 teaspoons chili powder
1 teaspoon salt
1/8 teaspoon garlic powder

In a large skillet, cook beef over medium heat until no longer pink; drain. In another skillet, saute the zucchini, mushrooms and onions in butter until tender; drain. Add to the beef. Stir in the rice, chilies, sour cream, 1/2 cup cheese and seasonings.

Transfer to a greased 2-qt. baking dish; sprinkle with remaining cheese. Bake, uncovered, at 350° for 20 minutes or until cheese is melted. **Yield:** 4 servings.

BEEF AND BISCUIT STEW

This easy-to-prepare dish is a meal in itself. That made it high on my mother's list of favorites— she had to cook for nine children! My brothers, sisters and I loved it, too.
—Sylvia Sonneborn, York, Pennsylvania

3 tablespoons all-purpose flour
2 pounds beef stew meat, cut into 1-inch cubes
2 tablespoons vegetable oil
2 teaspoons beef bouillon granules
2 cups boiling water
Salt and pepper to taste
6 to 8 small potatoes, peeled and quartered
3 small onions, quartered
4 medium carrots, sliced
1 package (10 ounces) frozen cut green beans, thawed
2 tablespoons cornstarch
1/4 cup cold water
BISCUIT DOUGH:
2 cups all-purpose flour
4 teaspoons baking powder
1/2 teaspoon salt
2 tablespoons vegetable oil
3/4 to 1 cup milk
Melted butter *or* margarine

Place the flour in a large resealable plastic bag; add beef in batches and shake to coat. In a Dutch oven, brown beef in oil over medium heat. Meanwhile, dissolve bouillon in boiling water; add to pan. Season with salt and pepper. Cover and simmer for 1-1/2 to 2 hours or until the meat is tender.

Add the potatoes, onions, carrots and beans; cover and cook until vegetables are tender, about 35 minutes. Combine cornstarch and cold water until smooth; stir into stew. Bring to a boil; cook and stir for 2 minutes or until thickened.

For biscuits, combine the flour, baking powder, salt and oil. Stir in enough milk to form a soft dough. Drop by tablespoonfuls over simmering stew. Brush dough with melted butter. Bake, uncovered, at 350° for 20-30 minutes or until a toothpick inserted into a biscuit comes out clean. **Yield:** 8-10 servings.

ONION-TOPPED HOT DISH

(Pictured above)

With ground beef, vegetables, potatoes and onion rings, one hearty serving of this dish satisfies hunger in a hurry.
—Marilisa Fagerlind, Glidden, Iowa

1-1/2 pounds ground beef
   1 package (16 ounces) frozen California-blend vegetables, thawed
   1 can (10-3/4 ounces) condensed cheddar cheese soup, undiluted
   1 cup (4 ounces) shredded mozzarella cheese
1/2 cup milk
1/2 teaspoon salt
1/4 teaspoon pepper
   1 package (32 ounces) frozen hash brown potatoes, thawed
1/4 cup butter *or* margarine, melted
1/2 teaspoon seasoned salt
 20 frozen large onion rings
   1 cup (4 ounces) shredded cheddar cheese

In a large skillet, cook beef over medium heat until no longer pink; drain. Stir in the vegetables, soup, mozzarella cheese, milk, salt and pepper. Transfer to a greased 13-in. x 9-in. x 2-in. baking dish. Sprinkle with potatoes; drizzle with butter. Top with seasoned salt and onion rings.

Cover and bake at 350° for 45-50 minutes or until heated through. Uncover; sprinkle with cheddar cheese. Bake 3-5 minutes longer or until cheese is melted. **Yield:** 6-8 servings.

COUNTRY GOULASH SKILLET

(Pictured below)

I've found that basic recipes like this never go out of style. My homegrown onions, peppers and corn make every bite extra-special.
—Lisa Neubert, South Ogden, Utah

1 pound ground beef
1 can (28 ounces) stewed tomatoes
1 can (10-3/4 ounces) condensed cream of mushroom soup, undiluted
2 cups fresh *or* frozen corn
1 medium green pepper, chopped
1 medium onion, chopped
1 tablespoon Worcestershire sauce
3 cups cooked elbow macaroni

In a large skillet, cook beef over medium heat until no longer pink; drain. Stir in the tomatoes, soup, corn, green pepper, onion and Worcestershire sauce. Bring to a boil. Reduce heat; cover and simmer for 20-25 minutes or until vegetables are tender. Stir in macaroni and heat through. **Yield:** 6-8 servings.

PEPPY POTATO CASSEROLE

Packaged potatoes give me a head start preparing this pizza-like dish.
Pepperoni adds just the right amount of spice.
—Joanna Goodman, Conway, Arkansas

2 cans (8 ounces *each*) tomato sauce
1-1/2 cups water
1-1/2 teaspoons Italian seasoning
1 package (5 ounces) scalloped
  potato mix
1/2 pound ground beef
24 pepperoni slices
4 ounces sliced provolone cheese
1/2 cup shredded mozzarella cheese
1 tablespoon grated Parmesan cheese

In a large saucepan, combine the tomato sauce, water and Italian seasoning; bring to a boil. Add potatoes with contents of sauce mix. Transfer to an ungreased 2-qt. baking dish.

In a skillet, cook beef over medium heat until no longer pink; drain. Spoon over potatoes; top with pepperoni. Bake, uncovered, at 400° for 20 minutes. Top with cheeses. Bake 15-20 minutes longer or until potatoes are tender. **Yield:** 4 servings.

PERFECT PARTNERS

Oven Stew and Biscuits is a super one-pot supper for a chilly night.
Serve with a tossed green salad and warm apple cider.

OVEN STEW AND BISCUITS

Soy sauce and sesame seeds give this hearty casserole a slight Oriental twist.
The recipe comes from my brother, who was a wonderful cook.
—Bertha Brookmeier, El Cajon, California

1/3 cup all-purpose flour
1 teaspoon salt
1/2 teaspoon pepper
2 pounds boneless beef top sirloin,
  cut into 1-inch cubes
1/4 cup vegetable oil
1 can (14-1/2 ounces) stewed
  tomatoes
1 jar (4-1/2 ounces) sliced
  mushrooms, drained
1 large onion, thinly sliced
3 tablespoons soy sauce
3 tablespoons molasses
1 medium green pepper, cut into
  1-inch pieces
1 tube (12 ounces) refrigerated
  buttermilk biscuits
1 tablespoon butter *or* margarine,
  melted
Sesame seeds

Combine the flour, salt and pepper in a large resealable plastic bag. Add beef in batches; shake to coat. In a large skillet, brown beef in oil over medium heat. Stir in the tomatoes, mushrooms, onion, soy sauce and molasses.

Transfer to a greased 13-in. x 9-in. x 2-in. baking dish. Cover and bake at 375° for 20 minutes. Stir in the green pepper. Cover and bake 10 minutes longer. Uncover; top with biscuits. Brush biscuits with butter; sprinkle with sesame seeds. Bake 15-18 minutes more or until the biscuits are golden brown. **Yield:** 6-8 servings.

Swiss Steak Dinner

(Pictured at right)

I came across this recipe in the 1950s, and it's served me well ever since. As this meaty meal bakes, the aroma gets our mouths watering!
—Gloria Cross, Cupertino, California

1/2 cup all-purpose flour
2 teaspoons salt, *divided*
1/2 teaspoon pepper
2 pounds boneless beef round steak (1/2 inch thick), cut into serving-size pieces
2 to 3 tablespoons vegetable oil
6 medium onions, thinly sliced
7 to 9 small red potatoes (about 1-1/4 pounds), halved
1 bay leaf
1 can (10-3/4 ounces) condensed tomato soup, undiluted
2 cups frozen cut green beans, thawed

In a large resealable plastic bag, combine the flour, 1-1/2 teaspoons salt and pepper. Add beef in batches and shake to coat. In a large skillet over medium heat, brown beef in oil on both sides. Transfer to a greased 3-qt. baking dish. Top with onions and potatoes. Sprinkle with remaining salt; gently toss to coat. Add the bay leaf. Spoon soup over top.

Cover and bake at 350° for 1-1/2 hours. Place beans around edge of dish. Bake 15-20 minutes longer or until meat and vegetables are tender. Discard bay leaf. **Yield:** 6 servings.

Super Supper

My children love the combination of ground beef, pasta and cheesy sauce in this dish. I especially appreciate its ease of preparation.
—Jane Hartery, Sarasota, Florida

1 pound ground beef
1 small onion, chopped
3/4 cup water
1 can (6 ounces) tomato paste
1 teaspoon salt
1/2 teaspoon garlic powder
1 package (8 ounces) cream cheese, cubed
3/4 cup milk
1/2 cup grated Parmesan cheese
7 cups cooked egg noodles

In a skillet, cook beef and onion over medium heat until meat is no longer pink; drain. Add the water, tomato paste, salt and garlic powder. Bring to a boil. Reduce heat; cover and simmer for 5-7 minutes or until heated through.

In a small saucepan, melt cream cheese over low heat, stirring constantly. Gradually stir in milk and Parmesan cheese until blended.

Place noodles in a greased 13-in. x 9-in. x 2-in. baking dish. Spread meat sauce over noodles. Spoon cream cheese mixture evenly over top. Bake, uncovered, at 350° for 30-35 minutes or until heated through. **Yield:** 6 servings.

Helpful Hint

Sliced or chopped onions can be frozen in a heavy-duty resealable plastic bag or airtight container for up to 3 months. Thaw and blot dry before sauteing.

SWISS STEAK DINNER

BEEF AND CORN CASSEROLE

(Pictured above)

*This recipe was passed down from my mother. It's now a stand-by for me as well as
our three grown daughters. It's a great dish to pass at potlucks.*
—Ruth Jost, Clear Lake, Iowa

1 package (10 ounces) fine egg
  noodles
1 pound ground beef
1 medium onion, chopped
1 can (15-1/4 ounces) whole kernel
  corn, drained
1 can (10-3/4 ounces) condensed
  tomato soup, undiluted
1 cup water
1 cup diced process cheese (Velveeta)
1/2 medium green pepper, chopped
1 medium carrot, thinly sliced
1 teaspoon salt
1/2 teaspoon pepper

Cook noodles according to package directions; drain. In a large skillet, cook beef and onion over medium heat until meat is no longer pink; drain. Add the noodles and remaining ingredients.

Transfer to a greased 13-in. x 9-in. x 2-in. baking dish. Cover and bake at 325° for 30 minutes. Uncover; bake 30-35 minutes longer or until bubbly. **Yield:** 8-10 servings.

WILD RICE HOT DISH

This recipe is actually a combination of two recipes I received from friends.
I've had many requests for it.
—Sandra McWithey, South St. Paul, Minnesota

3 cups boiling water
1 cup uncooked wild rice
1-1/2 pounds ground beef
1 medium onion, chopped
1 can (28 ounces) bean sprouts,
   drained
2 cans (10-3/4 ounces *each*)
   condensed cream of chicken soup,
   undiluted
1 can (10-1/2 ounces) condensed beef
   broth, undiluted
1-1/2 cups water
2 jars (4-1/2 ounces *each*) sliced
   mushrooms, drained
1/4 cup soy sauce
1 bay leaf
1 tablespoon dried parsley flakes
1/4 teaspoon *each* celery salt, onion
   salt, poultry seasoning, garlic
   powder, paprika and pepper
1/8 teaspoon dried thyme
1/2 cup sliced almonds

In a large bowl, pour boiling water over rice; let stand for 15 minutes. Meanwhile, in a skillet, cook beef and onion over medium heat until meat is no longer pink; drain. Drain rice. Stir in the beef mixture, bean sprouts, soup, broth, water, mushrooms, soy sauce and seasonings.

Transfer to a greased 13-in. x 9-in. x 2-in. baking dish. Cover and bake at 350° for 2 hours. Uncover; sprinkle with almonds. Bake 30 minutes longer or until rice is tender. Discard bay leaf. **Yield:** 8-10 servings.

SERVING SUGGESTION

A mixture of cauliflower, broccoli and carrots would add color to your table and complement the taste of Wild Rice Hot Dish.

SAUERKRAUT BEEF SUPPER

When I was growing up, my mother made this old-fashioned dish to mark the beginning of fall.
Her light-as-air rolls and creamy custard raisin pie were wonderful accompaniments.
—Carol Ann Cassaday, St. Louis, Missouri

1 pound uncooked lean ground beef
2/3 cup finely chopped fully cooked
   ham
2 cups cooked long grain rice
1-1/4 cups finely chopped onions, *divided*
1-1/4 teaspoons salt, *divided*
1/4 teaspoon pepper, *divided*
1 can (14 ounces) sauerkraut, rinsed
   and drained
1/2 teaspoon sugar
1 bacon strip, diced

In a bowl, combine the beef, ham, rice, 3/4 cup onions, 1 teaspoon salt and 1/8 teaspoon pepper; mix gently.

In a greased 2-1/2-qt. baking dish, place half of sauerkraut; sprinkle with half of the remaining onions. Top with meat mixture, remaining sauerkraut and onions. Sprinkle with sugar and remaining salt and pepper. Top with bacon. Cover and bake at 375° for 65-70 minutes or until hot and bubbly. **Yield:** 6 servings.

SLOPPY JOE CASSEROLE

As a working mom, I need all the time-saving recipes I can get. My two sons
prefer this all-in-one dish to sloppy joe sandwiches.
—Carol Knight, Norris City, Illinois

1 pound ground beef
3 cups cooked rice
1 can (15-1/2 ounces) sloppy joe
   sauce
1 can (15-1/4 ounces) whole kernel
   corn, drained
1 can (4 ounces) mushroom stems
   and pieces, drained
1 teaspoon seasoned salt
1/2 cup shredded mozzarella cheese

In a large skillet, cook beef over medium heat until no longer pink; drain. Stir in the rice, sloppy joe sauce, corn, mushrooms and seasoned salt.

Transfer to a greased 2-qt. baking dish. Cover and bake at 350° for 30 minutes. Uncover; sprinkle with cheese. Bake 5-10 minutes longer or until cheese is melted. **Yield:** 4-6 servings.

PERFECT PARTNERS

For a super side dish, steam 1 to 2 pounds of broccoli florets.
Melt 1/4 cup butter; add 1 tablespoon sesame seeds and
2 tablespoons soy sauce. Drizzle over broccoli.

CORN 'N' BEEF PASTA BAKE

I call this my "Friendship Casserole" because I often make it for new moms and other folks
who need a helping hand. The ingredients are easily assembled for a quick meal.
—Nancy Adams, Hancock, New Hampshire

1 pound ground beef
1 medium onion, chopped
1 medium green *or* sweet red pepper,
   chopped
2 garlic cloves, minced
2 cups frozen corn, thawed
1 can (14-1/2 ounces) diced tomatoes,
   undrained
1-1/2 cups uncooked bow tie pasta
1 cup buttermilk
1 package (3 ounces) cream cheese,
   cubed
1 to 2 teaspoons chili powder
Salt and pepper to taste
1 cup (4 ounces) shredded Monterey
   Jack Cheese

In a large skillet, cook the beef, onion, green pepper and garlic over medium heat until meat is no longer pink; drain. Stir in the corn, tomatoes, pasta, buttermilk, cream cheese, chili powder, salt and pepper.

Transfer to a greased 2-1/2-qt. baking dish; sprinkle with cheese. Cover and bake at 375° for 40 minutes. Uncover; bake 25-30 minutes longer or until the pasta is tender. **Yield:** 6-8 servings.

MEAT LOVER'S PIZZA CASSEROLE

(Pictured below)

*With three children, I need dishes that are sure to satisfy. This has been
a family favorite ever since a co-worker shared the recipe.*
—*Karin Ptak, Elburn, Illinois*

1 pound ground beef
1 medium onion, chopped
1 can (15 ounces) pizza sauce
8 ounces elbow macaroni, cooked
   and drained
2 cups (8 ounces) shredded
   mozzarella cheese
1 package (3-1/2 ounces) sliced
   pepperoni, quartered
1/2 teaspoon salt

In a large skillet, cook beef and onion over medium heat until meat is no longer pink; drain. Stir in remaining ingredients. Transfer to a greased 2-qt. baking dish. Bake, uncovered, at 350° for 40-45 minutes or until heated through. **Yield:** 6 servings.

BEEFY RICE SQUARES

My mother used to make this when I was growing up. Now I serve it to my family. It's one of my favorites because it's fast and easy.
—Barb Block, Tigerton, Wisconsin

1 pound uncooked lean ground beef
1 medium onion, chopped
3 cups Italian tomato sauce, *divided*
1/2 cup seasoned bread crumbs
1/4 teaspoon salt
1/8 teaspoon pepper
1-1/3 cups uncooked instant rice
1 cup (4 ounces) shredded cheddar cheese

In a bowl, combine the beef, onion, 1/2 cup tomato sauce, bread crumbs, salt and pepper. Press into a greased 8-in. square baking dish.

In a bowl, combine the rice, cheese and remaining tomato sauce. Pour over meat mixture. Cover and bake at 350° for 25 minutes. Uncover; bake 10-15 minutes longer or until rice is tender. Let stand for 5 minutes before cutting. **Yield:** 4 servings.

CORNED BEEF 'N' SAUERKRAUT BAKE

I love Reuben sandwiches, so this recipe was a dream come true! We especially like it with my husband's homemade sauerkraut.
—Susan Stahl, Duluth, Minnesota

1-3/4 cups sauerkraut, rinsed and well drained
1/2 pound thinly sliced deli corned beef, julienned
2 cups (8 ounces) shredded Swiss cheese
1/4 cup Thousand Island salad dressing
2 medium tomatoes, thinly sliced
6 tablespoons butter *or* margarine, *divided*
1 cup crushed seasoned rye crackers

In a greased 1-1/2-qt. baking dish, layer half of the sauerkraut, corned beef and cheese. Repeat layers. Drop salad dressing by teaspoonfuls over the cheese. Arrange the tomato slices over the top; dot with 2 tablespoons butter.

In a small saucepan, melt the remaining butter. Stir in the crumbs. Sprinkle over top of casserole. Bake, uncovered, at 400° for 30-35 minutes or until heated through. **Yield:** 6 servings.

SKIER'S STEW

This recipe got its name because you put it in the slow cooker...and head for the slopes! I like to prepare it two or three times a month in the fall and winter. When I come home after a busy day and get in out of the cold, a good hot dinner is waiting for me.
—Traci Gangwer, Denver, Colorado

5 large potatoes, peeled and cut into 1-inch cubes
8 medium carrots, cut into 1/4-inch slices
1-1/2 pounds beef stew meat, cut into 1-inch cubes
1 can (15 ounces) tomato sauce
1/2 cup water
1 envelope onion soup mix

In a 5-qt. slow cooker, layer potatoes, carrots and beef. In a bowl, combine the tomato sauce, water and soup mix; pour over meat. Cover and cook on high for 5-6 hours or until vegetables and meat are tender. **Yield:** 6 servings.

MEATBALL POTATO SUPPER

I'm frequently asked to bring this casserole to potluck dinners. Folks must enjoy it,
because there are never any leftovers to bring home!
—Sonya Morton, Molena, Georgia

2 eggs
1/2 cup dry bread crumbs
1 envelope onion soup mix
1-1/2 pounds lean ground beef
2 tablespoons all-purpose flour
6 medium potatoes, peeled and
  thinly sliced
1 can (10-3/4 ounces) condensed
  cream of celery soup, undiluted
1 cup milk
Paprika, optional

In a bowl, combine the eggs, bread crumbs and soup mix. Crumble beef over mixture and mix well. Shape into 1-in. balls. In a large skillet, brown meatballs in small batches over medium heat; drain. Sprinkle with flour; gently roll to coat.

Place half of the potatoes in a greased 2-1/2-qt. baking dish. Top with meatballs and remaining potatoes. In a bowl, combine soup and milk until blended; pour over potatoes. Sprinkle with paprika if desired. Cover and bake at 350° for 60-65 minutes or until the potatoes are tender. **Yield:** 6-8 servings.

CREAMY BEEF WITH BISCUITS

With 11 children, my mom had lots of cooking experience. She generously passed down
to me her knowledge and recipes. Mom usually served this dish to company.
—Mary Miller, Shreve, Ohio

2 pounds ground beef
1 medium onion, chopped
1 package (8 ounces) cream cheese,
  cubed
1 can (10-3/4 ounces) condensed
  cream of mushroom soup,
  undiluted
3/4 cup milk
1/2 cup ketchup
1/2 teaspoon salt
1/4 teaspoon pepper
1 tube (12 ounces) refrigerated
  buttermilk biscuits

In a large skillet, cook beef and onion over medium heat until meat is no longer pink; drain. Add cream cheese, stirring until melted. Add the soup, milk, ketchup, salt and pepper; mix well.

Transfer to a greased 13-in. x 9-in. x 2-in. baking dish. Cover and bake at 375° for 15 minutes. Uncover; arrange biscuits over top. Bake 20-25 minutes longer or until biscuits are golden brown. **Yield:** 8-10 servings.

HELPFUL HINTS

When buying potatoes, choose those that are firm, well-shaped and free of blemishes. Select the type by how you plan to use them:

• Russets or Idaho potatoes—with rough brown skin and numerous eyes—are excellent for baking and frying because they're high in starch and low in moisture.

• Long white potatoes have thinner, pale brown skin and imperceptible eyes. They are good boiled, baked or fried.

• Round red and round white potatoes are best suited for boiling.

• New potatoes are excellent boiled or roasted. They are frequently used in salads.

PORK CLASSICS

Versatile pork is a sure
family-pleaser, as the
44 flavorful combinations
in this chapter prove.
No matter what you
have on hand—ham,
ribs, chops, ground pork,
bacon or sausage—
you'll find a recipe
for a super supper.

VEGGIE NOODLE
HAM CASSEROLE (P. 89)

HAM 'N' CHEESE BOW TIES (P. 74)
MEXICAN-STYLE PORK CHOPS (P. 74)

HAM 'N' CHEESE BOW TIES

(Pictured on page 73)

*Everyone who tries this yummy casserole lists it as a favorite
from then on. Bow tie pasta makes it fun, and ham makes it hearty.*
—Stephanie Moon, Green Bay, Wisconsin

1 garlic clove, minced
1/4 cup butter *or* margarine
1/4 cup all-purpose flour
1/2 teaspoon salt
1/8 teaspoon pepper
2 cups milk
1/2 teaspoon prepared mustard
2-1/2 cups (10 ounces) shredded Colby cheese
2 cups bow tie pasta, cooked and drained
6 to 8 ounces fully cooked ham, julienned
1/4 cup grated Parmesan cheese

In a large saucepan, saute garlic in butter. Stir in flour, salt and pepper until blended. Gradually add milk. Bring to a boil; cook and stir for 2 minutes or until thickened and bubbly. Stir in the mustard and Colby cheese; cook and stir until cheese is melted. Add pasta and ham; stir until coated.

Transfer to a greased 2-qt. baking dish. Sprinkle with Parmesan cheese. Bake, uncovered, at 350° for 20-25 minutes or until heated through. **Yield:** 4-6 servings.

MEXICAN-STYLE PORK CHOPS

(Pictured on page 73)

*My family's fond of Mexican food, and I love to cook but not clean up.
This easy one-pot meal makes everybody happy.*
—Beverly Short, Gold Beach, Oregon

6 bone-in pork loin chops (1/2 inch thick)
2 tablespoons vegetable oil
1 medium onion, chopped
1 can (16 ounces) kidney beans, rinsed and drained
1 can (15-1/4 ounces) whole kernel corn, drained
1 can (10-3/4 ounces) condensed tomato soup, undiluted
1-1/4 cups water
1 cup uncooked instant rice
1/2 cup sliced ripe olives
2 to 3 teaspoons chili powder
1/2 teaspoon dried oregano
1/2 teaspoon salt
1/8 teaspoon pepper

In an ovenproof skillet, brown pork chops in oil on each side; remove and keep warm. In the same skillet, saute onion until tender. Stir in the remaining ingredients; bring to a boil. Place chops over top. Bake, uncovered, at 350° for 35-40 minutes or until meat is tender. **Yield:** 6 servings.

SMOKED SAUSAGE POTATO BAKE

(Pictured below)

My mom passed this recipe along to me. I often fix it for company because it's pleasing to the eye as well as the appetite. I rarely have leftovers, since second helpings are a given.
—Joanne Werner, La Porte, Indiana

1-3/4 cups water
2/3 cup milk
5 tablespoons butter *or* margarine, *divided*
1/2 teaspoon salt
2-2/3 cups mashed potato flakes
1 cup (8 ounces) sour cream
1 cup (4 ounces) shredded cheddar *or* Monterey Jack cheese
1 pound fully cooked smoked sausage links, halved lengthwise and cut into 1/2-inch slices
1 cup (4 ounces) shredded Monterey Jack *or* mozzarella cheese
2 tablespoons dry bread crumbs

In a large saucepan, bring water, milk, 4 tablespoons butter and salt to a boil. Remove from the heat; stir in potato flakes. Let stand for 30 seconds or until liquid is absorbed. Whip with a fork until fluffy. Stir in sour cream and cheddar cheese. Spoon half into a greased 2-qt. baking dish.

Top with sausage and remaining potatoes. Sprinkle with Monterey Jack or mozzarella cheese. Melt remaining butter and toss with bread crumbs; sprinkle over the top. Bake, uncovered, at 350° for 30-35 minutes or until heated through and edges are golden brown. **Yield:** 4-6 servings.

APPLE HAM BAKE

(Pictured above)

A great use for leftover ham, this dish has been served at countless church suppers.
A puffy topping covers a mixture of sweet potatoes, ham and apples.
—Amanda Denton, Barre, Vermont

3 medium tart apples, peeled and
  sliced
2 medium sweet potatoes, peeled
  and thinly sliced
3 cups cubed fully cooked ham
3 tablespoons brown sugar
1/2 teaspoon salt
1/4 teaspoon pepper
1/4 teaspoon curry powder
2 tablespoons cornstarch
1/3 cup apple juice
1 cup pancake mix
1 cup milk
2 tablespoons butter *or* margarine,
  melted
1/2 teaspoon ground mustard

In a large skillet, combine the apples, sweet potatoes, ham, brown sugar, salt, pepper and curry. Cook over medium heat until apples are crisp-tender; drain. Combine cornstarch and apple juice until smooth; stir into apple mixture. Bring to a boil; cook and stir for 1-2 minutes or until mixture is thickened. Transfer to a greased 2-qt. baking dish.

Cover and bake at 375° for 10 minutes or until sweet potatoes are tender. Meanwhile, in a bowl, whisk together pancake mix, milk, butter and mustard; pour over ham mixture. Bake, uncovered, for 25-30 minutes or until puffed and golden brown. **Yield:** 8 servings.

PANTRY PORK DISH

*I put this dish together one day when we had unexpected company for dinner.
I used ingredients from my pantry and tossed in some ground pork.
Our guests raved about the flavor.*
—Julia Trachsel, Victoria, British Columbia

1 pound ground pork
1 small onion, chopped, *divided*
1/2 teaspoon ground allspice
1/2 teaspoon dried oregano
1/2 teaspoon salt, *divided*
1/2 teaspoon pepper, *divided*
3 medium potatoes, peeled and
   sliced 1/4 inch thick
2 tablespoons all-purpose flour
2-1/2 cups julienned peeled butternut
   squash
1/4 teaspoon ground nutmeg
1-1/2 cups frozen cut green beans
1/4 cup sliced almonds, toasted

Combine pork, half of the onion, allspice, oregano, 1/4 teaspoon salt and 1/4 teaspoon pepper. Press into a greased 9-in. square baking dish. Top with potatoes and remaining onion. Combine the flour and remaining salt; sprinkle over potatoes.

Cover and bake at 350° for 40 minutes; drain. Uncover; layer with squash, nutmeg and remaining pepper. Top with the green beans. Cover and bake 30 minutes longer or until the vegetables are tender. Sprinkle with almonds; bake 5 minutes more or until golden brown. **Yield:** 4

CHEESY FRANKS AND POTATOES

*I came up with this recipe primarily because my husband loves hot dogs and I needed a break
from standard fare using franks. It was an instant hit. Even I enjoy the rich taste.*
—Shirley Bradley, Wildwood, Florida

6 jumbo hot dogs, halved lengthwise
   and cut into 1/2-inch pieces
1 tablespoon vegetable oil
1 medium onion, chopped
1/2 cup chopped green pepper
1 can (10-3/4 ounces) condensed
   cheddar cheese soup, undiluted
2/3 cup half-and-half cream
2 medium potatoes, cooked and
   cubed
1/4 teaspoon salt

In a large skillet over medium heat, brown hot dogs in oil for 2-3 minutes or until lightly browned. Remove with a slotted spoon. In the same skillet, saute onion and green pepper until tender.

In a small bowl, combine the soup, cream and onion mixture. Place potatoes in a greased 11-in. x 7-in. x 2-in. baking dish; sprinkle with salt. Top with hot dogs. Pour soup mixture over all. Bake, uncovered, at 350° for 30-35 minutes or until heated through. **Yield:** 6 servings.

TIMELY TIP

*Refrigerate cream in the coldest part of the refrigerator as
soon as you get home from the grocery store. Most creams will
keep up to a week past the date stamped on the carton.*

ITALIAN SAUSAGE FRIED RICE

*I created this dish one day when I wasn't in the mood for anything I'd tried before.
I used ingredients I had on hand. It's since become one of my family's most requested meals.
—Janet Wood, Windham, New Hampshire*

1 pound bulk Italian sausage
1 cup uncooked long grain rice
1 large onion, chopped
1 garlic clove, minced
2 cups water
1 teaspoon salt
1/4 teaspoon hot pepper sauce
1 can (14-1/2 ounces) diced tomatoes, undrained
1 cup frozen peas, thawed

In a large skillet, cook sausage over medium heat until no longer pink; drain. Add the rice, onion and garlic; cook and stir until onion is tender. Stir in the water, salt and hot pepper sauce. Bring to a boil. Reduce heat; cover and simmer for 18-20 minutes or until rice is tender.

Stir in tomatoes and peas; cover and cook 5-10 minutes longer or until peas are heated through. **Yield:** 4-6 servings.

SPARERIB CASSEROLE

*This is an old Southern recipe my mother passed on to me many, many years ago.
It's especially good for a Saturday night supper.
—Doris Voytovich, Inkster, Michigan*

4 to 5 pounds pork spareribs, cut into individual ribs
2 teaspoons salt, *divided*
1/2 teaspoon pepper, *divided*
5 tablespoons vegetable oil, *divided*
6 cups cubed potatoes
1 medium onion, sliced
2 garlic cloves, minced
4 teaspoons all-purpose flour
2 tablespoons dried parsley flakes
1 can (12 ounces) evaporated milk
1/8 teaspoon paprika

Sprinkle ribs with 1 teaspoon salt and 1/4 teaspoon pepper. In a large skillet, brown ribs in 3 tablespoons oil in batches. Place ribs on a rack in a shallow roasting pan. Bake, uncovered, at 350° for 20 minutes. Turn ribs; bake 20 minutes longer. Pat dry.

Place potatoes in a saucepan and cover with water; cover and bring to a boil over medium-high heat. Cook for 15-20 minutes or until tender. Meanwhile, in a saucepan, saute onion and garlic in remaining oil until tender. Stir in the flour, parsley, and remaining salt and pepper until blended. Gradually stir in milk. Bring to a boil; cook and stir for 2 minutes or until thickened.

Drain potatoes; place in a greased 13-in. x 9-in. x 2-in. baking dish. Top with sauce and ribs. Cover and bake at 350° for 15 minutes. Uncover; sprinkle with paprika. Bake 5-10 minutes longer or until ribs are tender and potatoes are heated through. **Yield:** 6 servings.

SPINACH LINGUINE WITH HAM

(Pictured below)

My grandmother used to make this for parties and potlucks. It was loved by all back then, and it still is today. If you don't have spinach linguine on hand, you can use all regular linguine.
—Mary Savor, Woodburn, Indiana

4 ounces uncooked spinach linguine, broken in half
4 ounces uncooked linguine, broken in half
2 cups cubed fully cooked ham
1 can (10-3/4 ounces) condensed cream of mushroom soup, undiluted
2-1/2 cups (10 ounces) shredded Swiss cheese, *divided*
1 cup (8 ounces) sour cream
1 medium onion, chopped
1/2 cup finely chopped green pepper
2 tablespoons butter *or* margarine, melted

Cook both types of linguine according to package directions; drain and place in a large bowl. Add the ham, soup, 2 cups cheese, sour cream, onion, green pepper and butter. Transfer to a greased 13-in. x 9-in. x 2-in. baking dish.

Cover and bake at 350° for 35 minutes. Uncover; sprinkle with remaining cheese. Bake 15-20 minutes longer or until cheese is melted. **Yield:** 8 servings.

PORK CHOP RICE BAKE

I love to cook, but I also love easy recipes like this one, which tastes like
you fussed. Canned soup makes the dish creamy and convenient.
—Brenda Henderson, Marshall, Missouri

2-1/4 cups uncooked instant rice
   1 can (10-3/4 ounces) condensed
      cream of celery soup, undiluted
   1 can (10-3/4 ounces) condensed
      cream of mushroom soup,
      undiluted
2-2/3 cups milk
   4 bone-in pork loin chops (1/2 inch
      thick)
   1 envelope onion soup mix

In a bowl, combine the rice, soups and milk. Transfer to a greased 13-in. x 9-in. x 2-in. baking dish. Arrange pork chops over rice. Sprinkle with soup mix. Cover and bake at 350° for 50-55 minutes or until meat juices run clear and rice is tender. **Yield:** 4 servings.

SERVING SUGGESTION

Bratwurst Potato Skillet tastes great with corn bread. Perk up
a store-bought mix by adding 1/2 to 1 cup shredded cheese,
chopped green onions or crumbled cooked bacon to the batter.

BRATWURST POTATO SKILLET

My husband, son and daughter request this supper on blustery fall and winter days.
Served with Italian bread, a crisp green salad and apple cider, it always satisfies.
—Alice Le Duc, Cedarburg, Wisconsin

   3 medium red potatoes
   1 pound fully cooked bratwurst *or*
      Polish sausage, cut into 1/2-inch
      slices
   2 teaspoons thinly sliced green onion
1-1/2 teaspoons vegetable oil
1-1/2 cups white wine *or* chicken broth
   1 teaspoon dried thyme
   1 teaspoon dried marjoram
   1 tablespoon sugar
   1 tablespoon Dijon mustard
   3 teaspoons minced fresh parsley,
      divided
   3 teaspoons snipped chives, *divided*
   1 to 2 teaspoons cider vinegar
1/2 teaspoon salt
1/4 teaspoon pepper
   2 egg yolks, lightly beaten

Place potatoes in a saucepan and cover with water; cover and bring to a boil over medium-high heat. Cook for 15-20 minutes or until tender; drain. Cool slightly; cut into cubes and keep warm.

In a large skillet, saute sausage and onion in oil until lightly browned; drain. Stir in wine or broth, thyme and marjoram. Bring to a boil. Reduce heat; simmer, uncovered, for 10 minutes.

Remove sausage; keep warm. Stir sugar, mustard, 1-1/2 teaspoons parsley, 1-1/2 teaspoons chives, vinegar, salt and pepper into pan juices; heat through. Whisk a small amount of hot liquid into egg yolks; return all to the pan. Cook and stir until thickened and bubbly. Stir in sausage and potatoes; heat through. Sprinkle with remaining parsley and chives. **Yield:** 3-4 servings.

STOVETOP HAM AND PENNE

(Pictured above)

A tangy garlic sauce pleasantly coats tender pasta and flavorful ham in this stovetop classic.
—Mary Bryant, Stanwood, Washington

12 ounces uncooked penne *or* other medium tube pasta
1/2 cup chopped green onions
5 to 7 garlic cloves, minced
2 tablespoons butter *or* margarine
2 tablespoons olive *or* vegetable oil
1 can (28 ounces) diced tomatoes, drained
1-1/2 cups cubed fully cooked ham
1 cup (8 ounces) sour cream
1/2 cup cubed cheddar cheese
1/2 cup cubed Monterey Jack cheese
1/2 cup chopped ripe olives, optional
1/2 cup white wine *or* tomato juice
1 tablespoon minced fresh basil *or* 1 teaspoon dried basil
Salt and pepper to taste

Cook pasta according to package directions. Meanwhile, in a saucepan, saute onions and garlic in butter and oil until tender. Stir in the remaining ingredients; heat through. Drain pasta and place in a bowl; add ham mixture and gently toss to coat. **Yield:** 4-6 servings.

ASPARAGUS HAM BAKE

This comforting casserole is a crowd-pleaser, so I often take it to church potluck suppers.
—Joan Nichols, Sarnia, Ontario

2 cups cubed fully cooked ham
2 cups cooked rice
1 can (10-3/4 ounces) condensed
  cream of mushroom soup,
  undiluted
3/4 cup evaporated milk
1/2 cup shredded process cheese
  (Velveeta)
3 tablespoons finely chopped onion
1 package (10 ounces) frozen
  asparagus spears, thawed
1/2 cup crushed cornflakes
3 tablespoons butter *or* margarine,
  melted

In a large bowl, combine the ham, rice, soup, milk, cheese and onion; mix well. Spoon half into a greased 2-qt. baking dish. Top with asparagus and remaining ham mixture. Combine cornflake crumbs and butter; sprinkle over top. Bake, uncovered, at 375° for 30-35 minutes or until heated through. **Yield:** 4-6 servings.

STICK-TO-YOUR-RIBS SUPPER

This sausage and bean skillet dish appears on my Sunday dinner menu at least once a month. For a little extra zest, add more chili powder and cayenne pepper.
—Cynthia Chapman, Allendale, South Carolina

2 medium green peppers, chopped
1 large onion, chopped
1 can (4 ounces) mushroom stems
  and pieces, drained
2 garlic cloves, minced
1 tablespoon vegetable oil
1 pound fully cooked kielbasa *or*
  Polish sausage, thinly sliced
1-1/2 cups water
1 can (16 ounces) kidney beans,
  rinsed and drained
1 can (15 ounces) pinto beans, rinsed
  and drained
1 can (14-1/2 ounces) diced tomatoes,
  undrained
2 teaspoons chili powder
1 teaspoon ground cumin
1/2 teaspoon salt
1/8 teaspoon cayenne pepper
3/4 cup uncooked long grain rice
1 cup (4 ounces) shredded mozzarella
  cheese

In a large skillet, saute the green peppers, onion, mushrooms and garlic in oil until tender. Add the sausage, water, beans, tomatoes, chili powder, cumin, salt and cayenne. Bring to a boil. Stir in the rice. Reduce heat; cover and simmer for 20-25 minutes or until rice is tender. Sprinkle with cheese; cover and cook for 5 minutes until cheese is melted. **Yield:** 10 servings.

CORNY PORK CHOPS

My grandmother began making this recipe in the 1950s, and it remains a family favorite today.
As simple as it seems, the corn dressing complements the pork beautifully.
—Ralph Petterson, Salt Lake City, Utah

4 bone-in pork loin chops (3/4 to
   1 inch thick)
1 teaspoon salt, *divided*
1/4 teaspoon pepper, *divided*
1 tablespoon vegetable oil
1 can (15-1/4 ounces) whole kernel
   corn, drained
2 celery ribs, diced
1 cup soft bread crumbs
1/3 cup ketchup
1 tablespoon chopped green onion

Season pork chops with 1/2 teaspoon salt and 1/8 teaspoon pepper. In a large skillet, brown the chops in oil on both sides.

Combine the corn, celery, bread crumbs, ketchup, onion, and remaining salt and pepper; place in a greased 11-in. x 7-in. x 2-in. baking dish. Top with chops. Cover and bake at 350° for 45-55 minutes or until meat juices run clear. **Yield:** 4 servings.

HOT DOGS 'N' RICE

When my husband was a child, his mother made this economical entree during the
lean times. It never failed to fill up her hungry family. Kids today like it, too.
—Susan Martin, Redwood City, California

1/2 cup chopped onion
1/2 cup chopped green pepper
2 tablespoons vegetable oil
1 cup uncooked long grain rice
1-1/2 cups water, *divided*
5 hot dogs, halved lengthwise and
   cut into 1/2-inch slices
1 can (14-1/2 ounces) stewed
   tomatoes, undrained
3 tablespoons ketchup

In a large skillet, saute onion and green pepper in oil until tender. Add rice; cook and stir for 2-3 minutes. Add 1-1/4 cups water and hot dogs. Bring to a boil. Reduce heat; cover and simmer for 20-25 minutes. Add the tomatoes, ketchup and remaining water. Cover and cook until rice is tender. **Yield:** 5 servings.

HELPFUL HINTS

Here's a quick explanation of common varieties of rice:
- *Rice is classified by size. Long grain rice, often called for in recipes, is four to five times longer than its width. When cooked, it produces light, dry granules that separate easily.*
- *Brown rice is the whole grain; only the inedible outer husk has been removed. Brown rice gets its light tan color, nutty flavor and chewy texture from its high-fiber, nutritious coating.*
- *White rice has had its hull and bran layers removed.*
- *Brown rice takes at least twice as long to cook as white long grain rice.*
- *Instant or quick-cooking rice has been fully or partially cooked, then dehydrated.*

BAKED ZITI AND SAUSAGE

(Pictured at right)

This is my husband's favorite casserole, and he requests it often.
He loves the combination of zesty Italian sausage and three types of cheese.
—Christina Ingalls, Manhattan, Kansas

3 cups uncooked ziti *or* other small
   tube pasta
1/2 pound Italian sausage links
1/4 cup butter *or* margarine
1/4 cup all-purpose flour
1-1/2 teaspoons salt, *divided*
1/4 teaspoon plus 1/8 teaspoon pepper,
   divided
2 cups milk
1/2 cup grated Parmesan cheese, *divided*
1 egg, lightly beaten
2 cups (16 ounces) small-curd
   cottage cheese
1 tablespoon minced fresh parsley
1 cup (4 ounces) shredded mozzarella
   cheese
Paprika

Cook pasta according to package directions. Drain; place in a bowl. In a skillet, cook sausage over medium heat until no longer pink; drain and cut into 1/2-in. slices.

In a saucepan, melt butter. Stir in the flour, 1 teaspoon salt and 1/4 teaspoon pepper until smooth; gradually add milk. Bring to a boil; cook and stir for 2 minutes or until thickened. Remove from the heat; stir in 1/4 cup Parmesan cheese. Pour over pasta; toss to coat.

In a bowl, combine the egg, cottage cheese, parsley, and remaining Parmesan cheese, salt and pepper. Spoon half of the pasta mixture into a greased 2-1/2-qt. baking dish. Top with cottage cheese mixture. Add sausage to the remaining pasta mixture; spoon over the top. Sprinkle with mozzarella cheese and paprika. Bake, uncovered, at 350° for 30-35 minutes or until hot and bubbly. **Yield:** 6 servings.

BACON TOMATO CASSEROLE

(Pictured at right)

This recipe from my mother is simple to make and can be a main dish or side dish.
Feel free to experiment with a variety of flavored stewed tomatoes.
—Mary McGair, Milwaukie, Oregon

6 ounces uncooked egg noodles
1 pound sliced bacon, diced
1/3 cup chopped green pepper
1/3 cup chopped onion
1 teaspoon salt
1/2 teaspoon dried marjoram
1/2 teaspoon dried thyme
1/8 teaspoon pepper
1 can (28 ounces) stewed tomatoes
1 cup (4 ounces) shredded cheddar
   cheese

Cook noodles according to package directions; drain. In a large skillet, cook bacon over medium heat until crisp. Remove to paper towels to drain, reserving 2 tablespoons drippings. In the drippings, saute green pepper, onion, salt, marjoram, thyme and pepper for 5 minutes. Stir in tomatoes. Bring to a boil. Reduce heat; simmer, uncovered, for 10 minutes. Stir in the noodles. Add half of the bacon.

Transfer to a greased 2-qt. baking dish. Top with cheese and remaining bacon. Bake, uncovered, at 350° for 10-15 minutes or until cheese is melted. **Yield:** 4-6 servings.

PORK CHOPS O'BRIEN

(Pictured below)

I like to make this recipe for small holiday gatherings, especially when folks are tired of ham and turkey. It's delicious and filling.
—Kathy Dustin, Bedford, Indiana

6 bone-in pork loin chops (1/2 inch thick)
1 tablespoon vegetable oil
1 can (10-3/4 ounces) condensed cream of celery soup, undiluted
1/2 cup milk
1/2 cup sour cream
1/4 teaspoon pepper
1 cup (4 ounces) shredded cheddar cheese, *divided*
1 can (2.8 ounces) french-fried onions, *divided*
1 package (24 ounces) frozen O'Brien hash brown potatoes, thawed
1/2 teaspoon seasoned salt

In a skillet, brown pork chops in oil on each side. In a large bowl, combine the soup, milk, sour cream, pepper, 1/2 cup cheese and 1/2 cup onions; fold in potatoes. Spread into a greased 13-in. x 9-in. x 2-in. baking dish. Arrange chops on top; sprinkle with seasoned salt.

Cover and bake at 350° for 40-45 minutes or until pork is tender. Uncover; sprinkle with remaining cheese and onions. Bake 5-10 minutes longer or until cheese is melted. **Yield:** 6 servings.

MICROWAVE CORN BREAD CASSEROLE

*I always seem to be short on time, so this quick-and-easy supper is just perfect for me.
You can find the ingredients in my kitchen any day of the week!*
—Cynthia Rodgers, Brewton, Alabama

2 cups frozen mixed vegetables
1-1/2 cups cubed fully cooked ham
1 package (6 ounces) corn bread
  stuffing mix
3 eggs
2 cups milk
1/4 teaspoon salt
1/4 teaspoon pepper
1 cup (4 ounces) shredded cheddar
  cheese

In a greased 11-in. x 7-in. x 2-in. microwave-safe dish, combine vegetables, ham and stuffing mix; mix well. In a bowl, combine eggs, milk, salt and pepper. Pour over corn bread mixture. Cover and refrigerate for at least 5 hours or overnight.

Remove from the refrigerator 30 minutes before cooking. Cover and microwave on high for 18-22 minutes or until a knife inserted in the center comes out clean. Sprinkle with cheese. Cover and let stand for 5 minutes before serving. **Yield:** 4-6 servings.

Editor's Note: This recipe was tested in an 850-watt microwave.

SIMPLE SUBSTITUTIONS

Microwave Corn Bread Casserole is just as tasty with cubed cooked chicken instead of ham. You can also try various frozen mixed vegetables. A combination of broccoli, red peppers, onions and mushrooms is a favorite of the cook who shared the recipe.

COUNTRY RIBS AND BEANS

This is one of my favorite ways to prepare pork spareribs. The celery and red pepper add color to this meaty meal, which always gets rave reviews from family and friends.
—Marlene Muckenhirn, Delano, Minnesota

3 to 3-1/2 pounds country-style pork
  spareribs
1/4 cup water
1 can (15 ounces) tomato sauce
1 envelope onion soup mix
1/3 cup packed brown sugar
2 tablespoons prepared mustard
1/8 teaspoon hot pepper sauce
2 cans (16 ounces *each*) kidney
  beans, rinsed and drained
2 cans (15-1/2 ounces *each*) great
  northern beans, rinsed and drained
3 celery ribs, thinly sliced
1 medium sweet red pepper, thinly
  sliced

Place ribs in an ungreased 13-in. x 9-in. x 2-in. baking dish; add water. Cover and bake at 350° for 1-1/2 hours. Remove ribs and keep warm.

Pour cooking juices into a measuring cup; skim fat. Add enough water to juices to measure 1 cup; pour into a saucepan. Add the tomato sauce, soup mix, brown sugar, mustard and hot pepper sauce. Simmer, uncovered, for 10 minutes; remove 1/2 cup.

To the remaining sauce, add beans, celery and red pepper. Transfer to the baking dish; add ribs. Pour reserved sauce over ribs. Cover and bake for 45 minutes or until the meat is tender. **Yield:** 6-8 servings.

Au Gratin Spinach 'n' Pork

This dish is nice and rich, which makes it a good choice when you crave comfort food.
It's a complete family meal all by itself. With rolls and a salad, it's a perfect company casserole.
—Sandy Szwarc, Albuquerque, New Mexico

2 large onions, sliced
1 tablespoon vegetable oil
1 tablespoon butter *or* margarine
2 bacon strips, diced
1 pound pork chop suey meat *or*
  boneless pork, cut into 1-inch cubes
1 package (10 ounces) fresh spinach,
  torn
2 garlic cloves, minced
2 teaspoons grated lemon peel
1 teaspoon fennel seed, crushed
1/2 teaspoon salt
1/2 teaspoon pepper
1 cup (4 ounces) shredded Swiss
  cheese, *divided*
2 tablespoons grated Parmesan
  cheese

In a large skillet, saute onions in oil and butter until golden. Remove to paper towels to drain. In the same skillet, cook bacon over medium heat until crisp; remove to paper towels to drain.

In the drippings, cook pork until browned. Add spinach and garlic; cook and stir for 6 minutes. Drain thoroughly. Stir in the lemon peel, fennel seed, salt, pepper, 1/3 cup Swiss cheese and bacon.

Place half of the onions in a greased 1-qt. baking dish; top with pork mixture and remaining onions (dish will be full). Sprinkle with Parmesan cheese and remaining Swiss cheese. Bake, uncovered, at 350° for 25-30 minutes or until pork is tender and cheese is melted. **Yield:** 4-6 servings.

SERVING SUGGESTION

Need a simple dessert? Layer lemon yogurt and fresh blueberries in
small clear glasses. Repeat layers. Top with crumbled oatmeal cookies.

Kielbasa Casserole for Two

I don't know if Mother made up this recipe or if it was handed down to her,
but it's scrumptious and can be made in small portions to satisfy two people.
—Kathryn Curtis, Lakeport, California

2 fully cooked kielbasa *or* Polish
  sausages (about 6 ounces)
1/4 cup sliced fresh mushrooms
1/4 cup finely chopped onion
1 tablespoon butter *or* margarine
2 tablespoons whipping cream
1-1/2 teaspoons Dijon mustard
1/8 teaspoon garlic powder
1/2 cup shredded cheddar cheese
4 tomato slices

Cut sausages in half lengthwise; place in a greased 1-1/2-qt. baking dish. In a saucepan, saute mushrooms and onion in butter until lightly browned. Stir in cream, mustard and garlic powder; bring to a boil. Cook and stir until slightly thickened. Pour over the sausages; top with cheese.

Bake, uncovered, at 450° for 15-20 minutes or until cheese is melted. Garnish with tomato slices. **Yield:** 2 servings.

VEGGIE NOODLE HAM CASSEROLE

(Pictured above and on page 72)

This saucy main dish is really quite versatile.
Without the ham, it can be a vegetarian entree or a hearty side dish.
—Judy Moody, Wheatley, Ontario

1 package (12 ounces) wide egg
   noodles
1 can (10-3/4 ounces) condensed
   cream of chicken soup, undiluted
1 can (10-3/4 ounces) condensed
   cream of broccoli soup, undiluted
1-1/2 cups milk
2 cups frozen corn, thawed
1-1/2 cups frozen California-blend
   vegetables, thawed
1-1/2 cups cubed fully cooked ham
2 tablespoons minced fresh parsley
1/2 teaspoon pepper
1/4 teaspoon salt
1 cup (4 ounces) shredded cheddar
   cheese, *divided*

Cook noodles according to package directions; drain. In a bowl, combine soups and milk; stir in the noodles, corn, vegetables, ham, parsley, pepper, salt and 3/4 cup of cheese. Transfer to a greased 13-in. x 9-in. x 2-in. baking dish.

Cover and bake at 350° for 45 minutes. Uncover; sprinkle with remaining cheese. Bake 5-10 minutes longer or until bubbly and cheese is melted. **Yield:** 8-10 servings.

BAKED CHOPS AND FRIES

A one-dish meal that's nice enough for company is a rare find, so this one's a treasure.
Pop it in the oven, chat with your guests and then serve them a delicious supper.
—Anita Bafik, Avonmore, Pennsylvania

1/2 teaspoon salt
1/8 teaspoon pepper
1/8 teaspoon paprika
4 bone-in pork loin chops (1/2 inch thick)
2 tablespoons vegetable oil
1 can (10-3/4 ounces) condensed cream of mushroom soup, undiluted
1/2 cup sour cream
2 tablespoons milk
1 teaspoon dried parsley flakes
4 cups frozen steak fries, thawed
2 cups frozen cut green beans, thawed

Combine the salt, pepper and paprika; sprinkle over pork chops. In a large skillet, brown chops in oil on each side; drain. Remove chops and keep warm. In the same skillet, combine the soup, sour cream, milk and parsley; cook and stir until heated through.

In a greased 11-in. x 7-in. x 2-in. baking dish, layer fries, beans and soup mixture. Top with chops. Cover and bake at 350° for 20 minutes. Uncover; bake 5-10 minutes longer or until meat is tender and vegetables are heated through. **Yield:** 4 servings.

SERVING SUGGESTION

For an all-green salad with extraordinary taste, toss together romaine or iceberg lettuce, cucumbers, green onion and chopped green apple.

CAMPFIRE CASSEROLE

With three different meats and four kinds of beans, this casserole really satisfies.
Serve it with cheese-topped corn bread for a complete meal.
—Flo Rahn, Hillsboro, Kansas

1/3 cup packed brown sugar
1/2 cup ketchup
1 teaspoon ground mustard
1/2 cup barbecue sauce
1/3 cup sugar
1/2 teaspoon chili powder
1/2 teaspoon salt
1/4 teaspoon pepper
1/2 pound ground beef, cooked and drained
1/2 pound bacon, cooked and crumbled
1/2 pound fully cooked bratwurst, cut into 1-inch slices
1 can (16 ounces) kidney beans, rinsed and drained
1 can (16 ounces) pork and beans
1 can (15-1/4 ounces) lima beans, rinsed and drained
1 can (15 ounces) chili beans

In a large bowl, combine the first eight ingredients; mix well. Add cooked beef, bacon and bratwurst. Stir in the beans. Pour into a greased 2-qt. baking dish. Bake, uncovered, at 350° for 1 hour or until heated through. **Yield:** 10-12 servings.

HAM NOODLE DINNER

(Pictured below)

*Whether I'm cooking for company or my own brood of five children,
this delicious casserole is always well-received.*
—Eileen Nilsson, Plymouth, Massachusetts

2-1/2 cups uncooked egg noodles
   1 celery rib, chopped
   1 medium onion, chopped
   1 tablespoon vegetable oil
   2 cups cubed fully cooked ham
   1 can (10-3/4 ounces) condensed
      cream of mushroom soup,
      undiluted
   1 package (10 ounces) frozen peas,
      thawed
   1 cup (4 ounces) shredded cheddar
      cheese
3/4 cup milk
   1 teaspoon ground mustard

Cook noodles according to package directions; drain. In a large skillet, saute celery and onion in oil until tender. Stir in the noodles and remaining ingredients. Transfer to a greased 2-qt. baking dish. Cover and bake at 350° for 50-60 minutes or until heated through. **Yield:** 4-6 servings.

POTATO LASAGNA

(Pictured above)

At our house, this is a regular—it's as much fun to fix as it is to eat! Sometimes we even make extras of the potatoes to serve as appetizers. It's great for potlucks, too.
—Mara Beaumont, South Milwaukee, Wisconsin

2 tablespoons olive *or* vegetable oil
2 garlic cloves, minced
1/2 teaspoon salt
1/2 teaspoon pepper
7 medium potatoes, sliced 1/4 inch thick
1 pound bulk Italian sausage
1 large onion, chopped
2 packages (10 ounces *each*) frozen chopped spinach, thawed and drained
1 cup ricotta cheese
1/4 cup seasoned bread crumbs
Dash cayenne pepper
Additional salt and pepper to taste
2 cups (8 ounces) shredded mozzarella cheese
1/2 cup chicken broth
2 tablespoons grated Parmesan cheese

In a large bowl, combine the oil, garlic, salt and pepper. Add the potatoes and toss to coat; spread evenly in an ungreased 15-in. x 10-in. x 1-in. baking pan. Cover and bake at 425° for 35-40 minutes or until tender. Cool for at least 15 minutes.

Meanwhile, in a large skillet, cook the sausage and onion over medium heat until meat is no longer pink; drain. Combine the spinach, ricotta, bread crumbs, cayenne, salt and pepper; mix well. In a greased 13-in. x 9-in. x 2-in. baking dish, layer a third of the potatoes, and half of the spinach mixture, sausage and mozzarella. Repeat layers. Pour broth over all. Top with remaining potatoes; sprinkle with Parmesan cheese.

Bake, uncovered, at 350° for 30-35 minutes or until the potatoes are tender. Let stand for 15 minutes before serving. **Yield:** 8-10 servings.

ZUCCHINI SAUSAGE SQUARES

*This dish is a great way to use up end-of-the-season squash, even when everyone
says they can't possibly look at another zucchini. It's simple yet tasty.*
—Fran Sawlaw, Paris, Illinois

5 small zucchini, cut into 1/4-inch
slices (about 4 cups)
1 large onion, chopped
1/2 cup butter *or* margarine
1 pound bulk Italian sausage, cooked
and drained
2 teaspoons minced fresh parsley
1/2 teaspoon pepper
1/4 teaspoon garlic powder
1/4 teaspoon dried basil
1/4 teaspoon dried oregano
2 eggs
2 cups (8 ounces) shredded
mozzarella cheese
1 tube (8 ounces) refrigerated
crescent rolls
2 tablespoons prepared mustard

In a large skillet, saute the zucchini and
onion in butter. Stir in the sausage, parsley
and seasonings. In a large bowl, combine
the eggs, cheese and sausage mixture.

Unroll crescent roll dough and place in a
greased 13-in. x 9-in. x 2-in. baking dish.
Press onto the bottom and up the sides to
form a crust; seal seams and perforations.
Brush with mustard. Spoon sausage mixture
over crust. Bake, uncovered, at 375° for
18-20 minutes or until crust is golden brown.
Yield: 6-8 servings.

SERVING SUGGESTION

*Herbs add flavor to simple salads. Scatter a generous amount of
freshly chopped parsley or chives over mixed greens.*

PORK CHOPS WITH APPLE STUFFING

*A friend shared this recipe from her Slovak mother back in the 1950s,
and my husband and children loved it. They still do.*
—Romaine Smith, Garden Grove, Iowa

6 bone-in pork loin chops (3/4 inch
thick)
4 tablespoons butter *or* margarine,
divided
6 cups stuffing croutons
3/4 cup chopped peeled apple
3/4 cup finely chopped celery
1/2 cup raisins
1/2 cup hot water
3 teaspoons rubbed sage
1 teaspoon salt
1/4 teaspoon pepper
4 teaspoons Dijon mustard

In a large skillet, brown pork chops in 2 tablespoons butter on each side. Melt remaining butter; stir in the croutons, apple, celery, raisins, water, sage, salt and pepper.
Place in a greased 3-qt. baking dish. Top with
pork chops. Spread mustard over chops. Cover and bake at 350° for 35 minutes. Uncover; bake 5-10 minutes longer or until meat
juices run clear. **Yield:** 6 servings.

SAUSAGE RICE PILAF

I serve this nicely seasoned rice casserole with a fresh green salad and some crusty bread or rolls. It's one of our favorite sausage recipes.
—Deborah Downing, Goshen, Indiana

2 pounds bulk Italian sausage
1 large onion, chopped
1 jar (7.3 ounces) sliced mushrooms, drained
2 cups uncooked long grain rice
2 cans (10-1/2 ounces *each*) condensed beef consomme, undiluted
2 cups water
2 teaspoons dried oregano
Grated Parmesan cheese, optional

In a large skillet, cook sausage, onion and mushrooms over medium heat until meat is no longer pink. Add rice, consomme, water and oregano; mix well. Transfer to an ungreased 13-in. x 9-in. x 2-in. baking dish. Cover and bake at 350° for 55-60 minutes or until rice is tender, stirring once. Sprinkle with Parmesan cheese if desired. **Yield:** 8 servings.

BARBECUED PORK WITH BEANS

Everyone raves about how tender these pork chops are.
—Donna Jordan, Hendersonville, North Carolina

4 bone-in pork loin chops (3/4 inch thick)
1 tablespoon vegetable oil
2 cans (11 ounces *each*) pork and beans
3 tablespoons Worcestershire sauce, *divided*
1/4 cup ketchup
1/4 to 1/2 teaspoon chili powder

In a large skillet, brown pork chops in oil on both sides. Combine pork and beans and 2 tablespoons Worcestershire sauce; place in a greased 11-in. x 7-in. x 2-in. baking dish. Top with chops.

Combine the ketchup, chili powder and remaining Worcestershire sauce; spoon over chops. Bake, uncovered, at 350° for 50-55 minutes or until meat is tender. **Yield:** 4 servings.

PORK SPANISH RICE

My family wasn't fond of pork roast until I used it in this yummy casserole.
—Betty Unrau, MacGregor, Manitoba

1 medium green pepper, chopped
1 small onion, chopped
2 tablespoons butter *or* margarine
1 can (14-1/2 ounces) diced tomatoes, drained
1 cup chicken broth
1/2 teaspoon salt
1/4 teaspoon pepper
1-3/4 cups cubed cooked pork
1 cup uncooked instant rice

In a large skillet, saute green pepper and onion in butter until tender. Stir in the tomatoes, broth, salt and pepper. Bring to a boil; stir in pork and rice. Transfer to a greased 2-qt. baking dish. Cover and bake at 350° for 20-25 minutes or until rice is tender and liquid is absorbed. Stir before serving. **Yield:** 4 servings.

HOT DOG CASSEROLE

(Pictured below)

When our children were small and I was busy trying to get all those extra things done that are part of a mom's normal schedule, I would make this quick hot dish. Kids love it.
—JoAnn Gunio, Franklin, North Carolina

3 tablespoons butter *or* margarine
2 tablespoons all-purpose flour
1 to 1-1/2 teaspoons salt
1/4 to 1/2 teaspoon pepper
1-1/2 cups milk
5 medium red potatoes, thinly sliced
1 package (1 pound) hot dogs, halved lengthwise and cut into 1/2-inch slices
1 medium onion, chopped
1/3 cup shredded cheddar cheese

In a saucepan, melt butter. Stir in flour, salt and pepper until smooth. Gradually add milk. Bring to a boil; cook and stir for 2 minutes or until thickened and bubbly.

In a greased 2-1/2-qt. baking dish, layer a third of the potatoes, half of the hot dogs and half of the onions. Repeat layers. Top with remaining potatoes. Pour white sauce over all. Cover and bake at 350° for 1 hour. Uncover; sprinkle with cheese. Bake 10-15 minutes longer or until potatoes are tender. **Yield:** 8 servings.

BAVARIAN WIENER SUPPER

This great family meal also goes over well at potluck suppers. The dish is always scraped clean and I'm asked for the recipe, which my daughter received from a friend.
—Helen Kendig, Lawrenceburg, Kentucky

1 can (10-3/4 ounces) condensed cream of mushroom soup, undiluted
1/2 cup mayonnaise*
1 jar (16 ounces) sauerkraut, rinsed and well drained
1 package (1 pound) hot dogs, halved lengthwise and cut into bite-size pieces
1 teaspoon caraway seeds
4 cups cubed cooked potatoes
1/4 cup soft bread crumbs
1 tablespoon butter *or* margarine, melted
1/4 teaspoon paprika

In a bowl, combine the soup and mayonnaise; mix well. In another bowl, combine sauerkraut, hot dogs, caraway seeds and half of the soup mixture. Spread into a greased shallow 2-qt. baking dish.

Combine potatoes and remaining soup mixture; mix well. Spoon over sauerkraut mixture. Combine the bread crumbs, butter and paprika; sprinkle over potatoes. Bake, uncovered, at 350° for 35-40 minutes or until heated through. **Yield:** 8 servings.

*Editor's Note: Reduced-fat or fat-free mayonnaise may not be substituted for regular mayonnaise.

SERVING SUGGESTION

Here's a tasty dessert that will keep you toasty.
Fill canned peach halves with a scoop of ricotta cheese;
sprinkle with cinnamon. Broil or grill until the cheese bubbles.

PORK NOODLE CASSEROLE

I learned to make this hearty dish from my grandmother. We never have a family get-together without it. It's a great addition to a buffet and makes a filling meal with warm rolls.
—Barbara Beyer, Two Rivers, Wisconsin

3 cups cubed cooked pork
1 cup chicken broth
1 can (14-3/4 ounces) cream-style corn
1 jar (4-1/2 ounces) whole mushrooms, drained
2/3 cup chopped green pepper
2/3 cup chopped onion
4 ounces process cheese (Velveeta), diced
2 tablespoons diced pimientos
1/2 teaspoon salt
1/4 teaspoon pepper
8 ounces uncooked egg noodles

In a large bowl, combine the first 10 ingredients; fold in the noodles. Spoon into a greased 2-1/2-qt. baking dish. Cover and bake at 325° for 1 hour or until the noodles are tender, stirring every 20 minutes. **Yield:** 6 servings.

HAM 'N' POTATOES AU GRATIN

(Pictured above)

*The comforting flavor of ham and potatoes can't be beat. This is a nice recipe
to share at covered-dish dinners—it's a meal in itself.*
—Leila Long, Rock Hill, South Carolina

1/4 cup chopped green onions
1/4 cup chopped green pepper
  2 tablespoons butter *or* margarine,
    divided
  3 cups cooked diced peeled potatoes
  2 cups cubed fully cooked ham
1/4 cup mayonnaise
  1 tablespoon all-purpose flour
1/8 teaspoon pepper
3/4 cup milk
  1 cup (4 ounces) shredded cheddar
    cheese

In a skillet, saute the onions and green pepper in 1 tablespoon butter until tender. In a bowl, combine the potatoes, ham, mayonnaise and onion mixture. Pour into an ungreased 11-in. x 7-in. x 2-in. baking dish.

In a saucepan, melt remaining butter. Stir in flour and pepper until smooth. Gradually add milk. Bring to a boil; cook and stir for 1 minute or until thickened. Stir in cheese just until melted. Pour over potato mixture. Cover and bake at 350° for 30 minutes or until bubbly. **Yield:** 4-6 servings.

SMOKED PORK CHOPS WITH SWEET POTATOES

Apple and sweet potato flavors combine so nicely with pork.
My family enjoys simple dinners like this one.
—Helen Sanders, Fort Myers, Florida

6 fully cooked smoked pork loin
  chops
1 tablespoon vegetable oil
4 large sweet potatoes, cooked,
  peeled and cut lengthwise into
  thirds
1/2 cup packed brown sugar
1/8 teaspoon pepper
2 large tart apples, peeled and thinly
  sliced
1/4 cup apple juice *or* water

In a large skillet, brown pork chops in oil on each side. Transfer to a greased 13-in. x 9-in. x 2-in. baking dish. Top with sweet potatoes. Combine brown sugar and pepper; sprinkle over sweet potatoes. Top with apples; drizzle with apple juice.

Cover and bake at 375° for 30 minutes. Uncover; bake 10-15 minutes longer or until the apples are tender. **Yield:** 6 servings.

TIMELY TIP

Store fresh pork that will be used within 6 hours of purchase in the refrigerator in its store packaging. For longer storage, remove the packaging and wrap loosely with waxed paper; store in the coldest part of the refrigerator for up to 2 days.

SCALLOPED POTATOES AND HAM

The nice thing about this creamy casserole is that the potatoes, eggs and ham can all be prepared ahead of time. Assembly is easy, and you can even use leftovers.
—Nancy Snyder, Albuquerque, New Mexico

1 cup (8 ounces) sour cream
1/2 cup whipping cream
1 tablespoon snipped chives
1-1/2 teaspoons salt
7-1/2 cups thinly sliced cooked peeled
  potatoes (about 6 medium)
3 hard-cooked eggs, sliced
1 cup diced fully cooked ham
1 cup soft bread crumbs
1 tablespoon butter *or* margarine,
  melted
1/4 teaspoon onion salt

In a bowl, combine the sour cream, whipping cream, chives and salt; mix well. In a greased 2-qt. baking dish, layer 2-1/2 cups potatoes, eggs and 3/4 cup sour cream mixture. Top with 2-1/2 cups of potatoes, ham and remaining potatoes. Pour the remaining cream mixture over top.

Combine bread crumbs, butter and onion salt; sprinkle over top. Bake, uncovered, at 350° for 55-60 minutes or until heated through. **Yield:** 6-8 servings.

CHILI CASSEROLE

*Even people who usually bypass casseroles can't stay away from this
zesty meat and rice dish. The seasonings make it irresistible.*
—Marietta Slater, Augusta, Kansas

1 pound bulk pork sausage
2 cups water
1 can (15-1/2 ounces) chili beans,
  undrained
1 can (14-1/2 ounces) diced tomatoes,
  undrained
3/4 cup uncooked long grain rice
1/4 cup chopped onion
1 tablespoon chili powder
1 teaspoon Worcestershire sauce
1 teaspoon prepared mustard
3/4 teaspoon salt
1/8 teaspoon garlic powder
1 cup (4 ounces) shredded cheddar
  cheese

In a skillet, cook the sausage over medium heat until no longer pink; drain. Transfer to a slow cooker. Add the next 10 ingredients; stir well. Cover and cook on low for 7 hours or until rice is tender. Stir in cheese; cook 10 minutes longer or until cheese is melted. **Yield:** 6 servings.

SLOW-COOKED HAM 'N' BROCCOLI

*This sensational dish is so wonderful to come home to, especially on a cool fall or winter day.
It's a delicious way to use up leftover holiday ham, too.*
—Jill Pennington, Jacksonville, Florida

3 cups cubed fully cooked ham
1 package (10 ounces) frozen
  chopped broccoli, thawed
1 can (10-3/4 ounces) condensed
  cream of mushroom soup,
  undiluted
1 jar (8 ounces) process cheese sauce
1 can (8 ounces) sliced water
  chestnut, drained
1-1/4 cups uncooked instant rice
1 cup milk
1 celery rib, chopped
1 medium onion, chopped
1/8 to 1/4 teaspoon pepper
1/2 teaspoon paprika

In a slow cooker, combine the first 10 ingredients; mix well. Cover and cook on high for 2-3 hours or until the rice is tender. Let stand for 10 minutes before serving. Sprinkle with paprika. **Yield:** 6-8 servings.

TIMELY TIP

*When using ham as a flavoring in soups, bean dishes or stir-fries,
finely chop the meat. You'll get more intense,
evenly distributed flavor than with a few large chunks.*

Sausage Potato Medley

*We raise our own meat and vegetables on our farm. I had few recipes
that used sausage, so I developed this one. I tried it out when my
Home Extension Club came for brunch, and everyone liked it and asked for
the recipe. Now, club members want me to serve this every time I'm the hostess!*
—Marie Clouse, Hope, Indiana

4 cups thinly sliced peeled potatoes
1 pound bulk pork sausage
3/4 cup chopped onion
1 cup (4 ounces) shredded cheddar
  cheese
3 tablespoons butter *or* margarine
1/4 cup all-purpose flour
1/2 teaspoon salt
1/4 teaspoon pepper
2 cups milk

Place potatoes in a saucepan and cover with water; cover and bring to a boil over medium-high heat. Cook for 5 minutes. Drain; place in a greased 2-qt. baking dish.

In a large skillet, cook sausage and onion over medium heat until meat is no longer pink; drain. Spoon over potatoes; sprinkle with cheese.

In a saucepan, melt butter; stir in flour, salt and pepper until smooth. Gradually add milk. Bring to a boil; cook and stir for 2 minutes or until thickened and bubbly. Pour over cheese. Cover and bake at 350° for 45-50 minutes or until potatoes are tender. **Yield:** 4-6 servings.

Serving Suggestion

*For a quick fruit salad, cube and combine watermelon,
honeydew and cantaloupe.*

Tangy Reuben Bake

*My husband's background is Czech, so just about everyone in the family loves sauerkraut,
especially in this casserole. When I want a bit more zip, I add a third cup of sliced green pepper.
My daughter won a purple ribbon at the state fair with this recipe.*
—Jewell Kronaizl, Vermillion, South Dakota

3 medium potatoes, peeled, sliced
  and cooked
8 ounces fully cooked kielbasa *or*
  Polish sausage, thinly sliced
1 can (8 ounces) sauerkraut, rinsed
  and drained
1/2 cup Thousand Island salad dressing
2 tablespoons sugar
2 tablespoons minced fresh parsley
1 tablespoon dried minced onion
1/2 to 1 teaspoon caraway seeds
3/4 cup shredded cheddar cheese

In a bowl, combine the first eight ingredients. Transfer to a greased 8-in. square baking dish. Bake, uncovered, at 350° for 25 minutes. Sprinkle with cheese. Bake 5 minutes longer or until cheese is melted. **Yield:** 4 servings.

PORK AND CORN CASSEROLE

A satisfying supper includes this casserole fresh from the oven, a garden salad and buttermilk biscuits. It's a winner every time!
—Karen Sesto, South Portland, Maine

7 cups uncooked egg noodles
1 pound ground pork
1 small green pepper, chopped
1 can (14-3/4 ounces) cream-style corn
1 can (11-1/2 ounces) condensed chicken with rice soup, undiluted
1 jar (2 ounces) diced pimientos, drained
8 ounces process cheese (Velveeta), cubed
1/2 cup dry bread crumbs
2 tablespoons butter *or* margarine, melted

Cook noodles according to package directions; drain. In a large skillet, cook pork and green pepper over medium heat until meat is no longer pink; drain. In a bowl, combine the noodles, corn, soup, pimientos, cheese and pork mixture; mix well.

Transfer to a greased shallow 2-1/2-qt. baking dish. Combine bread crumbs and butter; sprinkle over noodle mixture. Bake, uncovered, at 350° for 30-35 minutes or until bubbly and top is golden brown. **Yield:** 6-8 servings.

SEAFOOD CLASSICS

Seafood comes in many
varieties to suit differing
tastes and budgets. In this
chapter you'll find 23 delicious
recipes using fish fillets,
shrimp, canned salmon
and family-favorite tuna,
just to name a few.
Soon you'll be swimming
in compliments.

PADRE ISLAND SHELLS (P. 112)

CATCH-OF-THE-DAY CASSEROLE (P. 104)
BROCCOLI TUNA BAKE (P. 104)

CATCH-OF-THE-DAY CASSEROLE

(Pictured on page 103)

This super salmon recipe comes from my dear mother-in-law. She's one of the best cooks I know and one of the best mothers—a real gem.
—Cathy Clugston, Cloverdale, Indiana

4 ounces small shell pasta
1 can (10-3/4 ounces) condensed cream of celery soup, undiluted
1/2 cup mayonnaise*
1/4 cup milk
1/4 cup shredded cheddar cheese
1 package (10 ounces) frozen peas, thawed
1 can (7-1/2 ounces) salmon, drained, bones and skin removed
1 tablespoon finely chopped onion

Cook pasta according to package directions. Meanwhile, in a bowl, combine the soup, mayonnaise, milk and cheese until blended. Stir in peas, salmon and onion. Drain pasta; add to salmon mixture. Transfer to a greased 2-qt. baking dish. Bake, uncovered, at 350° for 30-35 minutes or until bubbly. **Yield:** 4 servings.

   ***Editor's Note:** Reduced-fat or fat-free mayonnaise may not be substituted for regular mayonnaise.

SERVING SUGGESTION

For a sweet, simple ending to a casserole dinner, mix together an 8-ounce package of cream cheese and a 7-ounce jar of marshmallow creme. Use as a dip for sliced apples, pears or other fruit.

BROCCOLI TUNA BAKE

(Pictured on page 103)

I remember the day I rushed home from school with this recipe in hand from my home economics class. My parents loved it then, and my husband and son do now. This recipe comes to mind on a busy evening, when I need a good quick meal.
—Pamela Tesoriero, Etiwanda, California

1 can (10-3/4 ounces) condensed cream of chicken soup, undiluted
1/3 cup milk
1 tablespoon lemon juice
1 can (12 ounces) albacore tuna, drained and flaked
1-1/2 cups cooked rice
1/4 teaspoon pepper
1 package (10 ounces) frozen broccoli florets, cooked and drained
1/2 cup shredded cheddar cheese

In a bowl, combine the soup, milk and lemon juice. Stir in tuna, rice and pepper. Transfer to a greased 10-in. pie plate or quiche dish. Bake, uncovered, at 375° for 25 minutes. Top with broccoli; sprinkle with cheese. Bake 5-10 minutes longer or until cheese is melted. **Yield:** 4-6 servings.

CHEDDAR SHRIMP AND PENNE

(Pictured above)

*My wife and I take turns in the kitchen. When I created this
creamy dish, it quickly became one of our favorites.*
—Brad Walker, Holt, Michigan

2 cups uncooked penne *or* other
　medium tube pasta
2 garlic cloves, minced
2 tablespoons butter *or* margarine
2 tablespoons all-purpose flour
1/2 teaspoon salt
1/4 teaspoon pepper
2 cups milk
1-1/2 cups (6 ounces) shredded cheddar
　cheese, *divided*
1 pound cooked medium shrimp,
　peeled and deveined
1 can (15-1/4 ounces) whole kernel
　corn, drained

Cook pasta according to package directions. Meanwhile, in a large saucepan, cook the garlic in butter over medium heat for 1 minute. Stir in flour, salt and pepper until blended. Gradually add milk. Bring to a boil; cook and stir for 2 minutes or until thickened. Reduce heat; stir in 1 cup of cheese until melted. Remove from the heat.

Drain pasta; add pasta, shrimp and corn to cheese sauce. Transfer to a greased 2-qt. baking dish. Cover and bake at 350° for 25 minutes. Uncover; sprinkle with remaining cheese. Bake 10-15 minutes longer or until bubbly. **Yield:** 4-6 servings.

BAKED FISH AND RICE

This simple-to-fix meal was an instant hit at our house. Fish and rice
are a tasty change of pace from traditional meat-and-potato fare.
—Jo Groth, Plainfield, Iowa

1-1/2 cups boiling chicken broth
  1/2 cup uncooked long grain rice
  1/4 teaspoon Italian seasoning
  1/4 teaspoon garlic powder
    1 package (10 ounces) frozen
      chopped broccoli, thawed and
      drained
    1 tablespoon grated Parmesan cheese
    1 can (2.8 ounces) french-fried
      onions, *divided*
    1 pound fish fillets
Dash paprika
  1/2 cup shredded cheddar cheese

In a greased 11-in. x 7-in. x 2-in. baking dish, combine the broth, rice, Italian seasoning and garlic powder. Cover and bake at 375° for 10 minutes. Add broccoli, Parmesan cheese and half of the onions. Top with fish fillets; sprinkle with paprika.

Cover and bake 20-25 minutes longer or until the fish flakes easily with a fork. Uncover; sprinkle with cheddar cheese and remaining onions. Bake 3 minutes longer or until cheese is melted. **Yield:** 4 servings.

PERFECT PARTNERS

Here's a simple salad idea. Sprinkle dried apricots or
cranberries over mixed greens for a burst of color and flavor.

TUNA NOODLE HOT DISH

This is an old recipe that I tweaked to suit my family's tastes.
I like to serve it with breadsticks and a veggie tray.
—Sheila Sjolund, Deer River, Minnesota

 12 ounces uncooked egg noodles
   2 cans (10-3/4 ounces *each*)
     condensed cream of chicken soup,
     undiluted
   1 cup (8 ounces) sour cream
 1/3 cup milk
   1 can (12 ounces) tuna, drained and
     flaked
   1 cup shredded process cheese
     (Velveeta)
   1 medium onion, chopped
   1 jar (2 ounces) diced pimientos,
     drained
   1 can (2-1/4 ounces) sliced ripe olives,
     drained
   1 cup crushed potato chips
Paprika

Cook noodles according to package directions; drain. In a large bowl, combine the soup, sour cream and milk. Stir in the noodles, tuna, cheese, onion, pimientos and olives. Pour into a greased 13-in. x 9-in. x 2-in. baking dish. Sprinkle with potato chips and paprika. Bake, uncovered, at 375° for 30-35 minutes or until heated through. **Yield:** 6-8 servings.

CRAB QUICHE

*The crab really comes through in this special quiche. If you like onions,
go heavy on the topping. If not, just garnish with a few.*
—Maryellen Hays, Wolcottville, Indiana

1 unbaked deep-dish pastry shell
   (9 inches)
3 tablespoons all-purpose flour
4 eggs
1 cup milk
1/4 teaspoon salt
1/8 teaspoon pepper
1/8 teaspoon ground nutmeg
1 can (6 ounces) crabmeat, drained,
   flaked and cartilage removed
1 can (4 ounces) mushroom stems
   and pieces, drained
1/2 cup shredded Swiss cheese
1/2 cup shredded cheddar cheese
1/2 cup grated Parmesan cheese
1/2 cup french-fried onions

Bake unpricked pastry shell at 425° for 5 minutes. Meanwhile, in a bowl, combine the flour, eggs, milk, salt, pepper and nutmeg until smooth. Add the crab, mushrooms and cheeses. Pour into pastry shell.

Bake at 350° for 35 minutes. Top with onions. Bake 10 minutes longer or until a knife inserted near the center comes out clean. Let stand for 10 minutes before serving. **Yield:** 8 servings.

SHRIMP CHICKEN SKILLET

*I'm a first-grade teacher who has hectic evenings, so I appreciate this dish. I can make it with
items I have on hand, plus it tastes great. My husband requests it often.*
—Kelly Corrigan, Crawfordville, Florida

1/2 pound fresh mushrooms, sliced
1/4 cup butter *or* margarine
1/2 cup sliced green onions
2 cans (10-3/4 ounces *each*)
   condensed cream of chicken soup,
   undiluted
1/2 cup half-and-half cream
1/4 cup chicken broth
1/4 cup sherry *or* additional chicken
   broth
1 cup (4 ounces) shredded cheddar
   cheese
2 cups cubed cooked chicken
2 cups cooked medium shrimp,
   peeled and deveined
2 tablespoons minced fresh parsley
Hot cooked rice

In a large skillet, saute mushrooms in butter for 5 minutes. Add onions; saute for 3 minutes or until tender. Stir in the soup, cream, broth and sherry or additional broth. Cook and stir over medium-low heat until blended; stir in cheese until melted. Add the chicken, shrimp and parsley; heat through. Serve over rice. **Yield:** 6 servings.

Tuna in the Straw Casserole

(Pictured above)

Shoestring potatoes give this main dish great flavor and crunch. Even my husband, who doesn't normally care for tuna, counts it among his favorites.
—Kallee McCreery, Escondido, California

1 can (10-3/4 ounces) condensed cream of mushroom soup, undiluted
1 can (5 ounces) evaporated milk
1 can (6 ounces) tuna, drained and flaked
1 can (4 ounces) mushroom stems and pieces, drained
1 cup frozen mixed vegetables, thawed
2 cups potato sticks, *divided*

In a bowl, combine the soup and milk until blended. Stir in the tuna, mushrooms, vegetables and 1-1/2 cups potato sticks. Transfer to a greased 1-1/2-qt. baking dish. Bake, uncovered, at 375° for 20 minutes. Sprinkle with the remaining potatoes. Bake 5-10 minutes longer or until bubbly and potatoes are crisp. **Yield:** 4 servings.

CRAB THERMIDOR

The taste of this dish is as impressive as its name. Imitation crabmeat keeps it affordable,
but it's fabulous with the real thing, especially for special occasions.
—Mary Rose Fedorka, Jamestown, New York

3 tablespoons butter *or* margarine
3 tablespoons all-purpose flour
1/4 teaspoon salt
1/8 teaspoon paprika
1/8 teaspoon ground nutmeg
1-1/2 cups half-and-half cream
2 ounces process cheese (Velveeta), cubed
1 tablespoon lemon juice
1/2 cup shredded cheddar cheese
2 packages (8 ounces *each*) imitation crabmeat, flaked
Additional paprika, optional

In a large saucepan, melt butter. Stir in the flour, salt, paprika and nutmeg until smooth. Gradually add cream. Bring to a boil; cook and stir for 2 minutes or until thickened. Reduce heat; stir in process cheese and lemon juice until cheese is melted. Remove from the heat; stir in cheddar cheese until melted. Stir in crab.

Transfer to a greased 1-qt. baking dish. Sprinkle with additional paprika if desired. Bake, uncovered, at 350° for 20-25 minutes or until bubbly. **Yield:** 4 servings.

BLEND OF THE BAYOU

My sister-in-law shared this recipe when I first moved to Louisiana. It's been
handed down in my husband's family for generations. It's quick to
prepare, nutritious and beautiful. I've passed it on to my children, too.
—Ruby Williams, Bogalusa, Louisiana

1 package (8 ounces) cream cheese, cubed
4 tablespoons butter *or* margarine, *divided*
1 large onion, chopped
2 celery ribs, chopped
1 large green pepper, chopped
1 pound cooked medium shrimp, peeled and deveined
2 cans (6 ounces *each*) crabmeat, drained, flaked and cartilage removed
1 can (10-3/4 ounces) condensed cream of mushroom soup, undiluted
1 jar (4-1/2 ounces) sliced mushrooms, drained
1 teaspoon garlic salt
3/4 teaspoon hot pepper sauce
1/2 teaspoon cayenne pepper
3/4 cup cooked rice
3/4 cup shredded cheddar cheese
1/2 cup crushed butter-flavored crackers (about 12 crackers)

In a small saucepan, cook and stir the cream cheese and 2 tablespoons butter over low heat until melted and smooth. In a large skillet, saute the onion, celery and green pepper in remaining butter until tender. Stir in the shrimp, crab, soup, mushrooms, garlic salt, hot pepper sauce, cayenne and rice.

Transfer to a greased 2-qt. baking dish. Combine cheese and cracker crumbs; sprinkle over the top. Bake, uncovered, at 350° for 25-30 minutes or until bubbly. **Yield:** 6-8 servings.

SEA SHELL CRAB CASSEROLE

(Pictured at right)

This was one of my favorite recipes when I was growing up.
These days I make it for my husband and our son.
—Brandi Jergenson, Vaughn, Montana

1-1/2 cups uncooked medium shell pasta
1 large onion, chopped
1 medium green pepper, chopped
3 celery ribs, chopped
3 tablespoons butter *or* margarine
1 can (12 ounces) evaporated milk
1/2 cup mayonnaise*
1 teaspoon salt
1 teaspoon ground mustard
1 teaspoon paprika
1 teaspoon Worcestershire sauce
1 can (2-1/4 ounces) sliced ripe olives, drained
2 packages (8 ounces *each*) imitation crabmeat, flaked

Cook pasta according to package directions. Meanwhile, in a large skillet, saute the onion, green pepper and celery in butter until tender. In a large bowl, combine milk and mayonnaise until blended. Stir in the salt, mustard, paprika and Worcestershire sauce. Drain pasta; add the pasta, olives and crab to the milk mixture.

Transfer to a greased shallow 2-qt. baking dish. Cover and bake at 350° for 25 minutes. Uncover; bake 5-10 minutes longer or until heated through. **Yield:** 6 servings.

*Editor's Note: Reduced-fat or fat-free mayonnaise may not be substituted for regular mayonnaise.

PINEAPPLE SHRIMP RICE BAKE

(Pictured at right)

The first time I made this casserole, my son begged me to make it again soon. That was more than 20 years ago, and it's still a favorite among family and friends. When I serve it at a luncheon, I add a fruit salad and warm breadsticks.
—Vi Manning, Spring Hill, Florida

2 cups chicken broth
1 cup uncooked long grain rice
1 garlic clove, minced
1 medium onion, chopped
1 medium green pepper, julienned
2 tablespoons vegetable oil
2 teaspoons soy sauce
1/4 teaspoon ground ginger *or* 1 teaspoon minced fresh gingerroot
1-1/2 pounds cooked medium shrimp, peeled and deveined
1-1/2 cups cubed fully cooked ham
1 can (8 ounces) pineapple tidbits, undrained

In a large saucepan, bring broth to a boil. Stir in rice. Reduce heat; cover and simmer for 25 minutes or until tender. Meanwhile, in a large skillet, saute the garlic, onion and green pepper in oil until tender. Stir in soy sauce and ginger. Add shrimp, ham and pineapple. Stir in rice.

Transfer to a greased 2-qt. baking dish. Bake, uncovered, at 350° for 15-20 minutes or until heated through. Stir before serving. **Yield:** 8 servings.

PADRE ISLAND SHELLS

(Pictured below and on page 102)

I'm asked to fix this dish over and over, so there's no doubt it's worth sharing.
—Dona Grover, Rockwall, Texas

1/2 cup chopped green pepper
 2 tablespoons thinly sliced green onion
 4 tablespoons butter *or* margarine, *divided*
 2 tablespoons all-purpose flour
1/2 teaspoon salt
 2 cups milk
 1 large tomato, peeled and chopped
 2 tablespoons minced fresh parsley
1-1/4 cups shredded pepper Jack *or* Monterey Jack cheese, *divided*
3-1/2 cups medium shell pasta, cooked and drained
 3 cans (6 ounces *each*) crabmeat, drained, flaked and cartilage removed *or* 1 pound imitation crabmeat, flaked
1/2 cup dry bread crumbs

In a large saucepan, saute green pepper and onion in 2 tablespoons butter until tender. Stir in the flour and salt until blended. Gradually stir in milk. Bring to a boil; cook and stir for 2 minutes or until thickened. Stir in tomato and parsley.

Remove from the heat; stir in 1 cup of cheese until melted. Stir in pasta and crab. Transfer to a greased shallow 2-1/2-qt. baking dish. Cover and bake at 350° for 20 minutes.

Melt the remaining butter; toss with bread crumbs. Sprinkle over casserole. Top with remaining cheese. Bake, uncovered, for 5-10 minutes or until golden brown.
Yield: 6-8 servings.

SEAFOOD LASAGNA

Everyone seems to enjoy this dish. I like to prepare it the day before and refrigerate it overnight. Just take it out of the fridge 30 minutes before popping it in the oven.
—Viola Walmer, Tequesta, Florida

3/4 cup chopped onion
2 tablespoons butter *or* margarine
1 package (8 ounces) cream cheese, cubed
1-1/2 cups (12 ounces) small-curd cottage cheese
1 egg, beaten
2 teaspoons dried basil
1 teaspoon salt
1/4 teaspoon pepper
1 can (10-3/4 ounces) condensed cream of shrimp soup, undiluted
1 can (10-3/4 ounces) condensed cream of mushroom soup, undiluted
1/2 cup white wine *or* chicken broth
1/2 cup milk
2 packages (8 ounces *each*) imitation crabmeat, flaked
1 can (6 ounces) small shrimp, rinsed and drained
9 lasagna noodles, cooked and drained
1/2 cup grated Parmesan cheese
3/4 cup shredded Monterey Jack cheese

In a large skillet, saute onion in butter until tender. Reduce heat. Add cream cheese; cook and stir until melted and smooth. Stir in cottage cheese, egg, basil, salt and pepper. Remove from the heat and set aside. In a bowl, combine the soups, wine or broth, milk, crab and shrimp.

Arrange three noodles in a greased 13-in. x 9-in. x 2-in. baking dish. Spread with a third of cottage cheese mixture and a third of the seafood mixture. Repeat layers twice. Sprinkle with Parmesan cheese.

Cover and bake at 350° for 40 minutes. Uncover; sprinkle with the Monterey Jack cheese. Bake 10 minutes longer or until cheese is melted and lasagna is bubbly. Let stand for 15 minutes before serving. **Yield:** 12 servings.

POTATO SALMON CASSEROLE

I like to experiment with cooking new things, which is how I came up with this tasty dish. It's a great way to work salmon into your menu.
—Laura Varney, Batavia, Ohio

2-1/2 cups cubed cooked potatoes
2 cups frozen peas, thawed
1 cup mayonnaise*
1 can (14-3/4 ounces) salmon, drained, bones and skin removed
5 ounces process cheese (Velveeta), cubed
1 cup finely crushed cornflakes
1 tablespoon butter *or* margarine, melted

Place potatoes in a greased 2-qt. baking dish. Top with peas; spread with mayonnaise. Top with salmon and cheese. Bake, uncovered, at 350° for 30 minutes. Combine cornflake crumbs and butter; sprinkle over top. Bake 5-10 minutes longer or until golden brown. **Yield:** 4-6 servings.

*Editor's Note: Reduced-fat or fat-free mayonnaise may not be substituted for regular mayonnaise.

CRUMB-TOPPED HADDOCK

With only five ingredients, this creamy dish with a crispy topping is a breeze to make.
—Debbie Solt, Lewistown, Pennsylvania

2 pounds haddock *or* cod fillets
1 can (10-3/4 ounces) condensed
    cream of shrimp soup, undiluted
1 teaspoon grated onion
1 teaspoon Worcestershire sauce
1 cup crushed butter-flavored
    crackers (about 25 crackers)

Arrange fillets in a greased 13-in. x 9-in. x 2-in. baking dish. Combine the soup, onion and Worcestershire sauce; pour over fish. Bake, uncovered, at 375° for 20 minutes. Sprinkle with cracker crumbs. Bake 15 minutes longer or until fish flakes easily with a fork. **Yield:** 6-8 servings.

OVEN JAMBALAYA

If you're looking for an easy but delicious version of jambalaya, this is it.
—Ruby Williams, Bogalusa, Louisiana

2-1/4 cups water
1-1/2 cups uncooked long grain rice
1 can (10-3/4 ounces) condensed
    cream of celery soup, undiluted
1 can (10-3/4 ounces) condensed
    cream of onion soup, undiluted
1 can (10 ounces) diced tomatoes and
    green chilies, undrained
1 pound fully cooked smoked
    sausage, cut into 1/2-inch slices
1 pound cooked medium shrimp,
    peeled and deveined

In a large bowl, combine the first five ingredients; mix well. Pour into a greased 13-in. x 9-in. x 2-in. baking dish. Cover and bake at 350° for 40 minutes. Stir in sausage and shrimp. Cover and bake 20-30 minutes longer or until the rice is tender. **Yield:** 8-10 servings.

FAVORITE HALIBUT CASSEROLE

I've been using this recipe since my college days. I even took it to Western Samoa, when I was teaching school there. You can substitute any whitefish for the halibut.
—Gayle Brown, Millville, Utah

5 tablespoons butter *or* margarine,
    divided
1/4 cup all-purpose flour
1/2 teaspoon salt
1/8 to 1/4 teaspoon white pepper
1-1/2 cups milk
1 small green pepper, chopped
1 small onion, chopped
2 cups cubed cooked halibut (about 1
    pound)
3 hard-cooked eggs, chopped
1 jar (2 ounces) diced pimientos,
    drained
1/3 cup shredded cheddar cheese

In a large saucepan, melt 4 tablespoons butter. Stir in flour, salt and pepper until smooth. Gradually add milk. Bring to a boil; cook and stir for 2 minutes or until thickened. Remove from the heat; cover and set aside. In a small skillet, saute green pepper and onion in remaining butter until tender. Stir into white sauce. Add the halibut, eggs and pimientos.

Transfer to a greased 1-1/2-qt. baking dish. Sprinkle with cheese. Bake, uncovered, at 375° for 15-20 minutes or until bubbly. **Yield:** 4 servings.

SHRIMP RICE CASSEROLE

I've been making this delicious dish for more than 30 years, and it hasn't failed me once.
It's fast to fix plus it always pleases family and guests.
—Marcia Urschel, Webster, New York

12 ounces cooked medium shrimp, peeled and deveined
2 cups cooked rice
1 can (10-3/4 ounces) condensed cream of mushroom soup, undiluted
1 can (4 ounces) mushroom stems and pieces, drained
1 cup (4 ounces) shredded cheddar cheese
4 tablespoons butter *or* margarine, melted, *divided*
2 tablespoons chopped green pepper
2 tablespoons chopped onion
1 tablespoon lemon juice
1/2 teaspoon white pepper
1/2 teaspoon ground mustard
1/2 teaspoon Worcestershire sauce
1 cup soft bread crumbs

In a large bowl, combine the shrimp, rice, soup, mushrooms, cheese, 2 tablespoons butter, green pepper, onion, lemon juice, pepper, mustard and Worcestershire sauce.

Transfer to a greased 1-1/2-qt. baking dish. Combine bread crumbs and remaining butter; sprinkle over top. Bake, uncovered, at 375° for 30-35 minutes or until lightly browned. **Yield:** 6 servings.

CHEESY TUNA LASAGNA

This wonderful casserole was added to my recipe collection many years ago.
The tuna and three-cheese blend wins over doubters who say they aren't fond of fish.
—Virginia Ferris, Lyons, Michigan

1 medium onion, chopped
2 tablespoons butter *or* margarine
1 can (12 ounces) tuna, drained and flaked
1 can (10-3/4 ounces) condensed cream of mushroom soup, undiluted
1/2 cup milk
1/2 teaspoon garlic salt
1/2 teaspoon dried oregano
1/4 teaspoon pepper
9 lasagna noodles, cooked and drained
1-1/2 cups small-curd cottage cheese
8 ounces sliced mozzarella cheese
1/4 cup grated Parmesan cheese

In a large saucepan, saute onion in butter until tender. Stir in the tuna, soup, milk, garlic salt, oregano and pepper until combined. Spread 3/4 cupful into a greased 11-in. x 7-in. x 2-in. baking dish.

Layer with three noodles (trimming if necessary), 3/4 cup tuna mixture, half of the cottage cheese and a third of the mozzarella cheese. Repeat layers. Top with remaining noodles, tuna mixture and mozzarella. Sprinkle with Parmesan cheese.

Bake, uncovered, at 350° for 25-30 minutes or until bubbly. Let stand for 10-15 minutes before serving. **Yield:** 6-8 servings.

CORN BREAD-TOPPED SALMON

There's no need to serve bread when you've already baked it into your main dish.
This economical casserole tastes great with tuna or chicken as well.
—Billie Wilson, Murray, Kentucky

2 cans (10-3/4 ounces *each*)
  condensed cream of mushroom
  soup, undiluted
1/4 cup milk
1 can (14-3/4 ounces) salmon,
  drained, bones and skin removed
1-1/2 cups frozen peas, thawed
1 package (8-1/2 ounces) corn
  bread/muffin mix
1 jar (4 ounces) diced pimientos,
  drained
1/4 cup finely chopped green pepper
1 teaspoon finely chopped onion
1/2 teaspoon celery seed
1/4 teaspoon dried thyme

In a large saucepan, bring the soup and milk to a boil. Add salmon and peas. Pour into a greased shallow 2-1/2-qt. baking dish. Prepare corn bread batter according to package directions; stir in the remaining ingredients. Spoon over salmon mixture.

Bake, uncovered, at 400° for 30-35 minutes or until a toothpick inserted in the corn bread comes out clean. **Yield:** 6-8 servings.

SERVING SUGGESTION

For a light, easy dessert that mixes sweet and tart,
drizzle chocolate syrup over orange or lemon sherbet.

BROCCOLI TUNA SQUARES

Family and friends always ask for this recipe because it's different than traditional tuna casserole.
I make it when I need something quick, which is often. We're always on the go.
—Janet Juncker, Geneva, Ohio

1 tube (8 ounces) refrigerated
  crescent rolls
1 cup (4 ounces) shredded Monterey
  Jack cheese
1 package (10 ounces) frozen chopped
  broccoli, cooked and drained
4 eggs
1 can (10-3/4 ounces) condensed
  cream of broccoli soup, undiluted
2 tablespoons mayonnaise
3/4 teaspoon onion powder
1/2 teaspoon dill weed
1 can (12 ounces) tuna, drained and
  flaked
1 tablespoon diced pimientos,
  drained

Unroll crescent roll dough into one long rectangle; place in an ungreased 13-in. x 9-in. x 2-in. baking dish. Seal seams and perforations; press onto bottom and 1/2 in. up the sides. Sprinkle with cheese and broccoli. In a bowl, combine the eggs, soup, mayonnaise, onion powder and dill; mix well. Stir in tuna and pimientos; pour over broccoli.

Bake, uncovered, at 350° for 35-40 minutes or until a knife inserted near the center comes out clean. Let stand for 10 minutes before serving. **Yield:** 8 servings.

NEW ENGLAND FISH BAKE

(Pictured above)

This is one of my favorite seafood dishes. My mother-in-law gave me the recipe.
—Norma DesRoches, Warwick, Rhode Island

4 medium potatoes, peeled
1 teaspoon all-purpose flour
1 small onion, sliced and separated
   into rings
1/2 teaspoon salt
1/4 teaspoon pepper
3/4 cup milk, *divided*
1-1/2 pounds cod, trout, catfish *or* pike
   fillets
3 tablespoons grated Parmesan
   cheese, optional
2 tablespoons minced fresh parsley
1/4 teaspoon paprika

Place potatoes in a saucepan and cover with water; cover and bring to a boil over medium-high heat. Cook for 15-20 minutes or until almost tender; drain. Cut into 1/8-in.-thick slices; place in a greased shallow 2-qt. baking dish. Sprinkle with flour. Top with onion; sprinkle with salt and pepper.

Pour half of the milk over potatoes. Top with fish and remaining milk. Sprinkle with Parmesan cheese if desired. Cover and bake at 375° for 20-30 minutes or until fish flakes easily with a fork. Sprinkle with parsley and paprika. **Yield:** 3-4 servings.

QUICK & EASY

These snappy dishes will please both you and your family. All 54 of them are short on preparation time but not short on flavor. You'll hear compliments every time you make one. A hearty, satisfying meal is just minutes away.

MICROWAVE TUNA 'N' CHIPS (P. 146)

CORN BREAD CHILI BAKE (P. 120)
ONE-DISH CHICKEN WITH VEGETABLES (P. 120)

CORN BREAD CHILI BAKE

(Pictured on page 119)

My husband has loved this recipe since the day we were married.
He requests it often. It's easy to make, and I usually have the ingredients on hand.
—Becky Grubaugh, Newton, Illinois

2 cans (15 ounces *each*) hot chili
  beans
1 small onion, chopped
3/4 cup shredded cheddar cheese
1 package (8-1/2 ounces) corn
  bread/muffin mix

Place chili beans in a greased 8-in. square baking dish. Top with onion and cheese. Prepare corn bread mix according to package directions; drop batter by spoonfuls over cheese. Bake, uncovered, at 350° for 30-35 minutes or until golden brown. Serve immediately. **Yield:** 4-6 servings.

PERFECT PARTNERS

For a quick dessert, spoon canned apricots or peaches into a custard cup.
Sprinkle with crumbled gingersnap or oatmeal cookies.

ONE-DISH CHICKEN WITH VEGETABLES

(Pictured on page 119)

I like to cook and try new recipes...my niece and I exchange the good ones. I made this dish,
and it looked so pretty that I got out my camera and took a picture of it.
—Katherine McKinley, New Albany, Indiana

1 envelope onion soup mix
1/2 teaspoon garlic powder
1/4 cup olive *or* vegetable oil
4 boneless skinless chicken breast
  halves
4 medium potatoes, cut into chunks
4 medium carrots, cut into 1/4-inch
  slices

In a large resealable plastic bag, combine the soup mix, garlic powder and oil. Add chicken, potatoes and carrots; toss to coat. Arrange in an ungreased 11-in. x 7-in. x 2-in. baking dish. Cover and bake at 425° for 15 minutes. Uncover; bake 15-20 minutes longer or until chicken juices run clear and vegetables are tender. **Yield:** 4 servings.

SERVING SUGGESTION

For a simple salad during cooler months, add halved mushrooms and sliced red
onions to a mixed green salad. Serve with prepared dressing of your choice.

HAM 'N' TATER BAKE

(Pictured above)

This casserole reminds me of a loaded baked potato. I usually make it several times a month—I've even served it to company. I'm always asked for the recipe, which I got from my sister.
—Peggy Grieme, Pinehurst, North Carolina

1 package (28 ounces) frozen steak fries
1 package (10 ounces) frozen chopped broccoli, thawed and drained
1-1/2 cups diced fully cooked ham
1 can (10-3/4 ounces) condensed cream of broccoli soup, undiluted
3/4 cup milk
1/2 cup mayonnaise*
1 cup (4 ounces) shredded cheddar cheese

Arrange the fries in a greased 3-qt. baking dish; layer with broccoli and then ham. Combine the soup, milk and mayonnaise until smooth; pour over ham. Cover and bake at 350° for 20 minutes. Uncover; sprinkle with cheese. Bake 20-25 minutes longer or until bubbly. **Yield:** 6-8 servings.

*Editor's Note: Reduced-fat or fat-free mayonnaise may not be substituted for regular mayonnaise.

RANCH CHICKEN 'N' RICE

*When I clipped this recipe from a neighborhood shopper a few years ago,
I couldn't wait to try it. Just as I expected, it quickly became a family favorite.*
—Erlene Crusoe, Litchfield, Minnesota

2 cups uncooked instant rice
1-1/4 cups milk
1 cup water
1 envelope ranch salad dressing mix
1 pound boneless skinless chicken breasts, cut into 1/2-inch strips
1/4 cup butter *or* margarine, melted
Paprika

Place rice in a greased shallow 2-qt. baking dish. In a bowl, combine the milk, water and salad dressing mix; set aside 1/4 cup. Pour remaining mixture over rice. Top with chicken strips. Drizzle with butter and reserved milk mixture. Cover and bake at 350° for 35-40 minutes or until rice is tender and chicken juices run clear. Sprinkle with paprika. **Yield:** 4 servings.

TURKEY ASPARAGUS CASSEROLE

*Convenient frozen asparagus lends bright color and garden flavor
while a sprinkling of french-fried onions provides a yummy crunch.*
—Cheryl Schut, Grand Rapids, Michigan

1 package (10 ounces) frozen chopped asparagus
2 cups cubed cooked turkey *or* chicken
1 can (10-3/4 ounces) condensed cream of chicken soup, undiluted
1/4 cup water
1 can (2.8 ounces) french-fried onions

In a small saucepan, cook asparagus in a small amount of water for 2 minutes; drain. Place in a greased 11-in. x 7-in. x 2-in. baking dish. Top with turkey. Combine soup and water; spoon over turkey. Bake, uncovered, at 350° for 25-30 minutes. Sprinkle with onions. Bake 5 minutes longer or until golden brown. **Yield:** 4 servings.

CHICKEN CROUTON HOT DISH

*This recipe has practically made my mom famous. When she takes it to a potluck, it's loved by all
who taste it. Whenever she serves it to family, the dish is empty at the end of the meal.*
—Beth Gramling, Warren, Pennsylvania

1 can (14-1/2 ounces) chicken broth
1 can (10-3/4 ounces) condensed cream of chicken soup, undiluted
1 cup (8 ounces) sour cream
1/2 cup butter *or* margarine, melted
1 package (14 ounces) seasoned stuffing croutons
4 cups shredded cooked chicken

In a large bowl, combine the broth, soup, sour cream and butter. Stir in croutons and chicken. Transfer to a greased 13-in. x 9-in. x 2-in. baking dish. Bake, uncovered, at 375° for 20-25 minutes or until heated through. **Yield:** 8 servings.

BEEFY PASTA AND RICE

*This wonderful recipe has two things going for it—it's good, and
it's inexpensive to make. I usually serve it with homemade applesauce and biscuits.*
—Heidi Butts, Streetsboro, Ohio

1 pound ground beef
1 medium onion, chopped
1 cup uncooked long grain rice
8 ounces uncooked spaghetti, broken
   into 1-inch pieces
1/4 cup butter *or* margarine
4 cups chicken broth
1 package (10 ounces) frozen peas
Salt and pepper to taste

In a large skillet, cook beef and onion over medium heat until meat is no longer pink; drain. In another skillet, brown rice and spaghetti in butter. Stir in the beef mixture, broth, peas, salt and pepper. Cover and simmer for 20 minutes or until the rice and spaghetti are tender. **Yield:** 8 servings.

SAUSAGE AND WILD RICE

*This hot dish is convenient because it's made in the microwave. It has nice flavor and looks good, too.
Even though I've been making it for more than 10 years, I still get requests for it.*
—Mary Bondegard, Brooksville, Florida

1 package (6 ounces) long grain and
   wild rice
1 pound bulk pork sausage
1 cup chopped green onions
1/2 pound fresh mushrooms, sliced
2 tablespoons all-purpose flour
1 cup chicken broth
1/4 cup half-and-half cream

Prepare rice according to package directions; set aside. Crumble sausage into an ungreased 2-qt. microwave-safe dish. Cover and microwave on high for 5-6 minutes or until no longer pink. Remove with a slotted spoon to paper towels to drain; reserve 2 tablespoons drippings.

Add onions and mushrooms to drippings. Cover and microwave on high for 4 minutes or until tender, stirring twice. Stir in the flour until blended. Gradually add broth and cream. Cover and cook on high for 4-6 minutes until slightly thickened, stirring twice. Stir in rice and sausage. Cover and microwave on high for 10-15 minutes or until liquid is absorbed. Let stand for 5 minutes before serving. **Yield:** 4 servings.

Editor's Note: This recipe was tested in an 850-watt microwave.

PERFECT PARTNERS

*For a light side dish, mix up a quick fruit salad. Add fresh green grapes
to canned mandarin oranges and pineapple tidbits.*

CRUNCHY CHICKEN CASSEROLE

(Pictured above)

*We enjoy this fast all-in-one meal often. I usually have chicken on hand,
but it also makes a great after-Thanksgiving meal using leftover turkey.*
—Patricia Sayers, Smyrna, Tennessee

1 package (6 ounces) instant
chicken-flavored stuffing mix
2 cups frozen mixed vegetables,
thawed
1 can (10-3/4 ounces) condensed
cream of chicken soup, undiluted
1 can (8 ounces) sliced water
chestnuts, drained
2 tablespoons water
1 cup shredded cooked chicken *or*
turkey

Prepare the stuffing mix according to package directions; set aside. In a bowl, combine the mixed vegetables, soup, water chestnuts and water. Transfer to an ungreased 2-qt. baking dish. Top with the chicken and prepared stuffing. Bake, uncovered, at 350° for 25-30 minutes or until heated through. **Yield:** 6 servings.

PORK CHOPS WITH APRICOT RICE

I came up with this recipe to use some of my favorite ingredients. I love the combination of apricots, golden raisins and celery with the crunch of almonds.
—Fayne Lutz, Taos, New Mexico

1 can (15-1/4 ounces) apricot halves, undrained
6 bone-in pork chops (1/2 inch thick)
3 tablespoons butter *or* margarine
1/4 cup chopped celery
2-1/2 cups uncooked instant rice
3/4 cup hot water
1/4 cup golden raisins
1/2 teaspoon ground ginger
1/2 teaspoon salt
1/4 teaspoon white pepper
1/4 cup slivered almonds

Place apricots in a blender or food processor; cover and process until smooth. Set aside. In a skillet over medium heat, brown pork chops in butter for 2-3 minutes on each side; remove and keep warm. In the same skillet, saute celery until tender. Add rice, water, raisins, ginger, salt, pepper and apricot puree; bring to a boil. Remove from the heat; stir in almonds.

Pour into an ungreased 13-in. x 9-in. x 2-in. baking dish. Place the pork chops on top. Cover and bake at 350° for 15-20 minutes or until meat juices run clear and rice is tender. **Yield:** 6 servings.

PERFECT PARTNERS

To complement Pork Chops with Apricot Rice, serve a simple tossed green salad and warm French bread.

HASTY HEARTLAND DINNER

This hearty microwave recipe from the American Egg Board comes in especially handy the week after Easter, when there are plenty of hard-cooked eggs to use up.

1 package (5-1/4 ounces) au gratin potato mix
4 hard-cooked eggs, chopped
1 cup chopped fully cooked ham
1 cup frozen peas

In a microwave, cook potatoes according to package directions. Add contents of sauce packet and milk as directed. Stir in the eggs, ham and peas. Cover with waxed paper. Cook on high for 6 minutes or until heated through, stirring occasionally. Let stand for 5 minutes before serving. **Yield:** 4 servings.

Editor's Note: This recipe was tested in a 700-watt microwave.

SERVING SUGGESTION

For a fast and flavorful dessert, top a scoop of vanilla ice cream or frozen yogurt with canned crushed pineapple.

EASY POTPIE

*The first time you make this recipe, you'll understand how it got its name.
Just about as fast as you can open a couple of cans and brown a crust, it's done.
It's great year-round, but it's especially suited to the winter months
because it comes out of the oven hearty and steaming hot.*
—Laura Odell, Eden, North Carolina

3 cups cubed cooked chicken *or* turkey
1 can (15 ounces) mixed vegetables, drained *or* 2 cups frozen mixed vegetables, thawed
1 can (10-3/4 ounces) condensed cream of celery soup, undiluted
1/4 cup chopped onion
2 tablespoons all-purpose flour
2 cups chicken broth
1/4 teaspoon dried rosemary, crushed
1/4 teaspoon pepper
BISCUIT TOPPING:
1 cup self-rising flour*
1/2 teaspoon pepper *or* lemon-pepper seasoning
1 cup buttermilk
1/2 cup butter *or* margarine, melted

In a large saucepan, combine chicken, vegetables, soup, onion and flour; mix well. Stir in broth, rosemary and pepper. Bring to a boil; cook and stir for 2 minutes or until thickened. Pour into an ungreased shallow 2-1/2-qt. baking dish.

For topping, combine the flour and pepper in a bowl. Stir in buttermilk and butter just until moistened. Spoon over chicken mixture. Bake, uncovered, at 425° for 25 minutes or until golden brown. **Yield:** 6 servings.

*Editor's Note: As a substitute for self-rising flour, place 1-1/2 teaspoons baking powder and 1/2 teaspoon salt in a measuring cup. Add all-purpose flour to measure 1 cup.

FETTUCCINE ALFREDO

*The original version of this recipe came from my sister, but I've added and
subtracted ingredients to suit my family's tastes. It's something I can whip up
at the last minute to feed guests who arrive unexpectedly. They always love it!*
—Nikki Best, Littleton, Colorado

1 package (9 ounces) refrigerated fettuccine
1 cup broccoli florets
1 cup cauliflowerets
1/2 small onion, chopped
2 tablespoons olive *or* vegetable oil
8 to 10 medium mushrooms, sliced
1 garlic clove, minced
2 cups diced fully cooked ham *or* chicken
1 jar (17 ounces) Alfredo sauce
Pepper to taste
Shredded Parmesan cheese

Cook fettuccine according to package directions. Meanwhile, in a large skillet, saute broccoli, cauliflower and onion in oil until tender. Add mushrooms and garlic; cook and stir for 3 minutes or until vegetables are crisp-tender.

Stir in the ham, Alfredo sauce and pepper. Cook until heated through. Drain fettuccine; toss with sauce. Sprinkle with Parmesan cheese. **Yield:** 4 servings.

STOVETOP HAMBURGER CASSEROLE

(Pictured below)

*This is quick comfort food at its best. It's hearty and mildly seasoned,
so it's great for a fast supper that everyone in the family will enjoy.*
—Edith Landinger, Longview, Texas

1 package (7 ounces) small shell pasta
1-1/2 pounds ground beef
1 large onion, chopped
3 medium carrots, chopped
1 celery rib, chopped
3 garlic cloves, minced
3 cups cubed cooked red potatoes
1 can (15-1/4 ounces) whole kernel
   corn, drained
2 cans (8 ounces *each*) tomato sauce
1-1/2 teaspoons salt
1/2 teaspoon pepper
1 cup (4 ounces) shredded cheddar
   cheese

Cook pasta according to package directions. Meanwhile, in a large skillet, cook beef and onion over medium heat until meat is no longer pink; drain. Add the carrots, celery and garlic; cook and stir for 5 minutes or until vegetables are crisp-tender.

Stir in the potatoes, corn, tomato sauce, salt and pepper; heat through. Drain pasta and add to skillet; toss to coat. Sprinkle with cheese. Cover and cook until cheese is melted. **Yield:** 6 servings.

WILD RICE CHICKEN CASSEROLE

My husband of 51 years loves to eat and I love to cook, so we're both happy
when I make this casserole. It's nice and creamy with a little crunch from almonds.
The chicken is canned, but you'd never know it from the taste.
—Mrs. Darrell Plinsky, Wichita, Kansas

1 package (6 ounces) long grain and
  wild rice
1/3 cup chopped onion
3 tablespoons chopped almonds
2 tablespoons dried parsley flakes
1/4 cup butter *or* margarine
1/3 cup all-purpose flour
2 cups milk
1-1/2 cups chicken broth
1/2 to 1 teaspoon salt
1/4 teaspoon pepper
1 can (10 ounces) chunk white
  chicken, drained

Prepare the rice according to package directions. Meanwhile, in a skillet, saute onion, almonds and parsley in butter for 4-5 minutes or until onion is tender and almonds are lightly toasted.

In a bowl, combine the flour, milk, broth, salt and pepper until smooth. Stir in the chicken, rice and vegetables. Pour into a greased 13-in. x 9-in. x 2-in. baking dish (mixture will be thin). Bake, uncovered, at 425° for 30-35 minutes or until bubbly and golden brown. **Yield:** 4-6 servings.

SIMPLE SUBSTITUTION

Wild Rice Chicken Casserole can easily be made with leftover
cooked chicken rather than canned. Just measure 1-1/3 cups cubed chicken.

TACO PIE

Crushed corn chips provide a lively crunch in this tasty main dish.
Cut into neat wedges, this pie is a fun and easy way to serve tacos without the mess.
It also adds variety to the buffet table at potluck dinners.
—Margery Bryan, Royal City, Washington

1-1/2 pounds ground beef
1 envelope taco seasoning
1/2 cup water
1 can (2-1/4 ounces) sliced ripe olives,
  drained
2 cups corn chips, crushed, *divided*
1 unbaked pastry shell (9 inches)
1 cup (8 ounces) sour cream
1 cup (4 ounces) shredded cheddar
  cheese
Shredded lettuce and sliced avocado,
  optional

In a skillet, cook beef over medium heat until no longer pink; drain. Stir in taco seasoning, water and olives. Simmer, uncovered, for 5 minutes, stirring frequently.

Sprinkle half of the corn chips into pie shell. Top with meat mixture, sour cream and cheese. Cover with remaining corn chips. Bake at 375° for 20-25 minutes or until crust is golden brown. Cut into wedges. Top with lettuce and avocado if desired. **Yield:** 6 servings.

GROUND BEEF STROGANOFF

This is one of the dishes my family requests most often whenever I ask what they'd like for dinner. It takes only minutes and it tastes great, so I always honor the request.
—Julie Curfman, Chehalis, Washington

1/2 pound ground beef
1 cup sliced fresh mushrooms
1 medium onion, chopped
1 garlic clove, minced
1 can (10-3/4 ounces) condensed cream of mushroom *or* cream of chicken soup, undiluted
1/4 teaspoon pepper
3 cups cooked egg noodles
1 cup (8 ounces) sour cream

In a large skillet, cook the beef, mushrooms, onion and garlic over medium heat until meat is no longer pink; drain. Stir in the soup and pepper. Cook for 2-3 minutes or until heated through. Reduce heat. Stir in the noodles and sour cream; cook until heated through. **Yield:** 3 servings.

SAUSAGE AND SAUERKRAUT CASSEROLE

This recipe has been in my family for more than 50 years. It has always been our favorite because it tastes so good. Plus, it's simple to prepare and reheats nicely.
—Deltie Tackette, Eubank, Kentucky

2 cups uncooked elbow macaroni
1 pound bulk pork sausage
1 can (14-1/2 ounces) diced tomatoes, undrained
1 cup sauerkraut, rinsed and drained
1 teaspoon sugar
4 to 5 tablespoons shredded cheddar cheese

Cook macaroni according to package directions. Meanwhile, in a skillet, cook sausage over medium heat until no longer pink; drain. Add tomatoes, sauerkraut and sugar to sausage and cook for 2 minutes. Drain macaroni; stir into skillet with cheese.
Spoon into a greased 8-in. square baking dish. Bake, uncovered, at 350° for 20 minutes or until heated through. **Yield:** 4-6 servings.

BEEF 'N' TOMATO MAC

For a quick casserole, this one is tops. It has only a handful of ingredients. To turn up the heat, use two 10-ounce cans of diced tomatoes and green chilies instead of plain tomatoes.
—Daria Wicinski, Round Lake, Illinois

3 cups uncooked elbow macaroni
1 pound ground beef
1 medium onion, chopped
2 cans (14-1/2 ounces *each*) chunky-style tomatoes, undrained
1 can (15-1/4 ounces) whole kernel corn, drained
Salt and pepper to taste

Cook macaroni according to package directions. Meanwhile, in a large skillet, cook beef and onion over medium heat until meat is no longer pink; drain. Stir in tomatoes and corn. Drain macaroni; stir into beef mixture. Cook, uncovered, for 12-15 minutes or until heated through; season with salt and pepper. **Yield:** 4-6 servings.

SMOKY POTATO SKILLET

(Pictured at right)

This dish is convenient because it uses packaged au gratin potatoes. You can alter the flavor by substituting a different mix, such as scalloped potatoes with sour cream and chives.
—Sue Ross, Casa Grande, Arizona

1 package (16 ounces) smoked
  sausage links, cut into 1-inch pieces
2 celery ribs, chopped
1 medium onion, chopped
1 tablespoon butter *or* margarine
2 cups water
2/3 cup milk
1 package (5-1/4 ounces) au gratin
  potatoes

In a large skillet, saute the sausage, celery and onion in butter until vegetables are tender. Stir in water, milk and contents of sauce mix from potatoes; bring to a boil. Stir in potatoes. Reduce heat; cover and simmer for 20-25 minutes or until potatoes are tender, stirring once. **Yield:** 4-6 servings.

DELUXE MACARONI AND CHEESE

This recipe is hearty, flavorful and easy to prepare. My husband loves it and even makes it himself from time to time. It appeals to the kid in all of us.
—Deborah Johnson, Woodbridge, Virginia

1 package (7-1/4 ounces) macaroni
  and cheese
1 pound diced fully cooked ham
1 package (10 ounces) frozen
  chopped broccoli, thawed and
  drained
1 can (10-3/4 ounces) condensed
  cream of celery soup, undiluted

Prepare macaroni and cheese according to package directions. Stir in ham, broccoli and soup; pour into a greased 2-qt. baking dish. Cover and bake at 350° for 30-45 minutes or until bubbly. **Yield:** 6 servings.

WESTERN CHILI CASSEROLE

(Pictured at right)

I'm a student and my husband is a truck driver. With three children going in three different directions every day, easy yet scrumptious meals are a must in our household. This one-dish dinner fits the bill.
—Terri Mock, American Falls, Idaho

1 pound ground beef
1 large onion, chopped
1 celery rib, chopped
1 can (15 ounces) chili with beans
1-1/2 cups corn chips, coarsely crushed,
  divided
3/4 cup shredded cheddar cheese

In a large skillet, cook the beef, onion and celery over medium heat until meat is no longer pink and vegetables are tender; drain. Stir in the chili and 1/2 cup of chips. Transfer to a greased 1-1/2-qt. baking dish. Sprinkle remaining chips around edge of dish; fill center with cheese. Bake, uncovered, at 350° for 10 minutes or until heated through. **Yield:** 4 servings.

SMOKY POTATO SKILLET
WESTERN CHILI CASSEROLE

BEEF 'N' BISCUIT BAKE

(Pictured below)

This dish is very satisfying and has the best flavor. It's a great example of Midwest cuisine.
—Erin Schneider, St. Peters, Missouri

1 pound ground beef
1 can (16 ounces) kidney beans,
  rinsed and drained
1 can (15-1/4 ounces) whole kernel
  corn, drained
1 can (10-3/4 ounces) condensed
  tomato soup, undiluted
1/4 cup milk
2 tablespoons dried minced onion
1/2 teaspoon chili powder
1/4 teaspoon salt
1 cup cubed process cheese (Velveeta)
1 tube (12 ounces) refrigerated
  buttermilk biscuits
2 to 3 tablespoons butter *or*
  margarine, melted
1/3 cup yellow cornmeal

In a large saucepan, cook beef over medium heat until no longer pink; drain. Add the beans, corn, soup, milk, onion, chili powder and salt; bring to a boil. Remove from the heat; stir in cheese until melted.

Transfer to a greased 2-1/2-qt. baking dish. Bake, uncovered, at 375° for 10 minutes. Meanwhile, brush all sides of biscuits with butter; roll in cornmeal. Place over hot meat mixture. Bake 10-12 minutes longer or until biscuits are lightly browned. **Yield:** 6-8 servings.

PERFECT PARTNERS

With meat, vegetables and bread, Beef 'n' Biscuit Bake is practically a meal in itself. All you need is a colorful salad. Here's a quick one:

To a bowl of mixed greens, add drained mandarin orange segments and sliced red onions.

For a refreshingly light dressing, combine 1/4 cup plain yogurt, 2 tablespoons reduced-fat mayonnaise and 2 tablespoons limeade concentrate.

HAM HOT DISH

*Parmesan cheese, ham and mushrooms make this a rich and tasty meal.
My family has come to expect this for dinner whenever I have leftover ham.*
—Judy Babeck, Bismarck, North Dakota

1/4 cup chopped onion
1/4 cup butter *or* margarine
3 tablespoons all-purpose flour
1/2 teaspoon salt
Dash ground nutmeg
Dash pepper
2-3/4 cups milk
1/4 cup chopped green pepper
1 can (4 ounces) mushroom stems
  and pieces, drained
1 jar (4 ounces) diced pimientos,
  drained
1 package (7 ounces) elbow
  macaroni, cooked and drained
1-1/2 cups cubed fully cooked ham
1/2 cup plus 2 tablespoons grated
  Parmesan cheese, *divided*

In a saucepan, saute onion in butter for 3 minutes or until tender. Stir in flour, salt, nutmeg and pepper. Gradually add milk, stirring constantly. Add the green pepper, mushrooms and pimientos. Bring to a boil; boil and stir for 2 minutes or until thickened. Remove from the heat; add macaroni and mix well.

Spoon half into a greased 13-in. x 9-in. x 2-in. baking dish. Sprinkle with ham and 1/2 cup of Parmesan cheese. Top with the remaining macaroni mixture. Sprinkle with remaining cheese. Bake, uncovered, at 375° for 20-30 minutes or until bubbly. **Yield:** 4-6 servings.

SERVING SUGGESTION

*Ham Hot Dish goes great with a tossed salad and hard rolls.
Dessert will take only minutes if you slice a purchased
angel food cake and top it with canned apricots and coconut.*

CREAMY BEAN GOULASH

*This stovetop supper gets you in and out of the kitchen in a jiffy. A friend served it to me
in the 1950s. I've been making it monthly for my family ever since.*
—Lois Joy Ardery, Murrieta, California

1 pound ground beef
1 medium onion, chopped
1 garlic clove, minced
2 cans (15-1/4 ounces *each*) butter
  beans, rinsed and drained
1 can (10-3/4 ounces) condensed
  tomato soup, undiluted
1 teaspoon salt
1 teaspoon Worcestershire sauce
1/4 teaspoon pepper
1/2 cup sour cream
Shredded cheddar cheese and minced
  fresh parsley, optional

In a large skillet, cook the beef, onion and garlic over medium heat until meat is no longer pink; drain. Stir in the beans, soup, salt, Worcestershire sauce, pepper and sour cream. Cover and simmer for 10 minutes or until heated through. Garnish with cheese and parsley if desired. **Yield:** 4 servings.

MASHED POTATO HOT DISH

(Pictured below)

My cousin gave me this simple but savory recipe. Whenever I'm making homemade mashed potatoes, I throw in a few extra spuds so I can make this dish for supper the next night.
—Tanya Abernathy, Yacolt, Washington

1 pound ground beef
1 can (10-3/4 ounces) condensed cream of chicken soup, undiluted
2 cups frozen French-style green beans
2 cups hot mashed potatoes (prepared with milk and butter)
1/2 cup shredded cheddar cheese

In a large skillet, cook beef over medium heat until no longer pink; drain. Stir in soup and beans. Transfer to a greased 2-qt. baking dish. Top with mashed potatoes; sprinkle with cheese. Bake, uncovered, at 350° for 20-25 minutes or until heated through and cheese is melted. **Yield:** 4 servings.

CHICKEN STROGANOFF

I concocted this recipe for those evenings when I'm running late and everyone is hungry. Even my finicky 4-year-old asks for seconds. For a no-fuss beef Stroganoff, substitute leftover steak.
—Phyllis Brittenham, Garwin, Iowa

4 cups uncooked egg noodles
2 cups cubed cooked chicken
1-1/2 cups (12 ounces) sour cream
1 can (10-3/4 ounces) condensed
    cream of mushroom soup, undiluted
1/2 teaspoon seasoned salt
1/4 teaspoon pepper
Minced fresh parsley, optional

Cook noodles according to package directions; drain. In a greased 2-qt. microwave-safe dish, combine the chicken, sour cream, soup, seasoned salt and pepper. Stir in the noodles. Cover and microwave on high for 5-7 minutes or until heated through. Sprinkle with parsley if desired. Let stand for 5 minutes before serving. **Yield:** 4-6 servings.

Editor's Note: This recipe was tested in an 850-watt microwave.

ITALIAN NOODLES

I seldom know if I'm going to have one, two or 15 people at the table for meals, so I need fast, simple recipes. This one's both—plus tasty. Kids seem to really like it.
—Barbara Thomas, Mankato, Kansas

4 cups uncooked egg noodles
1/2 pound ground beef
1/4 pound miniature smoked sausage
    links
2 cups frozen corn, thawed
1 jar (26 ounces) spaghetti sauce
1 cup (8 ounces) small-curd cottage
    cheese
1/4 teaspoon garlic powder
1/2 cup shredded mozzarella cheese

Cook noodles according to package directions. Meanwhile, in a large skillet, cook beef and sausage over medium heat until beef is no longer pink; drain. Add the corn, spaghetti sauce, cottage cheese and garlic powder; heat through. Drain noodles and stir into beef mixture. Sprinkle with cheese. Cover and cook for 5 minutes or until cheese is melted. **Yield:** 4-6 servings.

CRUNCHY TUNA SURPRISE

This recipe comes from my Grandma Mollie's kitchen. I work part-time, and we have a 2-year-old, so I appreciate quick and easy recipes like this.
—Lisa Le Sage, Wauwatosa, Wisconsin

1 can (12 ounces) tuna, drained and
    flaked
1-1/2 cups cooked rice
1 can (10-3/4 ounces) condensed
    cream of mushroom soup, undiluted
1/2 cup milk
1/4 cup minced fresh parsley
3/4 cup crushed cornflakes
2 tablespoons butter *or* margarine,
    melted

In a bowl, combine the first five ingredients. Transfer to a greased shallow 1-1/2-qt. baking dish. Combine the cornflake crumbs and butter; sprinkle over the top. Bake, uncovered, at 350° for 25-30 minutes or until bubbly. **Yield:** 4 servings.

SAUSAGE SKILLET SUPPER

After working all day, my husband referees high school basketball and football games.
I work part-time, volunteer in our town and am an all-season sports mom with four children.
If there ever was a need for quick cooking, it's in our house.
The men in my family say this fast dish is very satisfying.
—Cathy Williams, Aurora, Minnesota

1 pound smoked sausage links,
  cut into 1/2-inch slices
3/4 cup uncooked instant rice
1 can (10-3/4 ounces) condensed
  cream of celery soup, undiluted
3/4 cup water
1 tablespoon butter *or* margarine
1 package (10 ounces) frozen peas
1 can (4 ounces) mushroom stems
  and pieces, drained
1 cup (4 ounces) shredded Swiss
  cheese

In a large skillet, combine the sausage, rice, soup, water and butter. Bring to a boil. Reduce heat; cover and simmer for 5 minutes. Stir in peas and mushrooms. Cover and simmer for 20 minutes or until rice is tender. Sprinkle with cheese. **Yield:** 4 servings.

SIMPLE SUBSTITUTION

If you don't have cooked turkey on hand for Turkey Biscuit Stew, use chicken.
If you're in a hurry, you can buy cubed cooked chicken in the frozen foods
section of your supermarket or purchase a roasted chicken from the deli.

TURKEY BISCUIT STEW

This chunky stew makes a hearty supper, especially in the fall and winter.
Plus, it's a great way to use extra turkey during the holidays.
—Lori Schlecht, Wimbledon, North Dakota

1/3 cup chopped onion
1/4 cup butter *or* margarine
1/3 cup all-purpose flour
1/2 teaspoon salt
1/8 teaspoon pepper
1 can (10-1/2 ounces) condensed
  chicken broth, undiluted
3/4 cup milk
2 cups cubed cooked turkey
1 cup frozen peas
1 cup whole baby carrots, cooked
1 tube (12 ounces) refrigerated
  buttermilk biscuits

In a 10-in. ovenproof skillet, saute onion in butter until tender. Stir in flour, salt and pepper until blended. Gradually add broth and milk. Bring to a boil; cook and stir for 2 minutes or until thickened. Add the turkey, peas and carrots; heat through.

    Separate biscuits and arrange over the stew. Bake, uncovered, at 375° for 20-25 minutes or until biscuits are golden brown. **Yield:** 6-8 servings.

CHEDDAR CHICKEN SPIRALS

(Pictured above)

My granddaughters just love this chicken dish. I try to make it every time they come to visit. Lucky for me, it goes together quick as a wink in the microwave.
—Miriam Christophel, Battle Creek, Michigan

1-1/2 cups uncooked spiral pasta
  1/2 cup mayonnaise*
  1/3 cup milk
  1/2 teaspoon salt
  1/2 teaspoon dried basil
   2 cups frozen mixed vegetables, thawed
1-1/2 cups cubed cooked chicken
1-1/2 cups (6 ounces) shredded cheddar cheese, *divided*

Cook noodles according to package directions. Meanwhile, in a bowl, combine the mayonnaise, milk, salt and basil. Stir in the vegetables, chicken and 1 cup cheese. Drain pasta; stir into vegetable mixture. Transfer to a greased 1-1/2-qt. microwave-safe dish. Sprinkle with remaining cheese.

Cover and microwave on high for 5-6 minutes or until heated through and the cheese is melted. Let stand for 5 minutes before serving. **Yield:** 4 servings.

*Editor's Note: Reduced-fat or fat-free mayonnaise may not be substituted for regular mayonnaise. This recipe was tested in an 850-watt microwave.

CHICKEN BROCCOLI CASSEROLE

With plenty of tender chicken and broccoli, this cheese-topped dish is a real family-pleaser.
In fact, my clan would eat it any day of the week.
—Rachel Bywater, Holland, Michigan

4 cups cubed cooked chicken
3 cups frozen broccoli cuts, thawed
1 can (10-3/4 ounces) condensed
   cream of mushroom soup,
   undiluted
1 cup (8 ounces) sour cream
1 tablespoon lemon juice
1/2 cup shredded cheddar cheese

In a greased 2-qt. baking dish, layer chicken and broccoli. Combine the soup, sour cream and lemon juice; spread over broccoli. Sprinkle with cheese. Bake, uncovered, at 350° for 30-35 minutes or until bubbly and cheese is melted. **Yield:** 4-6 servings.

EASY BEEF AND RICE

When time is running short at dinnertime around our house, I rely on this microwave casserole.
Convenience foods like canned soup and instant rice make it a fast-to-fix meal.
—Doris Gill, Sargent, Nebraska

1 pound ground beef
1 can (10-3/4 ounces) condensed
   cream of celery soup, undiluted
1 can (10-3/4 ounces) condensed
   cream of chicken soup, undiluted
1 cup water
1 cup uncooked instant rice
3 tablespoons chopped onion
1/2 teaspoon salt
1/4 teaspoon pepper

Crumble beef into an ungreased 2-qt. microwave-safe dish. Cover and microwave on high for 5 minutes or until no longer pink; drain. Stir in the remaining ingredients. Cover and heat on high for 15 minutes or until rice is tender. Let stand for 5 minutes before serving. **Yield:** 4 servings.
   Editor's Note: This recipe was tested in a 700-watt microwave.

BARBECUE MACARONI BEEF

My husband's Grandma Curten used to make this meal for him when
he was a little boy. It's a regular around our house, which is fine with me, because
it's easy to fix and so good. The veggies add a nice crunch.
—Rose Curten, Modoc, Illinois

1 pound ground beef
1 bottle (28 ounces) barbecue sauce
8 ounces elbow macaroni, cooked
   and drained
1 medium onion, chopped
1 medium green pepper, chopped
3 celery ribs, chopped

In a large skillet, cook beef over medium heat until no longer pink; drain. Stir in barbecue sauce and macaroni; heat through. Add onion, green pepper and celery; mix well. **Yield:** 4 servings.

HEARTY PORK 'N' BEANS

This unusual recipe with apple and onion piqued my interest
when I found it. It's since become a family favorite.
—Anita Buzbee, Pensacola, Florida

1 pound ground beef
1 medium tart apple, peeled and
   diced
1 medium onion, chopped
1 can (16 ounces) pork and beans
4 bacon strips, cooked and diced
1/4 cup barbecue sauce
1/4 cup molasses
1 cup corn chips, coarsely crushed

Crumble beef into an ungreased shallow 2-qt. microwave-safe dish; add apple and onion. Cover and microwave on high for 4-6 minutes, stirring once; drain. Stir in the pork and beans, bacon, barbecue sauce and molasses. Cover and cook on high for 7-9 minutes or until heated through, stirring once. Let stand for 5 minutes. Just before serving, sprinkle with chips. **Yield:** 4-6 servings.

    Editor's Note: This recipe was tested in a 700-watt microwave.

SERVING SUGGESTION

For a tasty but time-saving dessert to accompany a
filling casserole, serve instant chocolate pudding sprinkled
with crumbled sandwich cookies or graham crackers.

LAYERED TORTILLA PIE

This is a nice dish for potluck dinners—my family really devours it whenever I serve it!
My sister used to serve tortilla pie at the hunting and fishing lodge she operated in Colorado.
It was a sure bet to win compliments from the men who came in
cold and hungry after spending the day tramping through the woods.
—Delma Snyder, McCook, Nebraska

1 pound ground beef
1 medium onion, chopped
1 can (8 ounces) tomato sauce
1 garlic clove, minced
3 teaspoons chili powder
1/2 teaspoon salt
1/4 teaspoon pepper
1 can (2-1/2 ounces) sliced ripe olives,
   drained, optional
1 tablespoon butter *or* margarine
6 corn tortillas (6 inches)
2 cups (8 ounces) shredded cheddar
   cheese
1/4 cup water

In a skillet, cook beef and onion over medium heat until meat is no longer pink; drain. Add tomato sauce, garlic, chili powder, salt, pepper and olives if desired; mix well. Simmer for 5 minutes.

    Lightly butter one side of each tortilla. Place one tortilla, buttered side down, in a greased 2-qt. baking dish. Top with about 1/2 cup of the meat mixture; sprinkle with about 1/3 cup cheese. Repeat layers, ending with cheese.

    Pour water around the sides of casserole (not over the top). Cover and bake at 400° for 20 minutes or until heated through. Let stand for 5 minutes before cutting. **Yield:** 4-6 servings.

REUBEN CASSEROLE

(Pictured at right)

I always get compliments when I take this wonderful casserole to a potluck dinner.
—Nita White, Cedar Springs, Michigan

1 can (14 ounces) sauerkraut, rinsed and drained
1 cup Thousand Island salad dressing
1 pound thinly sliced deli corned beef, cut into strips
2 cups (8 ounces) shredded Swiss cheese
4 to 6 slices rye bread, buttered

Combine sauerkraut and salad dressing; spread into a greased 13-in. x 9-in. x 2-in. baking dish. Top with corned beef and cheese. Place bread, buttered side up, over top. Bake, uncovered, at 375° for 25-30 minutes or until heated through and bubbly. **Yield:** 4 servings.

SIMPLE SUBSTITUTION

If you don't have cream of potato soup on hand for the Cheesy Hash Brown Bake, substitute cream of mushroom, celery, chicken or broccoli instead for equally satisfying results.

CHEESY HASH BROWN BAKE

(Pictured at right)

This recipe was so popular at the morning meetings of our Mothers of Preschoolers group that we published it in our newsletter. It's a great dish for busy moms because it can be prepared ahead of time. It's perfect for brunches or to serve on Christmas morning. It's creamy, comforting and tasty.
—Karen Burns, Chandler, Texas

1 package (30 ounces) frozen shredded hash brown potatoes, thawed
2 cans (10-3/4 ounces *each*) condensed cream of potato soup, undiluted
2 cups (16 ounces) sour cream
2 cups (8 ounces) shredded cheddar cheese, *divided*
1 cup grated Parmesan cheese

In a bowl, combine the potatoes, soup, sour cream, 1-3/4 cups of cheddar cheese and Parmesan cheese. Transfer to a greased 3-qt. baking dish. Sprinkle with remaining cheddar cheese. Bake, uncovered, at 350° for 40-45 minutes or until bubbly and cheese is melted. Let stand for 5 minutes before serving. **Yield:** 10 servings.

REUBEN CASSEROLE
CHEESY HASH BROWN BAKE

Enchilada Lasagna

Company was coming and I didn't have enough ground beef thawed, so the refried beans were a last-minute inspiration. They add extra goodness to this hearty, cheesy dish.
—Diane McCann, Sterling, Colorado

2 pounds ground beef
1 medium onion, chopped
2 garlic cloves, minced
1 can (10-3/4 ounces) condensed tomato soup, undiluted
1 cup picante sauce or salsa
1 can (16 ounces) refried beans
10 flour tortillas (6 inches)
4 cups (16 ounces) shredded cheddar cheese

In a large skillet, cook beef, onion and garlic over medium heat until no longer pink; drain. Stir in soup, picante sauce and refried beans; heat through.

Arrange five tortillas in a greased 11-in. x 7-in. x 2-in. baking dish, tearing as needed to cover the bottom. Layer with half of the meat mixture and half of the cheese. Repeat layers. Bake, uncovered, at 350° for 30 minutes or until heated through. Let stand for 5 minutes before serving. **Yield:** 10 servings.

Wild Rice Chicken Bake

I developed this recipe when I was low on groceries and in a hurry to get a good hot meal in the oven. The savory onion flavor bakes right into the chicken.
—Leslie Gillespie, Red Oak, Iowa

4 boneless skinless chicken breast halves
1 package (6 ounces) long grain and wild rice mix
1 envelope onion soup mix
2-1/3 cups water
1 tablespoon butter or margarine

Place chicken in a greased 13-in. x 9-in. x 2-in. baking dish. Combine the rice with contents of seasoning mix, soup mix, water and butter. Pour over chicken. Cover and bake at 350° for 55-60 minutes or until chicken juices run clear. **Yield:** 4 servings.

Hobo Hash

I came up with this recipe one day when I didn't have many groceries in the house. My kids named it Hobo Hash because it didn't have a lot in it and could be cooked in one pan.
—Linda Hendershott, St. Joseph, Michigan

1/2 pound sliced bacon, diced
1 medium onion, chopped
1 cup sliced fresh mushrooms
5 medium potatoes, peeled, cubed and cooked
1 can (10-3/4 ounces) condensed cream of mushroom soup, undiluted

In a large skillet, cook bacon over medium heat until crisp. Remove to paper towels to drain, reserving 3 tablespoons drippings. Saute onion and mushrooms in drippings until onion is tender. Stir in the potatoes and soup. Simmer, uncovered, for 5 minutes or until heated through. Sprinkle with bacon. **Yield:** 4 servings.

DEEP-DISH HAM PIE

*Whenever I have leftover ham to use up, my family can expect to
see this meaty pie on the table. It's loaded with ham and fabulous flavor.*
—Lucinda Walker, Somerset, Pennsylvania

1/4 cup butter *or* margarine
1/4 cup all-purpose flour
1/2 teaspoon salt
1/4 teaspoon ground mustard
1/8 teaspoon pepper
1 cup milk
1 teaspoon dried minced onion
2-1/2 cups cubed fully cooked ham
1 cup frozen peas
2 hard-cooked eggs, chopped
Pastry for single-crust pie

Melt butter in a saucepan; stir in flour, salt, mustard and pepper until smooth. Gradually add milk and onion. Bring to a boil; cook and stir for 2 minutes or until thickened. Stir in the ham, peas and eggs. Pour into an ungreased 11-in. x 7-in. x 2-in. baking dish.

On a floured surface, roll pastry to fit top of dish; place over filling. Seal and flute the edges; cut slits in the top. Bake at 425° for 25 minutes or until crust is golden brown and filling is bubbly. **Yield:** 6 servings.

PERFECT PARTNERS

*Beef and Potato Casserole is practically a meal in itself. Just put crusty
whole grain or sourdough bread on the table with it.*

BEEF AND POTATO CASSEROLE

*My husband goes to school and works full-time, and I'm the mother of a 1-year-old.
With a busy schedule like ours, this quick recipe of kitchen staples is just perfect!*
—Brenda Bradshaw, Oconto, Wisconsin

4 cups frozen potato rounds
1 pound ground beef
1 package (10 ounces) frozen
   chopped broccoli, thawed
1 can (10-3/4 ounces) condensed
   cream of celery soup, undiluted
1/3 cup milk
1 cup (4 ounces) shredded cheddar
   cheese, *divided*
1/4 teaspoon garlic powder
1/8 teaspoon pepper

Place potato rounds on the bottom and up the sides of a greased 13-in. x 9-in. x 2-in. baking dish. Bake, uncovered, at 400° for 10 minutes.

Meanwhile, in a skillet, cook beef over medium heat until no longer pink; drain. Place beef and broccoli over potatoes. Combine the soup, milk, 1/2 cup cheddar cheese, garlic powder and pepper; pour over beef mixture. Cover and bake at 400° for 20 minutes. Uncover; top with remaining cheese. Bake 2-3 minutes longer or until cheese is melted. **Yield:** 6 servings.

SPINACH RAVIOLI BAKE

(Pictured below)

This entree is unbelievably simple to prepare yet tastes delicious. The fact that you use frozen ravioli—straight from the bag without boiling or thawing—saves so much time.
—Susan Kehl, Pembroke Pines, Florida

2 **cups spaghetti sauce**
1 **package (25 ounces) frozen Italian sausage ravioli *or* ravioli of your choice**
2 **cups (8 ounces) shredded mozzarella cheese**
1 **package (10 ounces) frozen chopped spinach, thawed and squeezed dry**
1/4 **cup grated Parmesan cheese**

Place 1 cup spaghetti sauce in a greased 2-qt. baking dish. Top with half of the ravioli, mozzarella cheese, spinach and Parmesan cheese. Repeat layers. Bake, uncovered, at 350° for 40-45 minutes or until heated through and cheese is melted. **Yield:** 4-6 servings.

ZESTY PORK AND PASTA

On a cold Midwestern evening, this hot and spicy dish really warms us up.
It's a fun, festive change from spaghetti. Plus, everyone loves the leftovers...if there are any!
—Phyllis Brooks, Auburn, Illinois

1 pound bulk hot pork sausage
1 medium onion, chopped
1/2 cup chopped green pepper
1 can (14-1/2 ounces) stewed
  tomatoes
1 can (8 ounces) tomato sauce
1 cup uncooked spiral pasta
2 tablespoons brown sugar
1 to 2 teaspoons chili powder
1 teaspoon salt
Parmesan cheese, optional

In a large skillet, cook sausage until no longer pink; drain. Add onion and green pepper; cook until tender. Add tomatoes, tomato sauce, pasta, brown sugar, chili powder and salt; cover and simmer for 20 minutes or until pasta is tender. Sprinkle with Parmesan cheese if desired. **Yield:** 4 servings.

PERFECT PARTNERS

Keep the Italian theme going by serving Italian Chicken and Rice with garlic breadsticks and a purchased bag of Italian-blend salad greens. Toss in tomatoes and shredded Parmesan cheese, then top with Italian dressing.

ITALIAN CHICKEN AND RICE

I combined the best of three different recipes to come up with this tender and tasty chicken-rice dish. It's become my family's favorite way to eat chicken.
—Cathee Bethel, Lebanon, Oregon

2/3 cup biscuit/baking mix
1/3 cup grated Parmesan cheese
2 teaspoons Italian seasoning
1 teaspoon paprika
1 can (5 ounces) evaporated milk,
  divided
6 boneless skinless chicken breast
  halves
2 cups boiling water
2 cups uncooked instant rice
1 teaspoon salt
2 tablespoons butter *or* margarine,
  melted

In a large resealable plastic bag, combine the first four ingredients. Place 1/3 cup milk in a shallow bowl. Dip chicken in milk, then place in bag in batches and shake to coat.

In a greased 13-in. x 9-in. x 2-in. baking dish, combine water, rice, salt and remaining milk; mix well. Top with chicken. Drizzle with butter. Bake, uncovered, at 425° for 25-30 minutes or until the rice is tender and chicken juices run clear. **Yield:** 6 servings.

EASY AU GRATIN POTATOES

One taste of this comforting dish developed by our Test Kitchen and you'll never reach for a store-bought box of au gratin potatoes again! The thinly sliced "spuds" cook up tender in no time. Your family will request this recipe many times over.

3/4 cup half-and-half cream
1/2 cup milk
1/2 teaspoon salt
1/4 teaspoon garlic powder
  3 medium potatoes, peeled and
    thinly sliced
  1 cup seasoned salad croutons,
    divided
1/8 teaspoon pepper
1/2 cup shredded cheddar cheese

In a saucepan, bring cream, milk, salt and garlic powder to a boil. Add potatoes; reduce heat. Cover and simmer for 10-15 minutes or until potatoes are tender. Coarsely crush 1/4 cup of croutons.

Remove potatoes from the heat; stir in crushed croutons and pepper. Pour into a greased 1-1/2-qt. baking dish. Sprinkle with cheese and remaining croutons. Bake, uncovered, at 400° for 5-6 minutes or until cheese is melted. **Yield:** 4 servings.

MICROWAVE TUNA 'N' CHIPS

(Pictured at right and on page 118)

My kids like this so much, they could eat it every day. For a change of pace, use canned chicken and cream of chicken soup instead.
—Geraldine Clarke, Tuskegee Institute, Alabama

  1 can (10-3/4 ounces) condensed
    cream of celery soup, undiluted
1/4 cup milk
  1 can (12 ounces) tuna, drained and
    flaked
3/4 cup frozen peas, thawed
1/3 cup chopped celery
  1 tablespoon chopped onion
  1 teaspoon Worcestershire sauce
1-1/2 cups crushed potato chips, *divided*
  1 tablespoon shredded cheddar
    cheese

In a bowl, combine soup and milk. Stir in the tuna, peas, celery, onion and Worcestershire sauce. Place half in a greased shallow 1-qt. microwave-safe dish. Sprinkle with 1/2 cup chips. Top with remaining tuna mixture.

Microwave, uncovered, on high for 4 minutes or until bubbly. Top with remaining chips; sprinkle with cheese. Microwave 1 minute longer or until cheese is melted. Let stand for 5 minutes before serving. **Yield:** 3 servings.

Editor's Note: This recipe was tested in an 850-watt microwave.

HELPFUL HINTS

Potato chips and seasoned croutons add a satisfying crunch to the two casseroles on this page, but there are other tasty topping options:

• For a flavorful twist, try substituting crushed corn chips, french-fried onions, cornflakes, tortilla chips, chow mein noodles, butter-flavored crackers or bagel chips.

• To make a savory topping, add 1 tablespoon of melted butter to 1/2 cup bread, cracker or cereal crumbs. Sprinkle over the casserole and bake as directed.

POTLUCK CHICKEN CASSEROLE

(Pictured at right)

*I never bring home leftovers whenever I take this creamy, stick-to-your-ribs casserole
to a potluck. Its mild flavor has broad appeal. I especially like the way
the crumb topping adds a bit of crunch to each meaty serving.*
—Faye Hintz, Springfield, Missouri

8 cups cubed cooked chicken
2 cans (10-3/4 ounces *each*)
  condensed cream of chicken soup,
  undiluted
1 cup (8 ounces) sour cream
1 cup crushed butter-flavored crackers
  (about 25 crackers)
2 tablespoons butter *or* margarine,
  melted
1 teaspoon celery seed
Fresh parsley and sweet red pepper rings,
  optional

Combine the chicken, soup and sour cream; spread into a greased 13-in. x 9-in. x 2-in. baking dish. Combine cracker crumbs, butter and celery seed; sprinkle over the chicken mixture. Bake, uncovered, at 350° for 30-35 minutes or until bubbly. Garnish with parsley and red pepper if desired. **Yield:** 10-12 servings.

TIMELY TIP

*Instead of chopping the cabbage for Tuna Crunch Casserole,
use coleslaw mix from the produce department of your grocery store.
A 16-ounce bag contains about 6 cups.*

TUNA CRUNCH CASSEROLE

*This is a great everyday meal because it's exceptionally easy and economical to prepare.
If you have tuna on hand, you can decide to make this casserole
at the last minute without a trip to the store.*
—Alberta McKay, Bartlesville, Oklahoma

1/4 cup sliced almonds
1 small onion, chopped
1 celery rib, chopped
2 tablespoons butter *or* margarine
2 cups shredded cabbage
1 can (6 ounces) tuna, drained and
  flaked
1 can (10-3/4 ounces) condensed
  cream of mushroom soup,
  undiluted
1 can (3 ounces) chow mein noodles,
  divided

In a skillet, saute the almonds, onion and celery in butter. In a bowl, combine cabbage, tuna, soup and half of the chow mein noodles; stir in almond mixture. Spoon into an ungreased 11-in. x 7-in. x 2-in. baking dish. Sprinkle remaining noodles on top. Bake, uncovered, at 350° for 20 minutes or until bubbly. **Yield:** 4 servings.

POTLUCK CHICKEN CASSEROLE

BAKED MOSTACCIOLI

(Pictured below)

I created this recipe when I had a group to feed and only a few ingredients on hand.
—Andrea Warneke, St. Paul, Minnesota

1-1/2 pounds ground beef
   1 package (16 ounces) mostaccioli, cooked and drained
   1 jar (28 ounces) spaghetti sauce
   1 jar (24 ounces) salsa
1-1/2 cups (6 ounces) shredded cheddar cheese

In a Dutch oven, cook beef over medium heat until no longer pink; drain. Stir in the pasta, spaghetti sauce and salsa. Transfer to a greased 13-in. x 9-in. x 2-in. baking dish (dish will be full). Cover and bake at 350° for 40 minutes. Uncover; sprinkle with cheese. Bake 8-12 minutes longer or until heated through and cheese is melted. **Yield:** 6-8 servings.

SPEEDY CHILI MAC

This dish is a staple in our house on busy nights. Everything I need is handy in the pantry, plus everyone gobbles it up. I don't have to worry about any fussy eaters because no one complains.
—Shirley Burmeister, Glendale, Arizona

2 cups uncooked elbow macaroni
1-1/2 teaspoons dried minced onion
1 can (15 ounces) chili without beans
1 can (10-3/4 ounces) condensed
    cream of mushroom soup,
    undiluted
1 cup (4 ounces) shredded cheddar
    cheese, *divided*

In a saucepan, cook macaroni in boiling water for 5 minutes. Stir in onion. Cook 1-2 minutes longer or until macaroni is tender; drain.

In another saucepan, combine the chili and soup; heat through. Stir in macaroni and 3/4 cup of cheese. Transfer to a greased 11-in. x 7-in. x 2-in. baking dish. Cover and bake at 350° for 20 minutes. Uncover; sprinkle with remaining cheese. Bake 5-10 minutes longer or until cheese is melted. **Yield:** 4 servings.

PERFECT PARTNERS

Steamed green beans are a great side dish for Speedy Chili Mac or Tropical Chicken Bake. For a fast flavorful topping, melt 1/4 cup of butter; stir in 1/2 teaspoon garlic powder. Drizzle over hot beans.

TROPICAL CHICKEN BAKE

Cooking is a wonderful way to let your creativity come through. I start with basic recipes, then add my own personal touches to create meals like this one, which my family loves.
—Jane Bower, Normal, Illinois

4 boneless skinless chicken breast
    halves
1 tablespoon butter *or* margarine
3 medium sweet potatoes, cooked,
    peeled and quartered
2 medium firm bananas, cut into
    1/2-inch slices
1 can (11 ounces) mandarin oranges,
    drained
1 can (8 ounces) crushed pineapple,
    drained
1/2 cup sweet-and-sour sauce
1/3 cup chopped almonds *or* pecans

In a skillet over medium heat, brown chicken in butter. In an ungreased 2-qt. baking dish, combine sweet potatoes, bananas, oranges and pineapple. Top with chicken; pour sweet-and-sour sauce over all. Sprinkle with nuts. Bake, uncovered, at 350° for 20-25 minutes or until meat juices run clear. **Yield:** 4 servings.

POTLUCK PLEASERS

When you're cooking
for a crowd, you need plenty
of great-tasting food. In
this chapter you'll find 31
tried-and-true choices that
are sure to produce recipe
requests. Now all you have
to do is remember to
take home your empty pan!

SPAGHETTI GOULASH

(Pictured on page 153)

My mother always made this delicious dish when we had lots of company or we were going to a church dinner. She'd make two casseroles and save one in the freezer for another time.
—Jinger Newsome, Gainesville, Florida

1 package (16 ounces) thin spaghetti, broken in half
3/4 pound ground beef
3/4 pound bulk pork sausage
1 medium green pepper, chopped
1 medium onion, chopped
2 cans (14-1/2 ounces *each*) diced tomatoes, undrained
1 bottle (12 ounces) chili sauce
1 can (8 ounces) mushroom stems and pieces, drained
1 tablespoon Worcestershire sauce
1 teaspoon salt
1/4 teaspoon pepper
1 cup (4 ounces) shredded cheddar cheese, *divided*

Cook spaghetti according to package directions; drain. In a large skillet, cook beef, sausage, green pepper and onion over medium heat until meat is no longer pink; drain. Add the tomatoes; cover and simmer for 45 minutes. Remove from the heat. Stir in the chili sauce, mushrooms, Worcestershire sauce, salt, pepper and spaghetti.

Transfer to a greased 4-qt. baking dish or two greased 2-qt. baking dishes. Sprinkle with cheese. Cover and bake at 350° for 35-40 minutes or until heated through. **Yield:** 12-16 servings.

SERVING SUGGESTION

For a simple side dish that looks like you fussed, cut cabbage into single-serving-size wedges and steam until tender.

BROCCOLI SUPREME

I really don't know how long I've had this recipe, but it is a great favorite in our family. I've shared it with many friends, too.
—Lucy Parks, Birmingham, Alabama

2 tablespoons all-purpose flour
2 cans (10-3/4 ounces *each*) condensed cream of chicken soup, undiluted
1 cup (8 ounces) sour cream
1/2 cup grated carrot
2 tablespoons grated onion
1/2 teaspoon pepper
3 packages (10 ounces *each*) frozen broccoli cuts, thawed
1-1/2 cups crushed seasoned stuffing
1/4 cup butter *or* margarine, melted

In a large bowl, combine the flour, soup and sour cream. Stir in the carrot, onion and pepper. Fold in the broccoli.

Transfer to a greased 2-1/2-qt. baking dish. Combine stuffing and butter; sprinkle over top. Bake, uncovered, at 350° for 50-60 minutes or until bubbly and heated through. **Yield:** 12 servings.

CHICKEN NOODLE CASSEROLE

(Pictured below)

This tasty dish gets even better after it's been refrigerated a day or two, so the leftovers are always great. We eat it hot in the winter and cold in the summer.
—Cheryl Watts, Natural Bridge, Virginia

1 package (16 ounces) egg noodles
1 medium sweet red pepper, chopped
1 large onion, chopped
1 celery rib, chopped
2 garlic cloves, minced
1/4 cup butter *or* margarine
1-1/2 cups sliced fresh mushrooms
3 tablespoons all-purpose flour
3 cups chicken broth
3 cups half-and-half cream
2 packages (8 ounces *each*) cream cheese, cubed
12 cups cubed cooked chicken
1 to 1-1/2 teaspoons salt

TOPPING:
1 cup finely crushed cornflakes
2 tablespoons butter *or* margarine, melted
1 tablespoon vegetable oil
3 tablespoons minced fresh parsley
1/2 teaspoon paprika

Cook noodles according to package directions; drain. In a large skillet, saute the red pepper, onion, celery and garlic in butter until tender. Add mushrooms; cook 1-2 minutes longer or until tender. Remove vegetables with a slotted spoon; set aside. Add flour to the skillet; stir until blended. Gradually add broth. Bring to a boil; cook and stir for 2 minutes or until thickened. Reduce heat. Gradually stir in cream. Add the cream cheese; cook and stir until cheese is melted. Remove from the heat.

In a large bowl, combine the chicken, salt, noodles, vegetables and cheese sauce; mix well. Transfer to two ungreased shallow 3-qt. baking dishes. Combine topping ingredients. Sprinkle over top. Cover and bake at 350° for 20 minutes. Uncover; bake 15-20 minutes longer or until hot and bubbly. **Yield:** 2 casseroles (8-10 servings each).

HAM AND ASPARAGUS CASSEROLE

(Pictured on page 153)

We eat this tasty casserole often, so I like to change the ingredients now and then. I'll double the amount of rosemary, substitute green beans or broccoli for the asparagus or use chicken instead of ham.
—Kea Fisher, Bridger, Montana

1 package (16 ounces) spaghetti, broken into thirds
2 pounds fresh asparagus, trimmed and cut into 1-1/2 inch pieces
2 eggs, lightly beaten
1/2 cup grated Parmesan cheese, *divided*
1/4 cup butter *or* margarine
1/4 cup all-purpose flour
1 can (12 ounces) evaporated milk
1 cup milk
1/2 cup chicken broth
1/2 cup mayonnaise*
2 tablespoons lemon juice
2 teaspoons grated onion
2 teaspoons prepared mustard
2 teaspoons minced fresh parsley
1/4 teaspoon dried rosemary, crushed
1/2 cup shredded cheddar cheese
3 cups cubed fully cooked ham

Cook spaghetti according to package directions; rinse with cold water and drain. In a large saucepan, bring 2 cups of water to a boil. Add asparagus. Cover and cook for 3-5 minutes or until crisp-tender; drain.

In a bowl, toss spaghetti with eggs and 1/4 cup Parmesan cheese. Spread into two greased 2-qt. baking dishes.

In a large saucepan, melt butter. Stir in flour until smooth. Gradually add the evaporated milk, milk and broth. Bring to a boil; cook and stir for 1-2 minutes or until thickened. Remove from the heat. Whisk in the mayonnaise, lemon juice, onion, mustard, parsley and rosemary. Stir in cheddar cheese and remaining Parmesan until blended.

Sprinkle ham and asparagus over spaghetti crusts. Pour cheese sauce over top. Cover and bake at 350° for 40 minutes. Uncover; bake 5-10 minutes longer or until edges are bubbly. **Yield:** 2 casseroles (10 servings each).

*Editor's Note: Reduced-fat or fat-free mayonnaise may not be substituted for regular mayonnaise.

CHEESY COTTAGE POTATOES

This recipe is a real winner. Not only does my family like it, but it's popular at potlucks. It's also great to make ahead for a company dinner. Just remove it from the refrigerator 30 minutes before baking.
—Mary Louise Ireland, New Wilmington, Pennsylvania

3 slices bread, crusts removed and cubed
1/2 cup milk
10 medium potatoes, peeled, cubed and cooked
2 medium green peppers, chopped
1 large onion, chopped
1/2 cup minced fresh parsley
1-1/2 pounds process cheese (Velveeta), cubed
1/4 cup butter *or* margarine, melted

In a small bowl, soak bread in milk; set aside. In a large bowl, combine the potatoes, green peppers, onion, parsley and reserved bread mixture. Stir in cheese.

Transfer to a greased 13-in. x 9-in. x 2-in. baking dish. Drizzle with butter. Bake, uncovered, at 350° for 35-40 minutes or until bubbly. **Yield:** 16-20 servings.

COMPANY CASSEROLE

(Pictured above)

I concocted this recipe one day while trying to straighten up my canned goods cupboard. Friends and relatives have told me how much they like it. Many have asked for the recipe.
—Marcia McCutchan, Hamilton, Ohio

8 ounces process cheese (Velveeta), cubed
1/4 cup milk
2 cans (14-1/2 ounces *each*) diced tomatoes, undrained
3/4 cup mayonnaise *or* salad dressing*
1 tablespoon Worcestershire sauce
4 cups cubed fully cooked ham
4 cups cooked elbow macaroni
1 package (10 ounces) frozen chopped broccoli, thawed and drained
1 package (10 ounces) frozen peas, thawed
1 small green pepper, chopped
1 small onion, chopped
1/2 cup crushed stuffing mix
1 can (2.8 ounces) french-fried onions, chopped, optional
1 cup soft bread crumbs
1/4 cup butter *or* margarine, melted

In a large saucepan, cook and stir cheese and milk over low heat until cheese is melted. Stir in tomatoes until blended. Remove from the heat; stir in the mayonnaise and Worcestershire sauce until blended. Stir in the ham, macaroni, broccoli, peas, green pepper, onion, stuffing mix and onions if desired.

Transfer to two greased 2-1/2-qt. baking dishes. Toss bread crumbs and butter; sprinkle over the top. Bake, uncovered, at 350° for 35-40 minutes or until bubbly. **Yield:** 2 casseroles (8-10 servings each).

*Editor's Note: Reduced-fat or fat-free mayonnaise or salad dressing may not be substituted for regular mayonnaise or salad dressing.

SAUSAGE NOODLE CASSEROLE

(Pictured below)

The sausage makes this casserole meaty and hearty, and the blue cheese adds a special flavor.
It's easy to prepare, plus it only needs to bake for about 30 minutes.
—Julia Livingston, Frostproof, Florida

1 package (16 ounces) egg noodles
2 pounds bulk pork sausage
2 cans (10-3/4 ounces *each*)
   condensed cream of chicken soup,
   undiluted
2 cups (16 ounces) sour cream
1 cup crumbled blue cheese
2 jars (4-1/2 ounces *each*) sliced
   mushrooms, drained
1 jar (4 ounces) diced pimientos,
   drained
1/4 cup finely chopped green pepper
1 cup soft bread crumbs
2 tablespoons butter *or* margarine,
   melted

Cook noodles according to package directions; drain. In a large skillet, cook sausage over medium heat until no longer pink; drain.

In a Dutch oven, combine the soup, sour cream and blue cheese; cook and stir over medium heat until cheese is melted. Stir in the noodles, sausage, mushrooms, pimientos and green pepper.

Transfer to two greased 3-qt. baking dishes. Toss bread crumbs and butter; sprinkle over top. Bake, uncovered, at 350° for 30-35 minutes or until edges are bubbly. **Yield:** 2 casseroles (8 servings each).

DEEP-DISH BEEF BAKE

When tomatoes and green pepper are plentiful in my garden, I slice the tomatoes and chop the peppers, then freeze them on baking sheets. When they're frozen, I put them in heavy-duty bags and store for later use in this casserole.
—Karen Owen, Rising Sun, Indiana

1 pound ground beef
2 cups biscuit/baking mix
1/2 cup cold water
3 medium tomatoes, thinly sliced
1 medium green pepper, chopped
2 large onions, chopped
1 cup (4 ounces) shredded cheddar cheese, *divided*
1 cup (8 ounces) sour cream
2/3 cup mayonnaise*

In a skillet, cook beef over medium heat until no longer pink; drain. In a bowl, combine the biscuit mix and water until a soft dough forms. Spread into a greased 13-in. x 9-in. x 2-in. baking dish. Layer with the beef, tomatoes and green pepper.

Combine the onions, 1/2 cup cheese, sour cream and mayonnaise; spread over top. Bake, uncovered, at 375° for 30-35 minutes or until edges are browned. Sprinkle with remaining cheese. Bake 5 minutes longer or until the cheese is melted. **Yield:** 12 servings.

*Editor's Note: Reduced-fat or fat-free mayonnaise may not be substituted for regular mayonnaise.

LASAGNA CORN CARNE

My grandkids always ask me to make this dish, which is sort of like chili in a pan. I came up with the recipe one day using just ingredients I had on hand. It was an instant hit.
—Mary Lou Wills, La Plata, Maryland

1 pound ground beef
1 jar (16 ounces) salsa
1 can (16 ounces) kidney beans, rinsed and drained
1 can (14-3/4 ounces) cream-style corn
1 large onion, chopped
3/4 cup chopped green pepper
1 celery rib, chopped
1 tablespoon minced fresh basil *or* 1 teaspoon dried basil
1 teaspoon salt
1 teaspoon chili powder
3 garlic cloves, minced
12 lasagna noodles, cooked and drained
2 cups (8 ounces) shredded mozzarella cheese
1/2 cup grated Parmesan cheese

In a large skillet, cook beef over medium heat until no longer pink; drain. Add salsa, beans, vegetables and seasonings. Reduce heat; cover and simmer for 15 minutes.

Spread a fourth of the meat sauce in a greased 13-in. x 9-in. x 2-in. baking dish; top with four noodles. Repeat once. Top with half of the remaining sauce and half of the cheeses. Layer with the remaining noodles, sauce and cheeses.

Cover and bake at 350° for 30 minutes. Uncover; bake 15-20 minutes longer or until heated through. Let stand for 15 minutes before cutting. **Yield:** 12 servings.

GARDEN MEDLEY CASSEROLE

(Pictured above and on page 152)

This cheesy casserole includes a sunny combination of eggplant, zucchini and tomatoes.
—Phyllis Hickey, Bedford, New Hampshire

2 pounds eggplant
5 teaspoons salt, *divided*
1/4 cup olive *or* vegetable oil
2 medium onions, finely chopped
2 garlic cloves, minced
2 medium zucchini, sliced 1/2 inch thick
5 medium tomatoes, peeled and chopped
2 celery ribs, sliced
1/4 cup minced fresh parsley
1/4 cup minced fresh basil *or* 1 tablespoon dried basil
1/2 teaspoon pepper
1/2 cup grated Romano cheese
1 cup Italian bread crumbs
2 tablespoons butter *or* margarine, melted
1 cup (4 ounces) shredded mozzarella cheese

Peel eggplant and cut into 1/2-in.-thick slices; sprinkle both sides with 3 teaspoons salt. Place in a deep dish; cover and let stand for 30 minutes. Rinse with cold water; drain and pat dry. Cut into 1/2-in. cubes.

In a large skillet, saute eggplant in oil until lightly browned, about 5 minutes. Add the onions, garlic and zucchini; cook 3 minutes longer. Stir in the tomatoes, celery, parsley, basil, pepper and remaining salt; bring to a boil. Reduce heat; cover and simmer for 10 minutes. Remove from the heat; stir in Romano cheese.

Transfer to a greased 13-in. x 9-in. x 2-in. baking dish. Combine bread crumbs and butter; sprinkle over top. Bake, uncovered, at 375° for 15 minutes. Sprinkle with mozzarella cheese. Bake 5 minutes longer or until cheese is melted. **Yield:** 12 servings.

PINEAPPLE BAKED BEANS

Tangy pineapple dresses up these hearty baked beans. Brown the beef while you open cans and chop the vegetables, and it won't take long to get this side dish ready for the slow cooker.
—Gladys De Boer, Castleford, Idaho

1 pound ground beef
1 can (28 ounces) baked beans
1 can (8 ounces) pineapple tidbits, drained
1 jar (4-1/2 ounces) sliced mushrooms, drained
1 large onion, chopped
1 large green pepper, chopped
1/2 cup barbecue sauce
2 tablespoons soy sauce
1 garlic clove, minced
1/2 teaspoon salt
1/4 teaspoon pepper

In a skillet, cook beef over medium heat until no longer pink; drain. Transfer to a 5-qt. slow cooker. Stir in the remaining ingredients. Cover and cook on low for 4-8 hours or until bubbly. **Yield:** 12-16 servings.

BROCCOLI CHICKEN LASAGNA

As a working mother with four children, I often prepare casseroles.
This lasagna recipe doesn't have tomato sauce—just lots of chicken, ham and cheese.
—Dawn Owens, Palatka, Florida

1/2 pound fresh mushrooms, sliced
1 large onion, chopped
1/4 cup butter *or* margarine
1/2 cup all-purpose flour
1/2 teaspoon salt
1/4 teaspoon pepper
1/8 teaspoon ground nutmeg
1 can (14-1/2 ounces) chicken broth
1-3/4 cups milk
2/3 cup grated Parmesan cheese
1 package (16 ounces) frozen broccoli cuts, thawed
9 lasagna noodles, cooked and drained
1-1/3 cups julienned fully cooked ham, *divided*
2 cups (8 ounces) shredded Monterey Jack cheese, *divided*
2 cups cubed cooked chicken

In a large skillet, saute the mushrooms and onion in butter until tender. Stir in flour, salt, pepper and nutmeg until blended. Gradually stir in broth and milk. Bring to a boil; cook and stir for 2 minutes or until thickened. Stir in Parmesan cheese and broccoli; heat through.

Spread 1/2 cup broccoli mixture in a greased 13-in. x 9-in. x 2-in. baking dish. Layer with three noodles, a third of the remaining broccoli mixture, 1 cup ham and 1 cup Monterey Jack cheese. Top with three noodles, a third of the broccoli mixture, all of the chicken and 1/2 cup Monterey Jack cheese. Top with remaining noodles, broccoli mixture and ham.

Cover and bake at 350° for 45-50 minutes or until bubbly. Sprinkle with remaining cheese. Bake 5 minutes longer or until cheese is melted. Let stand for 15 minutes before cutting. **Yield:** 12 servings.

TURKEY RICE CASSEROLE

This creamy casserole is always one of the first to go in a buffet line. When I want to indicate serving size, I use sliced cheese squares on the top rather than shredded cheese.
—Ferne Carter Chapman, Tacoma, Washington

4 cups chicken broth
1/4 cup uncooked wild rice
1-3/4 cups uncooked long grain rice
2 cups sliced fresh mushrooms
1/2 cup fresh broccoli florets
1 small onion, chopped
1/4 cup grated carrot
1/4 cup sliced celery
2 tablespoons olive *or* vegetable oil
5 cups cubed cooked turkey
1 jar (2 ounces) diced pimientos, drained
1 teaspoon salt
1/2 teaspoon dried marjoram
1/2 teaspoon dried oregano
5 tablespoons all-purpose flour
3 cups milk
1/4 cup white wine *or* chicken broth
2 cups (8 ounces) shredded Swiss cheese
2 cups (8 ounces) shredded cheddar cheese, *divided*

In a large saucepan, bring broth to a boil; add the wild rice. Cover and simmer for 25 minutes. Add the long grain rice; simmer 25 minutes longer or until tender.

In a large skillet, saute the mushrooms, broccoli, onion, carrot and celery in oil until tender. Add the turkey, pimientos, salt, marjoram and oregano.

In a large saucepan, combine the flour, milk and wine or broth until smooth. Bring to a boil; cook and stir for 2 minutes or until thickened. Stir in the Swiss cheese and 1 cup cheddar cheese until melted. Add to turkey mixture.

Transfer to a greased 13-in. x 9-in. x 2-in. baking dish. Sprinkle with the remaining cheddar cheese. Bake, uncovered, at 350° for 25-30 minutes or until heated through. **Yield:** 12 servings.

MACARONI CHICKEN DINNER

My family considers this dish a complete dinner all by itself. When I'm having company, I add green beans, hot rolls and chilled mixed fruit for a quick yet nutritious meal.
—Zetta Harberts, Beattie, Kansas

2 cans (10-3/4 ounces *each*) condensed cream of mushroom soup, undiluted
1 cup chicken broth
1 cup milk
1/2 cup half-and-half cream
2-1/2 cups cubed cooked chicken
2 cups uncooked elbow macaroni
2 cups (8 ounces) shredded cheddar cheese
2 celery ribs, diced
4 hard-cooked eggs, chopped
3/4 cup dry bread crumbs
2 tablespoons butter *or* margarine, melted

In a large bowl, combine the soup, broth, milk and cream. Stir in the chicken, macaroni, cheese, celery and eggs. Transfer to a greased 3-qt. baking dish.

Cover and bake at 350° for 30 minutes. Uncover. Combine bread crumbs and butter; sprinkle over top. Bake 15-20 minutes longer or until macaroni is tender. Let stand for 5 minutes before serving. **Yield:** 10-12 servings.

HAWAIIAN PIZZA PASTA

I've been making this recipe since I discovered it and tweaked it to our family's liking more than 15 years ago. You can substitute chopped salami, pepperoni or cooked ground beef for the ham. Or add olives, red peppers—whatever you like on a pizza.
—Rose Enns, Abbotsford, British Columbia

1/2 pound fresh mushrooms, sliced
1 medium onion, chopped
1 medium green pepper, chopped
2 garlic cloves, minced
3 tablespoons vegetable oil
1 can (15 ounces) tomato sauce
2 bay leaves
1 teaspoon dried oregano
1 teaspoon dried basil
1/2 teaspoon sugar
3-1/2 cups uncooked spiral pasta
6 cups (24 ounces) shredded mozzarella cheese, *divided*
1 can (20 ounces) pineapple chunks, drained
1 cup cubed fully cooked ham

In a large saucepan, saute the mushrooms, onion, green pepper and garlic in oil for 5 minutes or until tender. Add the tomato sauce, bay leaves, oregano, basil and sugar. Bring to a boil. Reduce heat; simmer, uncovered, for 20-30 minutes or until thickened, stirring frequently. Meanwhile, cook pasta according to package directions; drain.

Discard bay leaves from sauce. Add the pasta, 5 cups of mozzarella cheese, pineapple and ham. Transfer to a greased shallow 3-qt. baking dish. Sprinkle with remaining cheese. Bake, uncovered, at 350° for 30-35 minutes or until heated through. **Yield:** 12-14 servings.

BAKED SPAGHETTI

This casserole is a standby for church suppers and other potluck functions. Keeping the cover on during most of the baking time keeps it moist.
—Doris Heath, Franklin, North Carolina

2 pounds ground beef
2 medium onions, chopped
2 cans (one 15 ounces, one 8 ounces) tomato sauce
1 can (8 ounces) sliced mushrooms, drained
1 teaspoon garlic powder
1 teaspoon dried oregano
2 packages (7 ounces *each*) spaghetti
1 package (8 ounces) cream cheese, softened
2 cups small-curd cottage cheese
1/2 cup sour cream
2 tablespoons minced chives
1/4 cup dry bread crumbs
1-1/2 teaspoons butter *or* margarine, melted

In a large skillet, cook beef and onions over medium heat until meat is no longer pink; drain. Add the tomato sauce, mushrooms, garlic powder and oregano. Bring to a boil. Reduce heat; simmer, uncovered, for 15 minutes, stirring occasionally. Meanwhile, cook the spaghetti according to package directions; drain.

In a mixing bowl, combine cream cheese, cottage cheese, sour cream and chives; beat well. Place half of spaghetti in a greased 4-qt. baking dish. Spoon cream cheese mixture evenly over top. Layer with remaining spaghetti and all of the beef mixture.

Toss bread crumbs and butter; sprinkle over the top. Cover and bake at 350° for 20 minutes. Uncover; bake 5-10 minutes longer or until heated through. **Yield:** 12 servings.

FOUR-CHEESE BOW TIES

(Pictured at right)

With its red tomatoes and green parsley, this dish always looks beautiful on a holiday buffet.
My daughter-in-law shared the recipe from her family, and it's now a favorite with our family, too.
—Mary Farney, Normal, Illinois

2 cans (14-1/2 ounces *each*) diced
    tomatoes
1 package (16 ounces) bow tie pasta
1/4 cup butter *or* margarine
1/4 cup all-purpose flour
1/4 teaspoon salt
1/4 teaspoon pepper
1-1/2 cups milk
1-1/2 cups (6 ounces) shredded
    mozzarella cheese
1-1/3 cups grated Romano cheese
1/2 cup shredded Parmesan cheese
1/4 cup crumbled blue *or* Gorgonzola
    cheese
1/2 cup minced fresh parsley

Drain tomatoes, reserving 1-1/4 cups juice; set aside. Cook pasta according to package directions; drain.

In a saucepan, melt butter over medium heat. Stir in the flour, salt and pepper until smooth; gradually add milk and reserved tomato juice. Bring to a boil; cook and stir for 2 minutes or until thickened. Remove from the heat.

In a large bowl, combine the pasta, sauce and reserved tomatoes. Stir in the cheeses and parsley; toss gently. Place in a greased 3-1/2-qt. baking dish. Bake, uncovered, at 375° for 30-35 minutes or until golden and bubbly. **Yield:** 12 servings.

SPECIAL HERB DRESSING

Our budget was tight when our children were small, so I cooked with hamburger often.
Nowadays I make this creative casserole because we love it!
—Trudy Williams, Shannonville, Ontario

1 pound ground beef
1 pound bulk pork sausage
1 pound fresh mushrooms, sliced
1 can (8 ounces) water chestnuts,
    drained and chopped
2 garlic cloves, minced
2 cups diced peeled apples
1 large onion, chopped
1/4 cup minced fresh parsley
1/4 cup chopped fresh celery leaves
1-1/2 teaspoons salt
1 teaspoon dried savory
1 teaspoon dried thyme
1 teaspoon rubbed sage
3/4 teaspoon pepper
Pinch nutmeg
1 cup chopped cranberries
12 cups cubed day-old bread
1 cup chicken broth

In a large skillet, cook beef and sausage over medium heat until no longer pink; drain. Add the mushrooms, water chestnuts, garlic, apples, onion, parsley and celery leaves; cook until mushrooms and apples are tender, about 6-8 minutes. Stir in seasonings and cranberries; mix well. Cook for 2 minutes.

Place bread cubes in a large bowl. Add meat mixture; stir in broth. Transfer to a greased 13-in. x 9-in. x 2-in. baking dish. Cover and bake at 350° for 35-45 minutes or until heated through. **Yield:** 14-16 servings.

BLACK-EYED PEA CASSEROLE

(Pictured above)

*This group-size dish is quick, simple and tasty. People always ask for "just a little more".
I guess you could call it one of my Southern favorites.*
—Kathy Rogers, Natchez, Mississippi

2 packages (6 ounces *each*) long grain
  and wild rice mix
2 pounds ground beef
2 medium onions, chopped
2 small green peppers, chopped
4 cans (15-1/2 ounces *each*)
  black-eyed peas with jalapenos,
  rinsed and drained
2 cans (10-3/4 ounces *each*)
  condensed cream of mushroom
  soup, undiluted
1-1/3 cups shredded cheddar cheese

In a large saucepan, cook the rice mixes according to package directions. Meanwhile, in a large skillet, cook the beef, onions and green peppers over medium heat until the meat is no longer pink; drain.

In a large bowl, combine the peas, soup, rice and beef mixture. Transfer to two greased 2-1/2-qt. baking dishes. Cover and bake at 350° for 20-25 minutes or until heated through. Uncover; sprinkle with cheese. Bake 5 minutes longer or until cheese is melted. **Yield:** 2 casseroles (10-12 servings each).

CROWD-PLEASING RICE BAKE

One of my favorite things to do when I have time is cook. This recipe is worth making time for because it offers such a comforting blend of flavors.
—Nadine Proffitt, Mechanicsville, Virginia

9 cups chicken broth
3 envelopes chicken noodle soup mix
2 cups uncooked long grain rice
1 pound bulk pork sausage
3 celery ribs, sliced
2 large onions, chopped
2 medium green peppers, chopped
1 can (10-3/4 ounces) condensed cream of mushroom soup, undiluted
6 cups cubed cooked chicken
1/2 cup slivered almonds, toasted

In a large saucepan, bring broth to a boil. Stir in soup mixes; cover and simmer for 10 minutes. Add rice; cover and simmer for 15 minutes. Remove from the heat.

In a large skillet, cook sausage over medium heat until no longer pink. Remove with a slotted spoon and set aside. Drain reserving 1 tablespoon drippings. In the drippings, saute celery, onions and green peppers until tender. Stir in the sausage, soup, chicken and rice mixture.

Transfer to two greased 2-1/2-qt. baking dishes. Cover and bake at 350° for 30 minutes or until rice is tender. Sprinkle with almonds. **Yield:** 2 casseroles (8 servings each).

TIMELY TIP

To reduce preparation time for Crowd-Pleasing Rice Bake on the day of the meal, cube the chicken and chop the celery, onions and green peppers the night before. Package each separately and store in the refrigerator.

ITALIAN BAKED BEANS

Even people who aren't wild about baked beans enjoy this dish—it puts a new twist on an old favorite. Sometimes I cook the beans on low in a slow cooker...easy and delicious!
—Betty Stucky, Hutchinson, Kansas

6 ounces sliced pepperoni
1 medium green pepper, chopped
1 large onion, chopped
1 tablespoon butter *or* margarine
1 can (12 ounces) tomato paste
2 cans (4 ounces *each*) mushroom stems and pieces, undrained
1/2 teaspoon salt
1/2 teaspoon pepper
1/2 teaspoon garlic powder
1/2 teaspoon dried basil
1/2 teaspoon dried oregano
4 cans (16 ounces *each*) pork and beans
1/4 cup grated Parmesan cheese

In a Dutch oven, cook the pepperoni, green pepper and onion in butter until vegetables are tender. Stir in the tomato paste, mushrooms, seasonings and beans; mix well. Sprinkle with Parmesan cheese. Cover and bake at 350° for 50-60 minutes or until heated through. **Yield:** 12-14 servings.

POTLUCK CHICKEN HOT DISH

(Pictured below)

With its down-home flavor, rich sauce and golden topping, this casserole brings folks back for seconds.
—Ruth Andrewson, Peck, Idaho

1/2 cup chopped fresh mushrooms
3 tablespoons finely chopped onion
2 garlic cloves, minced
4 tablespoons butter *or* margarine, *divided*
3 tablespoons all-purpose flour
1-1/4 cups milk
3/4 cup mayonnaise*
4 cups cubed cooked chicken
3 cups cooked long grain rice
2 celery ribs, chopped
1 cup frozen peas, thawed
1 jar (2 ounces) diced pimientos, drained
2 teaspoons lemon juice
1 teaspoon salt
1/2 teaspoon pepper
3/4 cup coarsely crushed cornflakes

In a large saucepan, saute mushrooms, onion and garlic in 3 tablespoons butter until tender. Stir in flour until blended. Gradually add milk. Bring to a boil; cook and stir for 2 minutes or until thickened. Remove from the heat; stir in mayonnaise. Add the chicken, rice, celery, peas, pimientos, lemon juice, salt and pepper; mix well.

Transfer to an ungreased 13-in. x 9-in. x 2-in. baking dish. Melt remaining butter; toss with cornflake crumbs. Sprinkle over top. Bake, uncovered, at 350° for 30-35 minutes or until bubbly. **Yield:** 8-10 servings.

*Editor's Note: Reduced-fat or fat-free mayonnaise may not be substituted for regular mayonnaise.

ASPARAGUS FLORENTINE

I am a native Missourian living near Frankfurt, Germany with my husband, Ralf.
I've had to learn how to adapt recipes because I can't always get ingredients here that I could
easily find back home. When I'm making this recipe in spring, I use mild white asparagus,
which is a German delicacy. It's just as good with green, however.
—Tiffiny Trump-Humbert, Raunheim, Germany

2-1/2 pounds fresh asparagus, trimmed
    and cut into 1-inch pieces
1 medium onion, chopped
1 garlic clove, minced
1/4 cup butter *or* margarine
1 can (10-3/4 ounces) condensed
    cream of celery soup, undiluted
1/2 cup water
3 egg yolks
1 tablespoon Worcestershire sauce
1/8 teaspoon ground mustard
Dash pepper
2 tablespoons lemon juice
1 package (8 ounces) cream cheese,
    cubed
1 package (10 ounces) frozen
    chopped spinach, thawed and
    squeezed dry

Place asparagus in a saucepan with a small amount of water; bring to a boil. Reduce heat; cover and simmer for 3-5 minutes or until crisp-tender. Drain and set aside. In a large saucepan, saute onion and garlic in butter until tender.

In a bowl, whisk together the soup, water, egg yolks, Worcestershire sauce, mustard and pepper. Whisk in the lemon juice. Add to onion mixture. Add cream cheese. Cook and stir over low heat until cheese is melted. Stir in spinach and asparagus; heat through.

Transfer to a greased 13-in. x 9-in. x 2-in. baking dish. Bake, uncovered, at 325° for 30-35 minutes or until a thermometer reads 160°. Let stand for 5 minutes before serving. **Yield:** 12 servings.

HOT CHICKEN SALAD

Rich and creamy with lots of chicken, this hot dish gets a nice crunch
from water chestnuts and toasted almonds.
—Ruth Burrus, Zionville, Indiana

4 cups cubed cooked chicken
8 celery ribs, sliced
2 cans (8 ounces *each*) sliced water
    chestnuts, drained
1 can (10-3/4 ounces) condensed
    cream of chicken soup, undiluted
1-1/2 cups mayonnaise*
1-1/2 cups (12 ounces) sour cream
1 cup sliced fresh mushrooms
1/2 cup slivered almonds, toasted
2 tablespoons finely chopped onion
2 tablespoons lemon juice
1/2 teaspoon salt
1/2 teaspoon pepper
1/2 cup shredded cheddar cheese
1/2 cup soft whole wheat bread crumbs

In a large bowl, combine the first 12 ingredients. Transfer to a greased 13-in. x 9-in. x 2-in. baking dish. Sprinkle with cheese and bread crumbs. Bake, uncovered, at 350° for 30-35 minutes or until heated through. **Yield:** 12 servings.

*Editor's Note: Reduced-fat or fat-free mayonnaise may not be substituted for regular mayonnaise.

CALIFORNIA CASSEROLE

This colorful casserole is named after the West Coast, but it always brings appreciative oohs and aahs when I serve it to fellow Texans. It's compatible with a variety of side dishes.
—Hope LaShier, Amarillo, Texas

  1 package (8 ounces) wide egg
    noodles
  2 pounds ground beef
  1 medium green pepper, chopped
3/4 cup chopped onion
  1 can (14-3/4 ounces) cream-style corn
  1 can (10-3/4 ounces) condensed
    tomato soup, undiluted
  1 can (10 ounces) diced tomatoes
    and green chilies, undrained
  1 can (8 ounces) tomato sauce
  1 can (4 ounces) mushroom stems
    and pieces, drained
  1 jar (4 ounces) diced pimientos,
    drained
  1 can (2-1/4 ounces) sliced ripe olives,
    drained
1-1/2 teaspoons celery salt
  1/2 teaspoon ground mustard
  1/2 teaspoon chili powder
  1/4 teaspoon pepper
  2 cups (8 ounces) shredded cheddar
    cheese

Cook noodles according to package directions; drain. In a Dutch oven, cook the beef, green pepper and onion over medium heat until meat is no longer pink; drain.

Stir in noodles and the next 11 ingredients. Cover and bake at 350° for 50 minutes. Uncover; sprinkle with cheese. Bake 10 minutes longer or until cheese is melted. **Yield:** 12-16 servings.

MAKE-AHEAD SCALLOPED POTATOES

When my husband and I got married, a dear friend, Sharon Kramer, fixed fabulous home-style food for our reception. Her tempting menu included these potatoes, which everybody loved.
—Linda Cox, Embarrass, Minnesota

  8 pounds potatoes, peeled and thinly
    sliced
  2 large onions, thinly sliced
1/3 cup all-purpose flour
  2 cans (10-3/4 ounces *each*)
    condensed cream of chicken soup,
    undiluted
2-2/3 cups milk
Salt and pepper to taste
  2 cups (8 ounces) shredded cheddar
    cheese

In two greased 13-in. x 9-in. x 2-in. baking dishes, layer potatoes and onions. Combine the flour, soup, milk, salt and pepper until blended; pour half over each dish.

Cover and bake at 325° for 1-1/4 to 1-1/2 hours or until potatoes are tender. Uncover; cool for 30 minutes. Cover and refrigerate overnight.

Remove from the refrigerator 30 minutes before reheating. Bake, covered, at 325° for 30-40 minutes. Uncover; sprinkle with the cheese. Bake 5 minutes longer or until the cheese is melted. **Yield:** 2 casseroles (10 servings each).

VEGGIE NOODLE CASSEROLE

(Pictured above)

This recipe combines nutritious vegetables and hearty noodles in a delectable cream sauce.
Whenever I serve this dish, it gets passed around until the pan is scraped clean.
—Jeanette Hios, Brooklyn, New York

1 package (16 ounces) wide egg
   noodles
1 can (10-3/4 ounces) condensed
   cream of chicken soup, undiluted
1 can (10-3/4 ounces) condensed
   cream of broccoli soup, undiluted
1-1/2 cups milk
1 cup grated Parmesan cheese,
   divided
3 garlic cloves, minced
2 tablespoons dried parsley flakes
1/2 teaspoon pepper
1/4 teaspoon salt
1 package (16 ounces) frozen
   broccoli, cauliflower and carrot
   blend, thawed
2 cups frozen corn, thawed

Cook noodles according to package directions; drain. In a bowl, combine the soups, milk, 3/4 cup Parmesan cheese, garlic, parsley, pepper and salt. Add the noodles and vegetables; mix well.

Pour into a greased 13-in. x 9-in. x 2-in. baking dish. Sprinkle with the remaining Parmesan. Cover and bake at 350° for 45-50 minutes or until heated through. **Yield:** 12-14 servings.

FIREFIGHTERS' CHICKEN SPAGHETTI

I'm usually in the kitchen most of the day making some kind of dish for my family, neighbors or the local fire department to pass around and try. My husband is a firefighter in our town, and this casserole is a favorite there.
—Krista Davis-Keith, New Castle, Indiana

12 ounces uncooked spaghetti, broken in half
1 can (10-3/4 ounces) condensed cream of chicken soup, undiluted
1 can (10-3/4 ounces) condensed cream of mushroom soup, undiluted
1 cup (8 ounces) sour cream
1/2 cup milk
1/4 cup butter *or* margarine, melted, *divided*
2 tablespoons dried parsley flakes
1/2 teaspoon garlic powder
1/2 teaspoon salt
1/4 teaspoon pepper
2 cups (8 ounces) shredded mozzarella cheese
1 cup grated Parmesan cheese
2 to 3 celery ribs, chopped
1 medium onion, chopped
1 can (4 ounces) mushroom stems and pieces, drained
5 cups cubed cooked chicken
1-1/2 cups crushed cornflakes

Cook spaghetti according to package directions; drain. In a large bowl, combine the soups, sour cream, milk, 2 tablespoons butter and seasonings. Add the cheeses, celery, onion and mushrooms. Stir in the chicken and spaghetti.

Transfer to a greased 3-qt. baking dish (dish will be full). Combine the cornflakes and remaining butter; sprinkle over top. Bake, uncovered, at 350° for 45-50 minutes or until bubbly. **Yield:** 12-14 servings.

HEARTY RICE CASSEROLE

You can see right away why this dish pleases a crowd. It's tasty and hearty—just like its name says. It's also easy on the cook, which I appreciate.
—Billie Bartlett, Monroe, Louisiana

1 can (10-3/4 ounces) condensed cream of mushroom soup, undiluted
1 can (10-3/4 ounces) condensed creamy onion soup, undiluted
1 can (10-3/4 ounces) condensed cream of chicken soup, undiluted
1 pound uncooked lean ground beef
1 pound uncooked bulk pork sausage
1 large onion, chopped
1 large green pepper, chopped
2 celery ribs, chopped
1-1/2 cups uncooked long grain rice

In a large bowl, combine all ingredients; mix well. Transfer to a greased 4-qt. baking dish. Cover and bake at 350° for 60-70 minutes or until the meat is no longer pink and the rice is tender. **Yield:** 12-16 servings.

POLISH REUBEN CASSEROLE

*People are always asking me for this recipe. It's easy to assemble and great
to take to potlucks, which we have a lot of in our farming community.*
—Imogene Peterson, Ontario, Oregon

1 package (8 ounces) egg noodles
2 cans (14 ounces *each*) Bavarian
  sauerkraut, drained
2 cans (10-3/4 ounces *each*)
  condensed cream of mushroom
  soup, undiluted
1-1/3 cups milk
1 medium onion, chopped
1 tablespoon prepared mustard
1-1/2 pounds Polish sausage *or* kielbasa,
  halved and cut into 1/2-inch slices
2 cups (8 ounces) shredded Swiss
  cheese
1/2 cup soft rye bread crumbs
2 tablespoons butter *or* margarine,
  melted

Cook noodles according to package directions; drain. Spread sauerkraut in a greased shallow 4-qt. baking dish. Top with noodles. In a bowl, combine the soup, milk, onion and mustard; pour over the noodles. Top with sausage; sprinkle with cheese.

Combine bread crumbs and butter; sprinkle over the top. Cover and bake at 350° for 30-35 minutes or until heated through. **Yield:** 12-14 servings.

SPAGHETTI PIZZA BAKE

Kids always go for this flavorful casserole, which is a cross between pizza and spaghetti.
—Jackie Heyer, Cushing, Iowa

2 pounds ground beef
1 medium onion, chopped
2 garlic cloves, minced
1 teaspoon salt
1/4 teaspoon pepper
1 package (7 ounces) thin spaghetti,
  broken into thirds
2 eggs
3/4 cup milk
1 jar (28 ounces) meatless spaghetti
  sauce
28 pepperoni slices
3/4 cup sliced fresh mushrooms
1/3 cup sliced ripe olives
2 cups (8 ounces) shredded
  mozzarella cheese

In a large skillet, cook the beef, onion and garlic over medium heat until meat is no longer pink; drain. Stir in salt and pepper; set aside. Cook spaghetti according to package directions; rinse in cold water and drain.

In a bowl, combine eggs and milk; stir in spaghetti. Transfer to a greased 13-in. x 9-in. x 2-in. baking dish. Top with spaghetti sauce, beef mixture, pepperoni, mushrooms and olives; sprinkle with cheese (dish will be full). Bake, uncovered, at 350° for 40-45 minutes or until bubbly. **Yield:** 12 servings.

TIMELY TIP

*Speed up salad making by washing, cutting and drying
all ingredients as soon as you buy them. Store in plastic bags.
At mealtime, pull out the bags and make a salad.*

PIES & PASTRIES

Fresh from the oven, a pie is a special treat, especially when it's the main course. This chapter features 40 tempting choices—from hearty meat pies to cheesy vegetable quiches to convenient handheld pastries. And each one tastes as good as it looks.

TUNA SPAGHETTI PIE (P. 184)

HOME-STYLE CHICKEN POTPIE (P. 176)
SPINACH BEEF PIE (P. 178)

HOME-STYLE CHICKEN POTPIE

(Pictured on page 175)

I served this potpie along with chili on Super Bowl Sunday. No one ate the chili.
In fact, one of my husband's single friends called the next day and asked for the leftover pie.
—Darlene Claxton, Brighton, Michigan

3/4 cup cold butter *or* margarine
2 cups all-purpose flour
1 cup (4 ounces) shredded cheddar
    cheese
1/2 cup plus 3 tablespoons cold water
FILLING:
2-1/2 cups halved baby carrots
3 celery ribs, sliced
6 tablespoons butter *or* margarine
7 tablespoons all-purpose flour
1 teaspoon salt
1/4 teaspoon coarsely ground pepper
2-1/2 cups chicken broth
1 cup whipping cream
4 cups cubed cooked chicken
1 cup frozen pearl onions, thawed
1 cup frozen peas, thawed
3 tablespoons minced chives
3 tablespoons minced fresh parsley
2 teaspoons minced fresh thyme
1 egg, lightly beaten

In a bowl, cut butter into flour until crumbly. Stir in cheese. Gradually add water, tossing with a fork until dough forms a ball. Cover and refrigerate for at least 1 hour.

In a saucepan, cook carrots and celery in a small amount of water until crisp-tender; drain and set aside. In another saucepan, melt butter. Whisk in the flour, salt and pepper until smooth. Gradually whisk in broth and cream. Bring to a boil; cook and stir for 2 minutes or until thickened. Stir in the carrots, celery, chicken, onions, peas, chives, parsley and thyme; heat through. Transfer to a greased 13-in. x 9-in. x 2-in. baking dish.

On a floured surface, roll out dough to fit top of dish. Place over filling; trim and flute edges. Cut slits in top. Brush with egg. If desired, cut leaf shapes out of remaining dough. Place over crust; brush with egg. Bake at 400° for 25-30 minutes or until bubbly and crust is golden brown. Let stand for 10 minutes before serving. **Yield:** 10-12 servings.

SOUTHWESTERN MEAT LOAF PIE

My family loves spicy foods, so my files are filled with recipes that call for salsa and cumin.
This pie can easily be taken to the harvest fields in summer and fall.
—Karen Ann Bland, Gove, Kansas

1 egg
2 cups salsa, *divided*
1/2 cup finely crushed saltines (about
    15 crackers)
1/2 teaspoon ground cumin
1/2 teaspoon salt
1/4 teaspoon pepper
1 pound ground beef
3 cups cooked rice
1 cup (4 ounces) shredded cheddar
    cheese, *divided*
Additional salsa, optional

In a large bowl, combine the egg, 3/4 cup salsa, cracker crumbs, cumin, salt and pepper. Crumble beef over mixture and mix well. Press onto the bottom and up the sides of a greased 9-in. pie plate. Bake, uncovered, at 350° for 25 minutes; drain.

Combine the rice, 1/2 cup cheese and remaining salsa; mix well. Spread over meat shell. Sprinkle with remaining cheese. Bake 10-15 minutes longer or until heated through. Let stand for 5-10 minutes before cutting. Serve with additional salsa if desired. **Yield:** 6 servings.

FIESTA CHICKEN 'N' STUFFING

(Pictured below)

My mother gave me this recipe at my bridal shower, and I've been making it ever since.
Mom knew that every new bride needs recipes for good food that is super easy to make.
—Angela Peppers, Memphis, Tennessee

3 eggs
3/4 cup milk
2 cups crushed stuffing mix
1-1/2 cups cubed cooked chicken
1 large tomato, chopped
3 tablespoons chopped green chilies
3 tablespoons chopped green onions
Sour cream and salsa, optional

In a bowl, combine the eggs and milk. Stir in the stuffing mix, chicken, tomato, chilies and onions. Transfer to a greased microwave-safe 9-in. pie plate. Cover with waxed paper. Microwave on high for 3 minutes; stir. Microwave for another 3 minutes; stir.

Cook 2-3 minutes longer or until set and a thermometer reads 160°. Let stand for 5 minutes before serving. Garnish with sour cream and salsa if desired. **Yield:** 4 servings.

Editor's Note: This recipe was tested in an 850-watt microwave.

SPINACH BEEF PIE

(Pictured on page 175)

I found this recipe about 15 years ago, and it's still one I turn to often. It's flavorful and pretty.
—Meg Stankiewicz, Garfield Heights, Ohio

1 cup all-purpose flour
1/3 cup old-fashioned oats
7 tablespoons cold butter *or* margarine
2 to 3 tablespoons cold water
1 pound ground beef
1 medium onion, chopped
1 medium green pepper, chopped
1 garlic clove, minced
1/4 cup ketchup
1 teaspoon salt
1 teaspoon dried oregano
1/2 teaspoon dried basil
1/2 teaspoon dried marjoram
1/4 teaspoon pepper
1 package (10 ounces) frozen chopped spinach, thawed and squeezed dry
3 eggs, lightly beaten
2 cups (8 ounces) shredded cheddar cheese, *divided*
1 large tomato, seeded and diced

In a bowl, combine flour and oats; cut in the butter until crumbly. Gradually add water, tossing with a fork until dough forms a ball. Roll out dough to fit a 9-in. pie plate. Transfer to plate; trim and flute edges.

In a skillet, cook the beef, onion, green pepper and garlic over medium heat until meat is no longer pink; drain. Stir in the ketchup and seasonings. Fold in the spinach; cool slightly. Stir in the eggs and 1 cup cheese until combined; spoon into crust.

Bake at 400° for 25-30 minutes or until the center is set. Top with 1-3/4 cups of cheese. Sprinkle the tomato and remaining cheese around edge of pie. Bake 5-10 minutes longer or until cheese is melted. Let stand for 5-10 minutes before cutting. **Yield:** 6-8 servings.

COUNTRY PIE

Men seem to really enjoy this simple yet tasty beef and rice pie. They always ask for seconds.
—Zelma Hartman, Franklin, North Carolina

1/2 cup tomato sauce
1/2 cup soft bread crumbs
1/4 cup chopped onion
1/4 cup chopped green pepper
1-1/2 teaspoons salt
1/4 teaspoon pepper
1/8 teaspoon dried oregano
1 pound lean ground beef
FILLING:
1-1/2 cups tomato sauce
1-1/3 cups instant rice
1 cup (4 ounces) shredded cheddar cheese, *divided*
1 cup water
1/2 teaspoon salt

In a large bowl, combine the first seven ingredients. Crumble beef over mixture and mix well. Press onto the bottom and up the sides of a greased 10-in. pie plate.

In a bowl, combine the tomato sauce, rice, 1/2 cup cheese, water and salt. Spoon into meat shell. Cover and bake at 350° for 25 minutes. Uncover; sprinkle with remaining cheese. Bake 15-20 minutes longer or until cheese is melted. Let stand for 15 minutes before cutting. **Yield:** 6 servings.

SAVORY CHICKEN PIE

(Pictured above)

Everyone will love the hearty combination of vegetables, chicken and sauce in this unique version of chicken potpie. The tasty homemade crust is so simple to prepare.
—Michelle Bentley, Niceville, Florida

1 cup (8 ounces) sour cream
1/2 cup butter *or* margarine, softened
1 egg
1 cup all-purpose flour
1 teaspoon baking powder
1 teaspoon salt
1 teaspoon rubbed sage
FILLING:
1/2 cup *each* chopped carrot, green pepper, sweet red pepper and onion
1/2 cup sliced fresh mushrooms
2 tablespoons butter *or* margarine
2 cups cubed cooked chicken
1 can (10-3/4 ounces) condensed cream of chicken soup, undiluted
1/2 cup shredded cheddar cheese

In a mixing bowl, beat the sour cream, butter and egg. Add the flour, baking powder, salt and sage; mix well (mixture will be sticky). Spread onto the bottom and up the sides of an ungreased 10-in. pie plate.

In a skillet, saute vegetables in butter until crisp-tender. Add chicken and soup; mix well. Spoon into the crust. Sprinkle with cheese. Bake at 400° for 30-35 minutes or until lightly browned. Let stand for 10 minutes before serving. **Yield:** 6-8 servings.

CHICKEN HAM 'N' MUSHROOM PIE

Parmesan cheese gives the crust of this pie an extra-special flavor. A co-worker back in Ohio shared the recipe. Friends and family talk about how good it is every time I make it.
—Darlene Tyktor, Glen Allen, Virginia

1 broiler/fryer chicken (3 to 4 pounds), cut up
3 cups water
1 medium carrot, cut into chunks
1 celery rib, cut into chunks
2 teaspoons salt
1/4 teaspoon dried thyme
1/4 pound fresh mushrooms, sliced
1/2 cup cubed fully cooked ham
1/4 cup butter *or* margarine
3 tablespoons all-purpose flour
1/8 teaspoon pepper
Dash ground nutmeg
1/2 cup frozen peas, thawed
PASTRY:
3/4 cup all-purpose flour
1/4 cup whole wheat flour
2 tablespoons grated Parmesan cheese
1/2 teaspoon salt
1/3 cup cold butter *or* margarine
1 egg yolk
1 teaspoon lemon juice
5 to 6 teaspoons cold water
GLAZE:
1 egg white
1 teaspoon water

In a Dutch oven or soup kettle, combine the first six ingredients; bring to a boil. Reduce heat; cover and simmer for 45-55 minutes or until chicken is tender. Remove chicken. When cool enough to handle, remove meat and skin from the bones; discard skin and bones. Cut the meat into chunks; set aside. Strain broth and set aside.

In a skillet, saute the mushrooms and ham in butter until mushrooms are tender. Sprinkle with flour, pepper and nutmeg; stir until blended. Gradually stir in 1-3/4 cups reserved broth (refrigerate any remaining broth for another use). Bring to a boil; cook and stir for 2 minutes or until thickened. Stir in peas and reserved chicken. Cool.

Meanwhile, combine the flours, Parmesan cheese and salt in a bowl. Cut in butter until crumbly. Stir in egg yolk and lemon juice. Gradually add cold water, tossing with a fork until dough forms a ball. On a floured surface, roll out dough into a 9-in. square.

Transfer chicken mixture to an ungreased 9-in. square baking dish. Place pastry over filling; trim and flute edges. Cut slits in top. Beat egg white and water; brush over pastry. Bake at 375° for 35-40 minutes or until bubbly and the crust is golden brown. Let stand for 10-15 minutes before cutting. **Yield:** 6-8 servings.

HELPFUL HINTS

Mushrooms add subtle flavor to many casseroles. Common cultivated mushrooms, ranging in color from white to light brown, can be found in most grocery stores. Here's how to choose and store them:
- *Look for mushrooms that are firm and evenly colored with tightly closed caps.*
- *Discard mushrooms that are damaged or soft. If the gills underneath are visible, the mushroom is past its prime but still usable.*
- *Store fresh mushrooms, unwashed, in the refrigerator for up to 3 days. Place them in a single layer on a tray and cover with a damp paper towel. Air helps mushrooms stay firm. Putting them in a plastic bag will speed up deterioration.*
- *Clean mushrooms just before using by rinsing under cold water and blotting dry. Don't immerse them or they'll become soft.*
- *To keep fresh mushrooms white, wipe them gently with a paper towel dipped in a mixture of lemon juice and water.*

FARMHOUSE PORK AND APPLE PIE

(Pictured below)

I've always loved pork and apples together, and this recipe combines them nicely.
It calls for a bit of preparation, but its wonderful flavor makes it well worth the extra effort.
—Suzanne Strocsher, Bothell, Washington

1 pound sliced bacon, cut into 2-inch
   pieces
3 medium onions, chopped
3 pounds boneless pork, cubed
3/4 cup all-purpose flour
Vegetable oil, optional
3 medium tart apples, peeled and
   chopped
1 teaspoon rubbed sage
1/2 teaspoon ground nutmeg
1 teaspoon salt
1/4 teaspoon pepper
1 cup apple cider *or* juice
1/2 cup water
4 medium potatoes, peeled and
   cubed
1/2 cup milk
5 tablespoons butter *or* margarine,
   divided
Additional salt and pepper
Minced fresh parsley, optional

In an ovenproof 12-in. skillet, cook bacon over medium heat until crisp. Remove with a slotted spoon to paper towels. In the drippings, saute onions until tender; remove with a slotted spoon and set aside.

Lightly coat pork with flour. Brown a third at a time in drippings, adding oil if needed. Remove from the heat; drain. Add bacon, onions, apples, sage, nutmeg, salt and pepper. Stir in the cider and water. Cover and bake at 325° for 2 hours or until pork is tender.

In a saucepan, cook potatoes in boiling water until tender. Drain; mash with milk and 3 tablespoons butter. Add salt and pepper to taste. Remove skillet from the oven; spread potatoes over pork mixture. Melt remaining butter; brush over potatoes. Broil 6 in. from the heat for 5 minutes or until topping is browned. Sprinkle with parsley if desired. **Yield:** 10 servings.

CHICKEN AND OYSTER PIE

I learned to cook traditional Dutch meals like this from my mother and grandmother.
—Mrs. Vernon Gergley, Lititz, Pennsylvania

1/4 cup all-purpose flour
  3 cups chicken broth, *divided*
  4 cups cubed cooked peeled potatoes
  3 cups cubed cooked chicken
  1 pint shucked oysters, drained and chopped *or* 2 cans (8 ounces *each*) whole oysters, drained and chopped
  1 package (16 ounces) frozen peas, thawed
  1 celery rib, chopped
  2 hard-cooked eggs, chopped
  1 tablespoon minced fresh parsley
Butter *or* margarine
Pastry for double-crust pie (9 inches)

In a large saucepan, stir the flour and 1/2 cup broth until smooth. Add the remaining broth. Bring to a boil; cook and stir for 2 minutes or until thickened. Remove from the heat. Add potatoes, chicken, oysters, peas, celery, eggs and parsley; mix gently.

Pour into a greased 13-in. x 9-in. x 2-in. baking dish. Dot with butter. Roll pastry into a 14-in. x 10-in. rectangle; place over chicken mixture and seal to edges of baking dish. Cut slits in pastry. Bake at 425° for 35 minutes or until golden brown. **Yield:** 8-10 servings.

HELPFUL HINT

You'll get about 1 cup of cooked meat per pound of whole chicken. A 3- to 4-pound broiler/fryer will provide 3 to 4 cups of meat after boning.

POTATO VEGETABLE QUICHE

When I can't decide what I'd like for supper, this hearty quiche comes to mind because it has a little bit of everything. It really hits the spot.
—Marion DeArmond, Sicamous, British Columbia

  5 medium potatoes (about 2 pounds), peeled and quartered
  2 tablespoons butter *or* margarine
  1 teaspoon salt
  1 teaspoon dried parsley flakes
1/4 teaspoon pepper
1/4 teaspoon ground nutmeg
  1 cup (4 ounces) shredded cheddar cheese
  1 medium onion, chopped
1/2 cup sliced fresh mushrooms
1/2 cup cooked crumbled bacon
1/4 cup chopped green pepper
1/4 cup chopped sweet red pepper
  3 eggs, lightly beaten
1/2 cup cream-style corn
1/4 cup milk
1/4 teaspoon paprika

Place potatoes in a large saucepan and cover with water; bring to a boil. Cover and cook until tender, about 20-30 minutes. Drain and place in a bowl; mash. Add the butter, salt, parsley, pepper and nutmeg. Mix well. Spread into a greased 9-in. pie plate. Combine the cheese, onion, mushrooms, bacon and peppers; spoon into potato crust.

Combine the eggs, corn and milk; pour over vegetables. Sprinkle with paprika. Bake at 375° for 45-50 minutes or until a knife inserted near the center comes out clean. Serve warm. **Yield:** 6-8 servings.

BEEF CHILI PIE

*I love to experiment with recipes to see what I can come up with, and
my husband is a willing guinea pig. He and I both called this one a success.*
—Trish Houff, Winchester, Virginia

1 pound ground beef
1 medium green pepper, chopped
1 can (16 ounces) kidney beans,
    rinsed and drained
1 can (14-1/2 ounces) stewed
    tomatoes, cut up
1/2 cup water
1 tablespoon dried minced onion
1 tablespoon chili powder
Dash ground cinnamon
Dash ground cloves
2 to 4 tablespoons brown sugar,
    optional
1/2 cup mashed potato flakes
Pastry for double-crust pie (9 inches)
3 cups shredded lettuce, *divided*
2 cups (8 ounces) shredded cheddar
    cheese
1 tablespoon butter *or* margarine,
    melted
1 tablespoon sesame seeds

In a skillet, cook beef and green pepper over medium heat until the meat is no longer pink; drain. Add the beans, tomatoes, water, onion, chili powder, cinnamon and cloves. Bring to a boil. Reduce heat; cover and simmer for 15 minutes. Stir in the brown sugar. Simmer, uncovered, for 12-15 minutes or until liquid is almost absorbed; stir in potato flakes.

Meanwhile, on a floured surface, roll one portion of pastry to fit the bottom and up the sides of an ungreased 8-in. square baking dish. Transfer pastry to dish; trim edges. Sprinkle lettuce and 1/2 cup cheese over crust. Top with half of the beef mixture and 3/4 cup cheese, then remaining beef mixture and cheese. Roll out remaining pastry to fit top of dish. Place over filling. Trim edges; seal with a fork. Cut slits in pastry. Brush with butter and sprinkle with sesame seeds.

Bake at 400° for 25-30 minutes or until golden brown. Let stand for 5 minutes before cutting. Serve with remaining lettuce. **Yield:** 6-8 servings.

CRESCENT CHEESEBURGER PIE

*I grab this recipe when I'm looking for a quick dinner that will bring smiles to
everyone at the table. Add a side salad, and presto, the meal is done!*
—Carolyn Hayes, Marion, Illinois

1 pound ground beef
1 small onion, chopped
1 can (8 ounces) tomato sauce
1/3 cup ketchup
1/2 teaspoon salt
1/4 teaspoon pepper
5 to 6 slices process American cheese
1 tube (8 ounces) refrigerated
    crescent rolls

In a skillet, cook the beef and onion over medium heat until the meat is no longer pink; drain. Stir in tomato sauce, ketchup, salt and pepper; heat through. Spoon into an ungreased 9-in. pie plate. Arrange the cheese on top.

Bake at 400° for 2-3 minutes or until cheese begins to warm. Unroll crescent roll dough and separate into triangles. Place over cheese, pressing down on edges of pie plate to seal. Bake 10-12 minutes longer or until golden brown. Let stand for 5 minutes before cutting. **Yield:** 8 servings.

TUNA SPAGHETTI PIE

(Pictured above and on page 174)

I'm a real pasta fan and I like fish as well, so I decided to combine the two.
When my granddaughters are over, I make this dish in tart tins, so each girl can have
her own pie. That works for both pint-size and senior-size appetites.
—Ruth Lee, Troy, Ontario

4 ounces spaghetti, broken into
    2-inch pieces
1/4 cup grated Parmesan cheese
1 egg, lightly beaten
1 tablespoon butter *or* margarine,
    melted
1 garlic clove, minced
1/4 teaspoon salt
1/8 teaspoon pepper
FILLING:
1 tablespoon finely chopped onion
1 teaspoon butter *or* margarine
1 tablespoon all-purpose flour
1/2 teaspoon salt
1/4 teaspoon celery salt
1/4 teaspoon garlic and herb seasoning
1/8 teaspoon pepper
1/4 cup milk
1/4 cup sour cream
1 egg, beaten
1 can (6 ounces) tuna, drained and
    flaked
1/4 cup grated Parmesan cheese,
    divided
1 small tomato, thinly sliced
Minced fresh parsley

Cook spaghetti according to package directions; rinse in cold water and drain. In a bowl, combine the spaghetti, Parmesan cheese, egg, butter, garlic, salt and pepper; mix well. Press onto the bottom and up the sides of a greased 9-in. pie plate; set aside.

In a skillet, saute onion in butter until tender. Remove from the heat. Stir in the flour and seasonings until blended. In a bowl, beat together the milk, sour cream and egg. Stir into the onion mixture until blended. Fold in the tuna; spoon into crust.

Sprinkle half of the Parmesan over pie. Arrange tomato slices over cheese; sprinkle with remaining Parmesan. Bake at 350° for 35-40 minutes or until crust is golden and filling is puffy. Sprinkle with parsley. Let stand for 5-10 minutes before cutting. **Yield:** 6 servings.

HEARTY PORK PIE

My family adores this pie, especially at holiday time. The dough is easy to work with, and the wonderful aroma calls everyone to the table, so I don't have to!
—Sue Bacon, Glencoe, Minnesota

2 cups all-purpose flour
1 teaspoon salt
1/2 cup shortening
1/2 cup sour cream
1 egg, lightly beaten
FILLING:
4 bacon strips, diced
1-1/2 pounds boneless pork, cut into
  1/2-inch cubes
3 small onions, chopped
1 garlic clove, minced
2 tablespoons all-purpose flour
1 teaspoon salt
1/4 to 1/2 teaspoon pepper
1/8 to 1/4 teaspoon ground allspice
3/4 cup water
1 teaspoon beef bouillon granules
3 tablespoons minced fresh parsley
1 tablespoon whipping cream

In a bowl, combine the flour and salt. Cut in shortening until the mixture resembles coarse crumbs. Combine sour cream and egg; add to crumb mixture, tossing with a fork until dough forms a ball. Cover and refrigerate for 2 hours.

Meanwhile, in a skillet, cook bacon over medium heat until crisp. Remove to paper towels; drain, reserving 2 tablespoons drippings. Brown pork in drippings. Add onions and garlic; cook and stir until tender. Sprinkle with flour, salt, pepper and allspice; stir until blended. Add the water, bouillon, parsley and bacon. Cover and cook over medium-low heat for 30 minutes or until meat is tender.

Divide dough in half; roll out one portion to fit a 9-in. pie plate. Transfer to pie plate; trim pastry even with edge. Spoon filling into crust. Roll out remaining pastry to fit top of plate; place over filling. Trim, seal and flute edges. Cut slits in pastry; brush with cream. Bake at 400° for 25-30 minutes or until golden brown. Let stand for 15 minutes before cutting. **Yield:** 6-8 servings.

CHEESEBURGER QUICHE

I'm a retired postmaster in our small farming town. I enjoy cooking, square dancing and doing volunteer work. This cheesy quiche is a recipe I pull out and enjoy often.
—Reta Ford, Chillicothe, Texas

3/4 pound ground beef
1 medium onion, chopped
1/3 cup chopped green pepper
1 tablespoon all-purpose flour
1 tablespoon dried parsley flakes
1/4 teaspoon garlic powder
1/4 teaspoon pepper
1 cup evaporated milk
2 eggs, beaten
1-1/2 cups (6 ounces) shredded cheddar
  cheese
1 unbaked pastry shell (9 inches)

In a large skillet, cook beef, onion and green pepper over medium heat until meat is no longer pink; drain. Stir in the flour, seasonings, milk, eggs and cheese. Transfer to pastry shell. Bake at 350° for 35-40 minutes or until a knife inserted near the center comes out clean. Let stand for 5 minutes before cutting. **Yield:** 6 servings.

BARBECUED PORK PIE

(Pictured at right)

I've had this recipe so long that I can't even remember where I got it. It's delicious, easy to prepare and unique because of the puff pastry crust. It's pretty, too, so you can't lose.
—Gigi Morgan, Indianapolis, Indiana

1 cup water
6 tablespoons butter (no substitutes)
1/2 teaspoon salt
Dash pepper
1 cup all-purpose flour
4 eggs
1-1/2 cups (6 ounces) shredded Swiss cheese
FILLING:
1 medium green pepper, chopped
1 small onion, chopped
1 garlic clove, minced
1 tablespoon butter
2 tablespoons minced fresh parsley
1 tablespoon cornstarch
1 can (8 ounces) tomato sauce
3/4 cup chicken broth
1 tablespoon Worcestershire sauce
1 teaspoon sugar
2-1/2 cups cubed cooked pork
1/2 cup shredded Swiss cheese

In a saucepan, bring the water, butter, salt and pepper to a boil. Add flour all at once; stir until a smooth ball forms. Remove from the heat; let stand for 5 minutes. Add eggs, one at a time, beating well after each addition. Continue beating until mixture is smooth and shiny. Stir in cheese.

Spread onto the bottom and up the sides of a greased 11-in. x 7-in. x 2-in. baking dish. Bake at 400° for 20 minutes.

Meanwhile, in a saucepan, saute green pepper, onion and garlic in butter until tender. Sprinkle with parsley and cornstarch; stir until blended. Stir in the tomato sauce, broth, Worcestershire sauce and sugar. Bring to a boil; cook and stir for 2 minutes or until thickened. Stir in the pork. Pour into crust; sprinkle with cheese. Bake 15-20 minutes longer or until puffed and golden. **Yield:** 6 servings.

SALMON BISCUIT BAKE

The combination of mayonnaise and milk makes the filling in this delicious pie extra creamy.
—Eleanor Mengel, Summerfield, Florida

1 can (14-3/4 ounces) salmon, drained, bones and skin removed
1 cup frozen peas, thawed
1/4 cup milk
1/4 cup mayonnaise*
2 tablespoons finely chopped green pepper
1/4 teaspoon lemon-pepper seasoning
1 cup (4 ounces) shredded cheddar cheese
TOPPING:
1 cup biscuit/baking mix
1/3 cup milk
2 tablespoons mayonnaise*

In a bowl, combine the salmon, peas, milk, mayonnaise, green pepper and lemon-pepper. Transfer to a greased 9-in. pie plate. Sprinkle with cheese. Combine the biscuit mix, milk and mayonnaise just until moistened. Drop eight mounds onto salmon mixture. Bake at 425° for 10-15 minutes or until bubbly and biscuits are golden brown. **Yield:** 4-6 servings.

*Editor's Note: Reduced-fat or fat-free mayonnaise may not be substituted for regular mayonnaise.

BARBECUED PORK PIE (P. 186)
CREAMED CHICKEN IN PASTRY SHELLS (P. 188)

CREAMED CHICKEN IN PASTRY SHELLS

(Pictured on page 187)

This recipe requires a little effort, but it's definitely worth the time. It's special enough to serve to guests, but if I saved it just for company, my family would not be happy.
—Dona Glover, Rockwall, Texas

2 packages (10 ounces *each*) frozen
  pastry shells
2 celery ribs, finely chopped
1 medium onion, chopped
2 tablespoons chopped green pepper
6 tablespoons butter *or* margarine,
  divided
6 tablespoons all-purpose flour
1/2 teaspoon salt
3 cups milk
1 can (10-3/4 ounces) condensed
  cream of mushroom soup,
  undiluted
4 cups cubed cooked chicken
1 can (4 ounces) mushroom stems
  and pieces, drained
1 jar (2 ounces) diced pimientos,
  drained
1/2 cup grated Parmesan cheese
1/2 cup sliced almonds

Bake pastry shells according to package directions; set aside. In a skillet, saute the celery, onion and green pepper in 1 tablespoon butter for 10 minutes or until tender. Remove from the heat and set aside.

In a large saucepan, melt the remaining butter over medium heat. Stir in flour and salt until smooth. Gradually add the milk. Bring to a boil; cook and stir for 2 minutes or until thickened. Stir in soup until blended. Add the chicken, mushrooms, pimientos and sauteed vegetables; mix well.

Transfer to a greased 3-qt. baking dish. Sprinkle with the Parmesan cheese and almonds. Bake, uncovered, at 350° for 20-25 minutes or until bubbly. Spoon into pastry shells. **Yield:** 6 servings (2 shells each).

HANDY MEAT PIES

These handheld pies make a great dinner entree, especially when time is short. They're also a favorite wintertime snack around our house.
—Amy Stumpf, Hampton, Virginia

3/4 pound ground beef
3/4 pound bulk pork sausage
1 medium onion, chopped
1/3 cup chopped green onions
1 garlic clove, minced
2 tablespoons minced fresh parsley
1 tablespoon water
2 teaspoons all-purpose flour
1/2 teaspoon baking powder
1/2 teaspoon salt
1/4 teaspoon pepper
2 tubes (12 ounces *each*) refrigerated
  buttermilk biscuits

In a large skillet, cook the beef and sausage over medium heat until no longer pink; drain. Add onions and garlic; cook until tender. Add the parsley, water, flour, baking powder, salt and pepper; mix well. Heat through. Cover and refrigerate for at least 1 hour.

On a floured surface, pat 10 biscuits into 4-in. circles. Top each with about 1/3 cup meat mixture. Pat remaining biscuits into 5-in. circles and place over filling; seal edges with water. Press edges together with a fork dipped in flour; pierce the top.

Place on an ungreased baking sheet. Bake at 375° for 12-14 minutes or until biscuits are golden brown and filling is hot. **Yield:** 10 servings.

TURKEY POTPIE

(Pictured below)

Family and guests rave about this hearty potpie and its flaky crust. The "secret"
crust ingredients are Parmesan cheese and instant mashed potato flakes.
—Cheryl Arnold, Lake Zurich, Illinois

1 can (10-3/4 ounces) condensed
  cream of mushroom soup,
  undiluted
1 can (5 ounces) evaporated milk
1/4 cup minced fresh parsley
1/2 teaspoon dried thyme
3 cups cubed cooked turkey
1 package (10 ounces) frozen mixed
  vegetables, thawed
1/4 teaspoon salt
1/4 teaspoon pepper
CRUST:
3/4 cup mashed potato flakes
3/4 cup all-purpose flour
1/4 cup grated Parmesan cheese
1/3 cup cold butter *or* margarine
1/4 cup ice water
Half-and-half cream

In a bowl, combine the first four ingredients. Stir in the turkey, vegetables, salt and pepper. Spoon into a greased 11-in. x 7-in. x 2-in. baking dish.

For crust, combine the potato flakes, flour and Parmesan cheese in a bowl; cut in butter until crumbly. Gradually add the water, tossing with a fork until dough forms a ball. On a lightly floured surface, roll out dough to fit baking dish. Cut vents in crust, using a small tree, star or other shape cutter if desired. Place over filling; trim and flute edges. Brush with cream.

Bake at 400° for 25-30 minutes or until golden brown. If necessary, cover edges of crust with foil to prevent overbrowning. **Yield:** 6 servings.

SHEPHERD'S PIE

*Of all the shepherd's pie recipes I've tried through the years, this version is my favorite.
I enjoy cooking and baking for friends and family, who agree this one is tops.*
—Mary Arthurs, Etobicoke, Ontario

PORK LAYER:
    1 pound ground pork
    1 small onion, chopped
    2 garlic cloves, minced
    1 cup cooked rice
    1/2 cup pork gravy *or* 1/4 cup chicken broth
    1/2 teaspoon salt
    1/2 teaspoon dried thyme
CABBAGE LAYER:
    1 medium carrot, diced
    1 small onion, chopped
    2 tablespoons butter *or* margarine
    6 cups chopped cabbage
    1 cup chicken broth
    1/2 teaspoon salt
    1/4 teaspoon pepper
POTATO LAYER:
    2 cups mashed potatoes
    1/4 cup shredded cheddar cheese

In a large skillet, cook pork, onion and garlic over medium heat until meat is no longer pink; drain. Stir in the rice, gravy, salt and thyme. Spoon into a greased 11-in. x 7-in. x 2-in. baking dish.

In the same skillet, saute carrot and onion in butter for 5 minutes. Stir in cabbage; cook for 1 minute. Add the broth, salt and pepper; cover and cook for 10 minutes. Spoon over the pork layer. Spoon or pipe mashed potatoes over top; sprinkle with cheese. Bake, uncovered, at 350° for 45 minutes or until browned. **Yield:** 6 servings.

SAUSAGE SPINACH POCKETS

I've found that these appetizing pockets are a great way to sneak vegetables into my kids' meals.
—Denise Stapleton, Fort Collins, Colorado

1/2 pound bulk pork sausage
1/3 cup chopped onion
  1 garlic clove, minced
  1 cup chopped fresh spinach
1/4 cup chopped fresh mushrooms
3/4 cup shredded mozzarella cheese
1/2 teaspoon salt
1/4 teaspoon pepper
  2 tablespoons grated Parmesan cheese, optional
  2 tubes (8 ounces *each*) refrigerated crescent rolls
  1 egg
  1 tablespoon water
  1 tablespoon cornmeal

In a large skillet, cook sausage, onion and garlic over medium heat until meat is no longer pink; drain. Remove from the heat; stir in the spinach and mushrooms. Add the mozzarella cheese, salt, pepper and Parmesan cheese if desired; mix well.

Separate crescent roll dough into eight rectangles; seal perforations and flatten into 5-in. x 4-1/2-in. rectangles. Place about 1/3 cup of sausage mixture on half of each rectangle to within 1/2 in. of edges. Beat egg and water; brush over edges of dough. Bring unfilled half of dough over filling; press edges with a fork to seal. Brush tops with egg mixture.

Sprinkle the cornmeal on a greased baking sheet; place pockets on pan. Bake at 350° for 15-20 minutes or until golden brown. **Yield:** 8 servings.

BEEF AND CHEDDAR QUICHE

(Pictured above)

This recipe is easy to prepare, so it's perfect for folks with a busy schedule, like me.
Ground beef adds a nice homey flavor to the quiche.
—Jeanne Lee, Terrace Park, Ohio

3/4 pound ground beef
  1 unbaked pastry shell (9 inches)
  3 eggs, beaten
1/2 cup mayonnaise*
1/2 cup milk
  1 medium onion, chopped
  4 teaspoons cornstarch
  1 teaspoon salt
1/2 teaspoon pepper
  2 cups (8 ounces) shredded cheddar
    cheese, *divided*

In a skillet, cook the beef over medium heat until no longer pink; drain. Line unpricked pastry shell with a double thickness of heavy-duty foil. Bake at 450° for 5 minutes. Remove foil and bake 5 minutes longer; set aside. Reduce heat to 350°.

Place beef in a large bowl. Add the eggs, mayonnaise, milk, onion, cornstarch, salt, pepper and 1 cup cheese. Pour into crust.

Bake for 35-40 minutes or until a knife inserted near the center comes out clean. If necessary, cover the edges of crust with foil to prevent overbrowning. Sprinkle with remaining cheese. Let stand for 5-10 minutes before cutting. **Yield:** 6-8 servings.

*Editor's Note: Reduced-fat or fat-free mayonnaise may not be substituted for regular mayonnaise.

SPEAR TIPS

Fresh asparagus can be substituted for frozen in Asparagus Spaghetti Pie.

Choose firm, bright green stalks with tight tips.

Wrap the stem ends in a wet paper towel, then seal in a plastic bag.

Asparagus will keep for up to 3 days in the refrigerator. Wash just before using.

ASPARAGUS SPAGHETTI PIE

(Pictured above)

I've served this attractive dish many times. It always receives many compliments and recipe requests.
—Lorraine Danz, Lancaster, Pennsylvania

1 package (7 ounces) spaghetti
2 eggs
1/2 cup grated Parmesan cheese
2 tablespoons butter *or* margarine, melted

FILLING:
1 cup cubed fully cooked ham
1 package (8 ounces) frozen asparagus spears, thawed and cut into 1-inch pieces
1 jar (4-1/2 ounces) sliced mushrooms, drained
1-1/2 cups (6 ounces) shredded Swiss cheese
2 eggs
1/2 cup sour cream
1 teaspoon dill weed
1 teaspoon minced chives

Cook spaghetti according to package directions; rinse in cold water and drain. In a large bowl, beat the eggs. Add spaghetti, Parmesan cheese and butter; mix well. Press onto the bottom and up the sides of a greased 10-in. pie plate.

Combine the ham, asparagus and mushrooms; spoon into crust. Sprinkle with Swiss cheese. Beat the eggs, sour cream, dill and chives; pour over cheese. Bake at 350° for 35-40 minutes or until crust is set and center is lightly browned. Let stand for 10 minutes before cutting. **Yield:** 6-8 servings.

SAVORY TOMATO PIE

*I describe this dish as a quiche without cheese. It's great for luncheons, brunches or breakfasts.
Don't skimp on the basil—it makes the pie!*
—Helen Marucci, Fergus, Ontario

  5 green onions, sliced
3/4 cup chopped sweet onion
  2 tablespoons butter *or* margarine
  2 pounds tomatoes, peeled, seeded
      and chopped
  1 unbaked pastry shell (9 inches)
  3 eggs
  1 cup half-and-half cream
1-1/2 teaspoons salt
  1 tablespoon minced fresh basil
      or 1 teaspoon dried basil
1/2 teaspoon white pepper

In a large skillet, saute onions in butter until tender. Add tomatoes; cook and stir over low heat until softened. Remove from the heat; cool.

Line unbaked pastry shell with a double thickness of heavy-duty foil. Bake at 450° for 5 minutes. Remove foil; bake 5 minutes longer. Reduce heat to 350°.

In a mixing bowl, beat the eggs, cream, salt, basil and pepper until smooth. Stir in the tomato mixture. Pour into pastry shell. Bake for 45-50 minutes or until a knife inserted near the center comes out clean. Let stand for 5 minutes before cutting. **Yield:** 6-8 servings.

CRANBERRY PORK PIE

*Pretty red cranberries give the tender pork a delightfully different taste.
This pie is a pleasure to serve—and eat—during the cold-weather months.*
—Elizabeth McJunkin, Toronto, Kansas

  2 bacon strips, diced
1/4 cup all-purpose flour
  1 teaspoon rubbed sage
1/2 teaspoon salt
  2 pounds pork chop suey meat
  1 tablespoon vegetable oil, optional
  1 cup finely chopped cranberries
1/3 cup sugar
3/4 cup hot chicken broth
BISCUIT CRUST:
  1 cup all-purpose flour
1-1/2 teaspoons baking powder
1/2 teaspoon salt
1/4 cup cold butter *or* margarine
1/3 cup milk

In a skillet, cook bacon over medium heat until crisp. Remove to paper towels. In a large resealable plastic bag, combine the flour, sage and salt. Add pork in batches; shake to coat.

In the bacon drippings, saute the pork in batches until browned, adding oil if needed. Transfer to a greased 1-1/2-qt. round baking dish. Sprinkle with bacon. Combine cranberries and sugar; sprinkle over pork. Pour broth over top. Cover and bake at 400° for 25 minutes.

Meanwhile, combine the flour, baking powder and salt in a bowl. Cut in butter until mixture resembles coarse crumbs. Stir in milk just until moistened. Turn onto lightly floured surface; knead 8-10 times. Roll into a circle the size of the baking dish. Cut into eight wedges; place over pork mixture. Bake, uncovered, for 20-25 minutes or until golden brown. **Yield:** 8 servings.

ZUCCHINI PIE

*This recipe is so good, you won't be thinking of zucchini as that "overabundant vegetable" anymore.
Instead, you'll be checking the garden, eager for the day you can start making this pie.*
—Lori Cardoza, Salem, Oregon

    1/2 cup butter *or* margarine, softened
      1 package (3 ounces) cream cheese,
        softened
      2 tablespoons whipping cream
1-1/2 cups all-purpose flour
    1/2 teaspoon salt
      1 egg white
    1/4 teaspoon water
FILLING:
      4 cups thinly sliced zucchini (about 1
        pound)
      1 cup chopped green onions
      2 garlic cloves, minced
      3 tablespoons butter *or* margarine
      1 teaspoon dried basil
      1 teaspoon dried oregano
    1/2 teaspoon salt
    1/4 teaspoon pepper
      2 eggs, lightly beaten
1-1/2 cups (6 ounces) shredded
        mozzarella cheese

In a mixing bowl, beat butter and cream cheese until smooth. Beat in the cream, flour and salt. On a lightly floured surface, knead dough until smooth. Cover and refrigerate for 1 hour.

On a lightly floured surface, roll out dough to fit a 9-in. pie plate or quiche dish. Transfer to pan; flute or trim edges. Prick dough. In a bowl, beat egg white and water; brush over bottom of crust. Bake at 425° for 13-15 minutes or until edges are golden brown. Reduce heat to 375°.

In a skillet, saute the zucchini, onions and garlic in butter for 10 minutes. Stir in the basil, oregano, salt and pepper. In a bowl, combine eggs and cheese; stir in zucchini mixture. Pour into the crust. Bake for 20-25 minutes or until crust is golden brown and a knife inserted near the center comes out clean. Let stand for 10 minutes before cutting. **Yield:** 6-8 serving

SUMMER VEGGIE PIE

*This is a favorite in late summer because family and friends grow the ingredients,
then pass them on to my sister and me. We have fun creating meals together.*
—Florence Palmer, Marshall, Illinois

    1/3 cup cold butter *or* margarine
1-1/3 cups all-purpose flour
      2 to 3 tablespoons cold water
      3 cups sliced zucchini
    1/2 cup sliced green onions
      2 tablespoons vegetable oil
      2 small tomatoes, seeded, chopped
        and drained
      1 cup (4 ounces) shredded cheddar
        cheese
      3 eggs
    3/4 cup milk
    1/2 teaspoon salt
    1/8 teaspoon pepper

In a bowl, cut butter into flour until crumbly. Gradually add the water, tossing with a fork until dough forms a ball. Cover with plastic wrap; let stand for 10 minutes. In a skillet, saute zucchini and onions in oil for 5 minutes; drain well and set aside.

On a floured surface, roll out dough to fit a 9-in. pie plate. Transfer to plate; trim and flute edges. Spoon tomatoes over crust. Top with zucchini mixture. Sprinkle with cheese. In a bowl, beat eggs, milk, salt and pepper; pour over cheese. Bake at 375° for 30-35 minutes or until a knife inserted near the center comes out clean. Let stand for 5 minutes before cutting. **Yield:** 6 servings.

CORNISH PASTIES

These are a bit different from traditional pasties, but the ingredients are probably already on your pantry shelf. I like to double the recipe and freeze the extras to have on hand as a quick meal when we're on the go.
—Judy Marsden, Ontario, California

1/2 pound ground beef
2 tablespoons all-purpose flour
1/2 to 1 teaspoon seasoned salt
1 tablespoon minced fresh parsley
1 teaspoon beef bouillon granules
1/4 cup water
1 cup diced peeled potato
1/2 cup diced carrot
2 tablespoons finely chopped onion
2 packages (11 ounces *each*) pie crust mix
Water

In a skillet, cook beef over medium heat until no longer pink; drain well. Stir in flour, seasoned salt and parsley until well coated. Dissolve bouillon in water; add to meat mixture. Add the potato, carrot and onion. Cover and cook over medium heat until the vegetables are crisp-tender. Cool.

Prepare pie crusts according to package directions. On a floured surface, roll each into a 12-in. square. Cut each square into four 6-in. squares. Place about 1/3 cup of meat mixture in the center of each square.

Moisten edges of pastry with water and fold over filling to form a triangle. Press edges with a fork to seal. Make a 1-in. slit in the top of each triangle. Place on two ungreased baking sheets. Bake at 400° for 20-25 minutes or until golden brown. **Yield:** 8 pasties.

CHEESEBURGER PIE

This is a meal my husband really enjoys, although it's a bit big for just the two of us. The good news is that it reheats nicely in the microwave.
—Sharon Scholl, Arlington, Indiana

1 cup plus 2 tablespoons biscuit/baking mix, *divided*
1/4 cup milk
1 pound ground beef
1 medium onion, chopped
1 tablespoon Worcestershire sauce
1/2 teaspoon salt
1/4 teaspoon pepper
1 can (14-1/2 ounces) diced tomatoes with garlic and onion, undrained
2 eggs, lightly beaten
2 cups (8 ounces) shredded cheddar cheese
Chili sauce, optional

In a bowl, combine 1 cup biscuit mix and milk; stir until a soft ball forms. Turn onto a floured surface; knead 5 times. Roll out dough to fit a 9-in. pie plate. Transfer to plate; trim and flute edges.

In a skillet, cook beef and onion over medium heat until meat is no longer pink; drain. Stir in Worcestershire sauce, salt, pepper and remaining biscuit mix. Pour into crust. Spoon tomatoes over top. Combine eggs and cheese; pour over tomatoes.

Bake at 375° for 30-35 minutes or until set and lightly browned. Let stand for 5 minutes before cutting. Serve with chili sauce if desired. **Yield:** 6-8 servings.

VEGETABLE BEEF PIE

(Pictured below)

*For more than a dozen years, this has been the No. 1 dish to serve company at our house.
So far, everyone who has tried it has given it a thumbs-up rating.
—Hannah McDowell, Penns Creek, Pennsylvania*

1 cup all-purpose flour
1/2 cup whole wheat flour
1/2 teaspoon salt
6 tablespoons shortening
2 tablespoons cold butter *or* margarine
1 cup (4 ounces) shredded cheddar cheese
1/4 cup cold water
FILLING:
1 pound ground beef
2 celery ribs, chopped
1 medium onion, chopped
1/4 cup chopped green pepper
1 can (8 ounces) tomato sauce
1 can (7 ounces) whole kernel corn, drained
1 tablespoon Worcestershire sauce
1/4 teaspoon salt
1/8 teaspoon pepper

In a bowl, combine flours and salt. Cut in shortening and butter until crumbly. Add cheese; toss to blend. Gradually add water, tossing with a fork until dough forms a ball. Divide dough in half. Cover and refrigerate.

For filling, in a skillet, cook the beef, celery, onion and green pepper over medium heat until meat is no longer pink and vegetables are tender; drain. Stir in the remaining ingredients. Bring to a boil. Reduce heat; cover and simmer for 15 minutes.

On a floured surface, roll out one portion of dough to fit the bottom of an ungreased 8-in. square baking dish. Transfer to dish. Spoon filling over crust. Roll out remaining dough to fit top of dish; cut slits or shapes with cookie cutters. Place over filling; trim and flute edges. Arrange cutouts over pastry. Bake at 375° for 35-40 minutes or until bubbly and crust is golden brown. Let stand for 10-15 minutes before cutting. **Yield:** 4-6 servings.

CHICKEN POTPIE

(Pictured below and on the front cover)

Our neighbors and a friend from back home are always after me to make "those yummy potpies".
That's all the encouragement I need, since we really like 'em, too!
—Ada-May Smith, Citrus Springs, Florida

1 package (16 ounces) frozen mixed
    vegetables, thawed
2-1/4 cups cubed cooked chicken
1 cup frozen pearl onions, thawed
1 jar (4-1/2 ounces) sliced
    mushrooms, drained
1/4 cup butter *or* margarine
1/4 cup all-purpose flour
3/4 teaspoon dried thyme
1 can (14-1/2 ounces) chicken broth
2 teaspoons chicken bouillon
    granules
Pastry for a single-crust pie

In a greased deep 2-1/2-qt. baking dish, combine the vegetables, chicken, onions and mushrooms; set aside. In a small saucepan, melt butter. Stir in flour and thyme until smooth. Gradually add broth and bouillon. Bring to a boil; cook and stir for 2 minutes or until thickened. Pour over vegetable mixture.

Roll out pastry to fit top of dish. Place over filling; trim and flute edges. Cut slits in top. Bake at 450° for 18-20 minutes or until golden brown. Let stand for 5 minutes before cutting. **Yield:** 6-8 servings.

TURKEY BROCCOLI BAKE

This crustless quiche is a great way to use up leftover turkey. The golden cheese topping
is creamy and inviting. The broccoli blends well with the other flavors.
—Lorraine Damm, Essex, Ontario

1 package (10 ounces) frozen
    chopped broccoli, thawed
2-1/2 cups (10 ounces) shredded cheddar
    cheese, *divided*
1-1/2 cups cubed cooked turkey
2/3 cup chopped onion
3/4 cup biscuit/baking mix
3/4 teaspoon salt
1/4 teaspoon pepper
3 eggs, beaten
1-1/3 cups milk

In a bowl, combine the broccoli, 2 cups of cheese, turkey and onion. Spoon into a greased 9-in. deep-dish pie plate.

In a bowl, combine the biscuit mix, salt, pepper, eggs and milk. Pour over broccoli mixture; sprinkle with remaining cheese. Bake at 400° for 30-35 minutes or until a knife inserted near the center comes out clean. Let stand for 5 minutes before cutting. **Yield:** 6-8 servings.

STEAK POTPIE

When I hear "meat and potatoes", this is the recipe that comes to mind. I've made it for years and still get compliments on it. Most often, friends comment how hearty the pie is.
—Pattie Bonner, Cocoa, Florida

3/4 cup sliced onion
4 tablespoons vegetable oil, *divided*
1/4 cup all-purpose flour
1 teaspoon salt
1/2 teaspoon pepper
1/2 teaspoon paprika
Pinch ground allspice
Pinch ground ginger
1 pound boneless beef round steak, cut into 1/2-inch pieces
2-1/2 cups boiling water
3 medium potatoes, peeled and diced
Pastry for single-crust pie (9 inches)

In a large skillet, saute the onion in 2 tablespoons oil until golden. Drain; set onion aside. In a large resealable plastic bag, combine the dry ingredients; add beef in batches and shake to coat. In the same skillet, brown meat in remaining oil. Add water; cover and simmer until meat is almost tender, about 1 hour.

Add the potatoes; simmer, uncovered, for 15-20 minutes or until the meat and potatoes are tender. Pour into a greased 1-1/2-qt. baking dish. Top with sauteed onions.

Roll out pastry to fit baking dish. Place over hot filling; seal to edges of dish. Cut slits in pastry. Bake at 450° for 25-30 minutes or until golden brown. If necessary, cover edges of crust with foil to prevent overbrowning. **Yield:** 4-6 servings.

BROCCOLI BEEF PIE

Twenty years ago, I ran my own restaurant. For the last 15, I've been a cook at our local school, so I'm always in the kitchen cooking. Whenever I fix this for my husband and me, I give half to my single brother, who shares it with his friends.
—JoLynn Keller, Glasco, Kansas

2 cups all-purpose flour
3/4 teaspoon salt
2/3 cup shortening
6 to 8 tablespoons cold water
FILLING:
1 pound ground beef
1 small onion, chopped
2 cups chopped broccoli, cooked and drained
2 cups (8 ounces) shredded Swiss cheese
4 ounces cream cheese, cubed
1 egg, beaten
1/2 cup plus 1 teaspoon milk, *divided*
1 tablespoon all-purpose flour
1/2 teaspoon garlic powder
1/2 teaspoon salt
1/2 teaspoon pepper

In a bowl, combine flour and salt; cut in shortening until crumbly. Gradually add water, tossing with a fork until dough forms a ball. Roll out dough to fit a 9-in. pie plate. Transfer to plate; trim even with edge.

In a skillet, cook beef and onion over medium heat until meat is no longer pink; drain. Stir in the broccoli, Swiss cheese, cream cheese, egg, 1/2 cup milk, flour, garlic powder, salt and pepper. Spoon into crust.

Roll out remaining dough to fit top of dish; place over filling. Trim, seal and flute edges; cut slits in top. Brush pastry with remaining milk. Bake at 350° for 50-55 minutes or until the crust is golden brown. Let stand for 5 minutes before cutting. **Yield:** 6-8 servings.

CORNMEAL SOMBRERO PIE

*I've been making this dish in winter instead of chili for the last 20 years.
Although there's just the two us, we rarely have much left over.*
—Elaine Seevers, Cordova, Illinois

1/2 pound ground beef
1/2 pound ground pork
1 large onion, sliced
2-1/2 cups tomato juice
1 package (10 ounces) frozen corn
1 to 2 tablespoons chili powder
1 teaspoon salt
1/4 teaspoon pepper
PASTRY:
1 cup all-purpose flour
1/4 cup cornmeal
1/2 teaspoon salt
1/3 cup plus 1 tablespoon shortening
3 tablespoons cold water

In a skillet, cook beef, pork and onion over medium heat until meat is no longer pink; drain. Stir in the tomato juice, corn, chili powder, salt and pepper. Bring to a boil. Reduce heat; simmer, uncovered, for 10 minutes. Pour into a greased 11-in. x 7-in. x 2-in. baking dish.

In a bowl, combine the flour, cornmeal and salt. Cut in shortening until crumbly. Gradually add water, tossing with a fork until dough forms a ball. Roll out into a 12-in. x 8-in. rectangle; place over the meat mixture. Bake at 400° for 30-35 minutes or until golden brown. **Yield:** 4-6 servings.

PERFECT PARTNERS
A mixed green salad goes well with meat pies. Add crunch by sprinkling toasted sesame seeds or sunflower kernels over the greens.

BEEF PASTIES

Our Test Kitchen staff came up with this recipe for pasties as a way to put leftover pot roast to good use. Just tuck the cooked beef, carrots, potatoes and onion into pie pastry...your family will be amazed at the tender and flaky results!

2 cups cubed cooked roast beef
(1/4-inch pieces)
1-1/2 cups cubed cooked potatoes
1 cup beef gravy
1/2 cup diced cooked carrot
1/2 cup diced cooked onion
1 tablespoon minced fresh parsley
1/4 teaspoon dried thyme
1/2 teaspoon salt
1/8 to 1/4 teaspoon pepper
Pastry for double-crust pie (9 inches)
Half-and-half cream

In a large bowl, combine the first nine ingredients; set aside. Divide pastry into fourths; on a lightly floured surface, roll out each portion into an 8-in. circle. Mound about 1 cup filling on half of each circle. Moisten edges with water; fold dough over filling and press edges with a fork to seal.

Place on an ungreased baking sheet. Cut slits in top of pasties; brush with cream. Bake at 450° for 20-25 minutes or until golden brown. **Yield:** 4 servings.

POPOVER WITH HOT TURKEY SALAD

(Pictured above)

I first tasted this turkey salad at a club dinner. Now I make it at home, and there are never any leftovers. The popover "bowl" is a unique way of serving that always draws comments.
—Mary Anne Mayberry, Fairmont, Minnesota

2 eggs
1 cup milk
1 cup all-purpose flour
1/2 teaspoon salt
4 cups cubed cooked turkey
4 celery ribs, diced
2 cups (8 ounces) shredded cheddar cheese
1 can (2-1/4 ounces) sliced ripe olives, drained
1 cup mayonnaise *or* salad dressing*
1/4 cup milk
1/8 teaspoon pepper
Pinch onion powder
1-1/2 cups crushed potato chips
Tomato wedges, optional

Let eggs and milk stand at room temperature for 30 minutes. In a mixing bowl, beat eggs until lemon-colored and foamy. Add milk, flour and salt; beat just until smooth (do not overbeat). Pour into a greased 10-in. pie plate. Bake at 400° for 35-40 minutes or until deep golden brown. Immediately prick with a fork in the center to allow steam to escape.

In a saucepan, combine the turkey, celery, cheese, olives, mayonnaise, milk, pepper and onion powder; cook and stir over low heat until heated through. Stir in potato chips. Spoon into popover. Garnish with tomato wedges if desired. Serve immediately. **Yield:** 10-12 servings.

Editor's Note: Reduced-fat or fat-free mayonnaise or salad dressing may not be substituted for regular mayonnaise or salad dressing.

HAM 'N' CHEESE PIE

There's no need to make a crust for this delicious and easy quiche.
My family and friends love it for dinner, brunch or any other time.
—*Iris Posey, Albany, Georgia*

1 cup diced fully cooked ham
3/4 cup shredded Swiss cheese
5 bacon strips, cooked and crumbled
3/4 cup shredded sharp cheddar cheese
3 tablespoons chopped onion
3 tablespoons chopped green pepper
1 cup milk
1/4 cup biscuit/baking mix
2 eggs
1/4 teaspoon salt
1/8 teaspoon pepper

In a greased 10-in. quiche dish or pie plate, layer the ham, Swiss cheese, bacon, cheddar cheese, onion and green pepper. Place the remaining ingredients in a blender in the order listed; blend for 30-40 seconds. Pour over filling; do not stir.

Bake, uncovered, at 350° for 30-35 minutes or until a knife inserted near the center comes out clean. Let stand for 5 minutes before cutting. **Yield:** 6-8 servings.

SERVING SUGGESTION

For a simple, nutritious dessert, create your own fruit and yogurt parfaits. Drain an 8-ounce can of pineapple tidbits and combine with 1/2 cup of orange or vanilla yogurt. Add a heaping spoonful to four parfait glasses. Top each with a handful of fresh blueberries and a sprinkling of granola. Repeat layers twice.

PORK POTPIE

What a great way to use up leftover pork roast—and it sure doesn't taste like leftovers.
It's one of those down-home comfort foods that really warms up a cold night.
—*Dlores DeWitt, Colorado Springs, Colorado*

2 medium carrots, thinly sliced
1 small onion, chopped
1/4 cup water
2 cups cubed cooked pork
1 can (10-3/4 ounces) condensed
    cream of celery soup, undiluted
2 tablespoons minced fresh parsley
1/4 teaspoon salt
1/8 teaspoon dried savory
1/8 teaspoon garlic powder
Pastry for single-crust pie (9 inches)
1 tablespoon grated Parmesan cheese

In a saucepan, cook carrots and onion in water until tender; drain. Add the pork, soup, parsley, salt, savory and garlic powder. Transfer to a greased 9-in. pie plate.

On a lightly floured surface, roll out pastry into a 10-in. circle; place over pork mixture. Cut slits in top; flute edges. Sprinkle with Parmesan cheese. Bake at 425° for 18-20 minutes or until golden brown. Let stand for 5 minutes before cutting. **Yield:** 4-6 servings.

MEATLESS CLASSICS

Whether you're looking for a
one-meal change of pace
or your family prefers
meatless dishes all the time,
this chapter offers 32
satisfying choices. You'll find
casseroles packed with
garden-fresh produce
as well as hearty grains.

PINTO BEANS AND RICE (P. 223)

VEGGIE-PACKED STRATA (P. 204)

VEGGIE-PACKED STRATA

(Pictured on page 203)

This is a wonderful, colorful casserole that everyone enjoys.
I'm sure you'll be hooked on it after one bite, too.
—Jennifer Unsell, Tuscaloosa, Alabama

2 medium sweet red peppers, julienned
1 medium sweet yellow pepper, julienned
1 large red onion, sliced
3 garlic cloves, minced
3 tablespoons olive *or* vegetable oil, *divided*
2 medium yellow summer squash, thinly sliced
2 medium zucchini, thinly sliced
1/2 pound fresh mushrooms, sliced
1 package (8 ounces) cream cheese, softened
1/4 cup whipping cream
2 teaspoons salt
1 teaspoon pepper
6 eggs
8 slices bread, cubed, *divided*
2 cups (8 ounces) shredded Swiss cheese

In a large skillet, saute the peppers, onion and garlic in 1 tablespoon oil until tender. Drain; pat dry and set aside. In the same skillet, saute yellow squash, zucchini and mushrooms in remaining oil until tender. Drain; pat dry and set aside.

In a large mixing bowl, beat the cream cheese, cream, salt and pepper until smooth. Beat in eggs. Stir in vegetables, half of the bread cubes and Swiss cheese. Arrange the remaining bread cubes in a greased 10-in. springform pan. Place on a baking sheet. Pour egg mixture into pan.

Bake, uncovered, at 325° for 60-70 minutes or until a knife inserted near the center comes out clean. Let stand for 10 minutes before serving. Run a knife around edge of pan to loosen; remove sides. Cut into wedges. **Yield:** 8-10 servings.

BAKED ZITI

Many of my casserole recipes have been frowned upon by my children, but they give a cheer when they hear we're having Baked Ziti for supper. I've tried to incorporate more meatless meals into our menus. No one misses the meat in this one. Even the leftovers are well-liked.
—Charity Burkholder, Pittsboro, Indiana

3 cups uncooked ziti *or* small tube pasta
1-3/4 cups meatless spaghetti sauce, *divided*
1 cup (8 ounces) small-curd cottage cheese
1-1/2 cups (6 ounces) shredded mozzarella cheese, *divided*
1 egg, lightly beaten
2 teaspoons dried parsley flakes
1/2 teaspoon dried oregano
1/4 teaspoon garlic powder
1/8 teaspoon pepper

Cook pasta according to package directions. Meanwhile, in a large bowl, combine 3/4 cup spaghetti sauce, cottage cheese, 1 cup mozzarella cheese, egg, parsley, oregano, garlic powder and pepper. Drain pasta; stir into cheese mixture.

In a greased 8-in. square baking dish, spread 1/4 cup of spaghetti sauce. Top with pasta mixture, and remaining sauce and mozzarella. Cover and bake at 375° for 45 minutes. Uncover; bake 5-10 minutes longer or until bubbly. **Yield:** 6 servings.

MEATLESS CHILI BAKE

(Pictured above)

My husband is a farmer, and this delicious dish is easy and quick to fix whenever he decides to come in and eat. Our children all like it, too.
—Lisa Flamme, Gladbrook, Iowa

2-1/2 cups uncooked spiral pasta
  1 can (15 ounces) vegetarian chili with beans
  1 jar (12 ounces) chunky salsa
  1 can (11 ounces) whole kernel corn, drained
1/2 cup shredded cheddar cheese

Cook pasta according to package directions; drain. In a large bowl, combine the chili, salsa and corn. Add pasta; toss to coat. Transfer to a greased shallow 2-qt. baking dish; sprinkle with cheese. Bake, uncovered, at 400° for 25-30 minutes or until bubbly. **Yield:** 4-6 servings.

HERBED VEGETABLE SQUARES

Flavorful veggies form the foundation of this colorful casserole. You can serve it as an entree, as a side dish with beef or chicken or as an appetizer.
—Dorothy Pritchett, Wills Point, Texas

1 package (10 ounces) frozen chopped spinach, thawed and squeezed dry
2 tablespoons vegetable oil
1-1/2 cups chopped zucchini
1 package (10 ounces) frozen cut green beans, thawed
1 large onion, chopped
1/4 cup water
1 garlic clove, minced
1-1/2 teaspoons dried basil
1-1/2 teaspoons salt
1/8 teaspoon pepper
1/8 teaspoon ground nutmeg
4 eggs
1/4 cup grated Parmesan cheese
Paprika

In a skillet, saute spinach in oil for 2 minutes. Stir in the zucchini, beans, onion, water, garlic, basil, salt, pepper and nutmeg. Cover and simmer for 10 minutes, stirring occasionally. Remove from the heat.

In a bowl, beat eggs; gradually stir in 1-1/2 cups vegetable mixture. Return all to the pan and mix well. Transfer to a greased 11-in. x 7-in. x 2-in. baking dish. Place in a 13-in. x 9-in. x 2-in. baking dish; fill the larger dish with hot water to a depth of 1 in.

Bake at 350° for 25-30 minutes or until a knife inserted near the center comes out clean. Sprinkle with Parmesan cheese and paprika. Let stand for 10 minutes before cutting. **Yield:** 6-8 servings.

SIMPLE SUBSTITUTION

When zucchini and yellow summer squash are both plentiful, use 3/4 cup of each instead of 1-1/2 cups of zucchini in the Herbed Vegetable Squares. You'll add a rich new color to the dish.

GRILLED CHEESE IN A PAN

My cousin served this dish at a shower years ago, and my daughter and I immediately asked for the recipe. If you don't have the exact cheeses it calls for, you can switch a couple and it still tastes absolutely delicious.
—Mary Ann Wendt, Ada, Michigan

1 tube (8 ounces) refrigerated crescent rolls
4 cups (1 cup *each*) shredded Muenster, Monterey Jack, Swiss and cheddar cheese
1 package (8 ounces) cream cheese, sliced
1 egg, lightly beaten
1 tablespoon butter *or* margarine, melted
1 tablespoon sesame seeds

Unroll crescent roll dough; divide in half. Seal perforations. Line an ungreased 8-in. square baking pan with half of the dough. Layer with the Muenster, Monterey Jack, Swiss, cheddar and cream cheese. Pour egg over all.

Top with remaining dough. Brush with butter; sprinkle with sesame seeds. Bake, uncovered, at 350° for 30-35 minutes or until golden brown. **Yield:** 9 servings.

PIZZA PASTA PIE

(Pictured below)

I received this recipe years ago at a party. When I try a new recipe and like it,
I write the date, who was at the meal and any comments about the dish right on the card.
That makes it fun when I go back through my recipes later.
—Harriet Stichter, Milford, Indiana

2 eggs
1-1/2 cups cooked spaghetti
4 tablespoons grated Parmesan cheese, *divided*
1 tablespoon butter *or* margarine, melted
1 package (10 ounces) frozen chopped spinach, thawed and squeezed dry
3/4 cup small-curd cottage cheese
1 cup pizza sauce
1/2 cup finely shredded carrot
1/4 cup chopped fresh mushrooms
1 teaspoon dried oregano
1/2 teaspoon dried basil
1/4 teaspoon garlic powder
1/2 cup shredded mozzarella cheese

In a bowl, beat one egg. Stir in the spaghetti, 2 tablespoons Parmesan cheese and butter; mix well. Spread onto the bottom and up the sides of a greased 9-in. pie plate. Spread spinach over top.

In a bowl, lightly beat the remaining egg. Stir in cottage cheese and remaining Parmesan. Spread over spinach. Combine pizza sauce, carrot, mushrooms, oregano, basil and garlic powder; pour over cottage cheese mixture.

Bake, uncovered, at 350° for 25-30 minutes. Sprinkle with mozzarella cheese; bake 5 minutes longer or until cheese is melted. Let stand for 5 minutes before cutting. **Yield:** 6 servings.

TORTELLINI BROCCOLI BAKE

(Pictured above)

I usually make this dish for birthdays or holiday dinners. It's a great main dish or side dish.
Everyone—even my young granddaughters—enjoys the combination of broccoli, cheese and tortellini.
—Esther McCoy, Dillonvale, Ohio

1 package (19 ounces) frozen cheese
  tortellini, cooked and drained
1 package (16 ounces) frozen
  chopped broccoli, thawed
1 jar (2 ounces) diced pimientos,
  drained
2 tablespoons chopped onion
CHEESE SAUCE:
  1 garlic clove, minced
  2 tablespoons butter *or* margarine
  2 tablespoons all-purpose flour
1/4 teaspoon salt
1/8 teaspoon pepper
1/8 teaspoon ground nutmeg
  1 cup milk
1/3 cup plus 1/4 cup grated Parmesan
  cheese, *divided*

In a large bowl, combine the tortellini, broccoli, pimientos and onion; set aside. In a saucepan, saute garlic in butter for 1 minute. Stir in the flour, salt, pepper and nutmeg. Gradually stir in milk until blended. Bring to a boil; cook and stir for 2 minutes or until thickened. Remove from the heat; stir in 1/3 cup Parmesan cheese until melted. Fold into broccoli mixture.

Transfer to a greased 2-qt. baking dish. Cover and bake at 350° for 40-45 minutes or until hot and bubbly, stirring twice. Top with remaining Parmesan. Cover and let stand for 5 minutes or until cheese is melted. **Yield:** 4-6 servings.

VEGETARIAN QUICHE

When your garden is full of fresh veggies, this is the recipe to reach for.
All you need is a salad and you have a terrific late-summer meal.
—Debbie Jones, California, Maryland

1 unbaked pastry shell (9 inches)
1-1/2 cups chopped onion
1 medium green pepper, chopped
1 cup chopped tomatoes
1/2 cup chopped zucchini
1/2 cup sliced fresh mushrooms
2 tablespoons butter *or* margarine
1/4 to 1/2 teaspoon curry powder
1/2 teaspoon salt
1/4 teaspoon pepper
Pinch ground cinnamon
5 eggs
1/4 cup milk
1/4 cup grated Parmesan cheese

Line unpricked pastry shell with a double thickness of heavy-duty foil. Bake at 450° for 5 minutes. Remove foil; bake 5 minutes longer. Reduce heat to 350°.

In a skillet, saute the onion, green pepper, tomatoes, zucchini and mushrooms in butter. Add the curry powder, salt, pepper and cinnamon; mix well. Spoon into crust.

In a bowl, beat eggs. Add the milk and cheese; mix well. Carefully pour over vegetables. Bake for 40-45 minutes or until a knife inserted near the center comes out clean. Let stand for 5 minutes before cutting. **Yield:** 6-8 servings.

SERVING SUGGESTION

To round out the meal, serve Vegetarian Quiche with a simple fruit salad.
Combine cubed melon, sliced bananas and red grapes. Toss with orange juice.

ZIPPY MACARONI AND CHEESE

When I was asked to teach an advanced 4-H foods class, I included this recipe.
The kids loved it and have been making it for their families ever since.
—Glenda Schwarz, Morden, Manitoba

1-1/3 cups uncooked elbow macaroni
1 cup (8 ounces) small-curd cottage cheese
1 cup (4 ounces) shredded mozzarella cheese
1/2 cup shredded cheddar cheese
1 teaspoon cornstarch
1 cup milk
1 small onion, grated
1/4 cup finely chopped green pepper
1 teaspoon Dijon mustard
1/2 teaspoon salt
1/4 to 1/2 teaspoon crushed red pepper flakes
1/2 cup crushed cornflakes
1 tablespoon butter *or* margarine, melted

Cook macaroni according to package directions; drain. Add cottage cheese, mozzarella cheese and cheddar cheese; set aside.

In a saucepan, combine cornstarch and milk until smooth. Stir in the onion, green pepper, mustard, salt and red pepper flakes. Bring to a boil; cook and stir for 2 minutes or until thickened. Pour over macaroni mixture; gently stir to coat.

Transfer to a greased 2-qt. baking dish. Combine cornflakes and butter; sprinkle over the top. Bake, uncovered, at 350° for 25-30 minutes or until bubbly and the top is golden brown. **Yield:** 4 servings.

CHEESY CORN CASSEROLE

(Pictured at right)

*I've had this recipe for years, and my family still asks for it all the time.
Our son, who is not a big vegetable eater, says it's one of his favorites.*
—Joan Hallford, North Richland Hills, Texas

3 eggs, beaten
1 cup (8 ounces) sour cream
1/2 cup cornmeal
1/2 cup butter *or* margarine, melted
1 can (8-3/4 ounces) cream-style corn
1 can (7 ounces) whole kernel corn, drained
1 can (4 ounces) chopped green chilies
1 cup cubed Monterey Jack cheese
1 cup cubed cheddar cheese
1/2 teaspoon salt
1/4 teaspoon Worcestershire sauce

In a bowl, combine all ingredients; mix well. Transfer to a greased shallow 2-qt. baking dish. Bake, uncovered, at 350° for 45-55 minutes or until a knife inserted near the center comes out clean. Let stand for 5-10 minutes before serving. **Yield:** 6 servings.

BLACK BEAN LASAGNA

(Pictured at right)

*I'm a schoolteacher who loves exchanging recipes with my colleagues.
This is a great recipe for a crowd. It's tasty, nutritious and feeds plenty.*
—Deborah Kolek, Winchester Center, Connecticut

1 large onion, chopped
1 medium green pepper, chopped
4 to 6 garlic cloves, minced
2 tablespoons vegetable oil
1 can (28 ounces) crushed tomatoes
1-1/2 teaspoons salt
1-1/2 teaspoons chili powder
1 teaspoon ground cumin
1/8 teaspoon cayenne pepper
1 can (15 ounces) black beans, rinsed and drained
1 cup canned pinto beans, rinsed and drained
1 carton (15 ounces) ricotta cheese
1 egg white, beaten
2 tablespoons minced fresh parsley
1 tablespoon chopped seeded jalapeno pepper*
2 cups (8 ounces) shredded cheddar cheese
4 flour tortillas (7 inches), halved

In a saucepan, saute the onion, green pepper and garlic in oil until tender. Stir in the tomatoes, salt, chili powder, cumin and cayenne. Bring to a boil. Reduce heat; simmer, uncovered, for 10 minutes. Stir in the black beans and pinto beans. Heat through.

In a bowl, combine the ricotta cheese, egg white, parsley and jalapeno. Spread a third of the bean mixture in a greased 13-in. x 9-in. x 2-in. baking dish. Top with half of the cheddar cheese, tortillas and ricotta mixture. Repeat layers. Spread remaining bean mixture over top.

Cover and bake at 350° for 30-35 minutes or until bubbly. Let stand for 15 minutes before cutting. **Yield:** 12 servings.

*Editor's Note: When cutting or seeding hot peppers, use rubber or plastic gloves to protect your hands. Avoid touching your face.

CHEESY CORN CASSEROLE
BLACK BEAN LASAGNA

MUSHROOM BROCCOLI QUICHE

I've taken this dish to many family picnics—everyone enjoyed it.
—Edie DeSpain, Logan, Utah

1 unbaked pastry shell (9 inches)
3 eggs
2 cups milk
1 tablespoon Worcestershire sauce
1/2 teaspoon salt
1/8 teaspoon cayenne pepper
1 cup chopped fresh broccoli
1/4 cup chopped green onions
1/2 cup sliced fresh mushrooms
1 cup (4 ounces) shredded Swiss cheese

Line unpricked pastry shell with a double thickness of heavy-duty foil. Bake at 450° for 5 minutes. Remove foil; bake 5 minutes longer or until light golden brown. Reduce heat to 350°.

In a bowl, whisk together the eggs, milk, Worcestershire sauce, salt and cayenne. Stir in the broccoli, onions and mushrooms. Sprinkle cheese over crust. Pour egg mixture over cheese. Bake for 60-65 minutes or until a knife inserted near the center comes out clean. Let stand for 5 minutes before cutting. **Yield:** 6-8 servings.

BARLEY BAKE

This is a delicious change of pace from potato casseroles. Slivered almonds give it a nice crunch.
—Lamar Lyons Parker, Peoria, Illinois

1/2 pound fresh mushrooms, sliced
1 celery rib, chopped
1/2 cup chopped green onions
5 tablespoons butter *or* margarine
1 cup uncooked quick-cooking barley
2 cups vegetable broth, *divided*
1/2 cup minced fresh parsley
1/2 cup slivered almonds

In a large skillet, saute the mushrooms, celery and onions in butter until tender. Add barley; cook and stir until barley is golden, about 6-7 minutes.

In a greased 2-qt. baking dish, combine barley mixture, 1 cup broth and parsley. Cover and bake at 350° for 30 minutes. Uncover; stir in almonds and remaining broth. Bake 45-50 minutes longer or until barley is tender. **Yield:** 8 servings.

WINTER SQUASH QUICHE

I always get compliments when I serve this quiche to my hungry crew.
—Mary Detweiler, West Farmington, Ohio

2 tablespoons chopped onion
2 teaspoons vegetable oil
2 cups (8 ounces) shredded Swiss cheese
1-1/2 cups milk
1 cup mashed cooked butternut *or* acorn squash
3 eggs
1/4 teaspoon salt
1/8 teaspoon pepper
1/8 teaspoon ground nutmeg

In a skillet, saute onion in oil until tender. Transfer to a greased 9-in. pie plate. Sprinkle with cheese. In a bowl, whisk the milk, squash, eggs, salt, pepper and nutmeg until smooth; pour over cheese. Bake at 325° for 50-60 minutes or until a knife inserted near the center comes out clean. Let stand for 5 minutes before cutting. **Yield:** 6 servings.

TORTILLA TORTE

This dish tastes much too good to be good for you, but it is. The beans provide protein and fiber.
I've served it over and over at my house, and we never tire of it.
—Terri Webber, Miami, Florida

1 medium onion, chopped
1 garlic clove, minced
2 tablespoons vegetable oil
1 can (15 ounces) pinto beans, rinsed
   and drained
1/4 teaspoon ground cumin
1/4 teaspoon chili powder
2 tablespoons chili sauce
4 flour tortillas (8 inches)
1/4 cup salsa
1 can (4 ounces) chopped green
   chilies, drained
3/4 cup shredded Monterey Jack cheese
Shredded lettuce, chopped tomatoes,
   sour cream *and/or* additional salsa,
   optional

In a skillet, cook onion and garlic in oil over medium heat until the onion is tender. Add the beans, cumin and chili powder. Reduce heat; simmer, uncovered, for 5 minutes, mashing the beans with a wooden spoon. Stir in chili sauce; set aside.

Wrap tortillas in foil; bake at 350° for 10 minutes. Unwrap; place one tortilla in a greased 9-in. deep-dish pie plate. Spread with a third of the bean mixture. Combine the salsa and chilies; spoon a third over the bean mixture. Top with 1/4 cup cheese. Repeat layers twice. Top with the remaining tortilla.

Cover and bake at 350° for 15-20 minutes or until heated through. Cut into wedges. Serve with lettuce, tomatoes, sour cream and salsa if desired. **Yield:** 4 servings.

OREGANO POTATO CASSEROLE

Seasonings, cottage cheese, sour cream and eggs dress up ordinary
mashed potatoes. This fluffy casserole is tops with my family.
—Barbara Stewart, Portland, Connecticut

2-1/2 cups mashed potatoes (prepared
   with milk)
1 cup (8 ounces) small-curd cottage
   cheese
1/2 cup sour cream
3 eggs, *separated*
2 tablespoons minced fresh oregano
   or 2 teaspoons dried oregano
2 tablespoons minced fresh parsley
   or 2 teaspoons dried parsley flakes
1/2 teaspoon seasoned salt
2 tablespoons butter *or* margarine

In a large bowl, combine the potatoes, cottage cheese, sour cream, egg yolks, oregano, parsley and seasoned salt. In a mixing bowl, beat egg whites until stiff peaks form; fold into potato mixture.

Transfer to a lightly greased 2-1/2-qt. baking dish. Dot with butter. Bake, uncovered, at 350° for 1 hour or until lightly browned. **Yield:** 6-8 servings.

PERFECT PARTNERS

Serve Oregano Potato Casserole with a tossed spinach and
apple salad and a loaf of fresh-from-the-oven garlic bread.

CHEESY VEGETABLE EGG DISH

(Pictured below)

I'm a cook at a Bible camp, and this is one of my most popular recipes.
Everyone who tries it raves about it. The one that touched me the most was when
a 10-year-old boy asked me for the recipe so he could have his mom make it at home.
—Elsie Campbell, Dulzura, California

1 medium zucchini, diced
1 medium onion, chopped
1 can (4 ounces) mushroom stems
   and pieces, drained
1/4 cup chopped green pepper
1/2 cup butter *or* margarine
1/2 cup all-purpose flour
1 teaspoon baking powder
1/2 teaspoon salt
10 eggs, lightly beaten
2 cups (16 ounces) small-curd cottage
   cheese
4 cups (1 pound) shredded Monterey
   Jack cheese

In a skillet, saute the zucchini, onion, mushrooms and green pepper in butter until tender. Stir in the flour, baking powder and salt until blended. In a bowl, combine the eggs and cottage cheese. Stir in the vegetables and Monterey Jack cheese.

Transfer to a greased 2-1/2-qt. baking dish. Bake, uncovered, at 350° for 35-45 minutes or until set and a thermometer reads 160°. **Yield:** 8-10 servings.

GARDEN LASAGNA

*As soon as we have ripe tomatoes and zucchini in the garden,
my family asks for this dish. I'm always happy to oblige, since it tastes so good.
—Harriet Stichter, Milford, Indiana*

3-1/2 cups meatless spaghetti sauce
1 can (6 ounces) tomato paste
1 cup sliced fresh mushrooms
2 tablespoons vegetable oil
3 cups (24 ounces) small-curd cottage cheese
1 cup grated Parmesan cheese
2 eggs, beaten
1 to 2 tablespoons minced fresh oregano *or* 1 to 2 teaspoons dried oregano
1 tablespoon minced fresh basil *or* 1 teaspoon dried basil
1-1/2 teaspoons minced fresh parsley *or* 1/2 teaspoon dried parsley flakes
1 garlic clove, minced
1/2 teaspoon seasoned salt
1/2 teaspoon lemon-pepper seasoning
10 lasagna noodles, cooked and drained
3 cups shredded zucchini (about 2 medium), *divided*
3 cups (12 ounces) shredded mozzarella cheese
3 large tomatoes, cut into 1/2-inch slices

In a saucepan, combine spaghetti sauce, tomato paste, mushrooms and oil. Bring to a boil. Reduce heat; simmer, uncovered, for 20 minutes. In a bowl, combine the next nine ingredients.

In a greased 13-in. x 9-in. x 2-in. baking dish, layer five noodles and half of the cottage cheese mixture. Top with 2-1/2 cups zucchini. Layer with a third of the sauce and half of the mozzarella. Repeat layers of noodles, cottage cheese mixture and sauce. Top with tomato slices and remaining sauce and mozzarella.

Cover and bake at 350° for 35-40 minutes. Uncover; bake 10 minutes longer. Sprinkle with remaining zucchini. Let stand for 15-20 minutes before cutting. **Yield:** 8-10 servings.

SWISS POTATO KUGEL

*I'd rather read a cookbook than a best-selling novel. I thoroughly enjoy planning a
sumptuous dinner for my family. We have a daughter who loves potatoes of any kind.
I believe she could eat this dish and pass over all the other goodies on the table.
—Judy Wilson, Placentia, California*

1 large onion, finely chopped
2 tablespoons butter *or* margarine
4 cups shredded *or* diced cooked peeled potatoes (about 4 medium)
2 cups (8 ounces) shredded Swiss cheese
1/4 cup all-purpose flour
1 teaspoon salt
1/4 teaspoon pepper
3 eggs
3/4 cup half-and-half cream
Tomato slices and fresh thyme, optional

In a large skillet, saute onion in butter until tender. Remove from the heat; add potatoes. Toss cheese with flour, salt and pepper; add to skillet and blend well.

In a small bowl, combine the eggs and cream. Stir into the potato mixture. Spoon into a greased 9-in. square baking dish. Bake, uncovered, at 350° for 20-30 minutes or until golden brown. Let stand for 5 minutes; cut into squares. Garnish with tomato and thyme if desired. **Yield:** 9 servings.

ZIPPY CORN BAKE

This satisfying hot dish resembles an old-fashioned spoon bread with zip. My family and friends agree this recipe really dresses up corn. It's a convenient dish to transport to a potluck.
—Laura Kadlec, Maiden Rock, Wisconsin

4 eggs
1 can (15-1/4 ounces) whole kernel corn, drained
1 can (14-3/4 ounces) cream-style corn
1-1/2 cups cornmeal
1-1/4 cups buttermilk
1 cup butter *or* margarine, melted
2 cans (4 ounces *each*) chopped green chilies
2 medium onions, chopped
1 teaspoon baking soda
3 cups (12 ounces) shredded cheddar cheese, *divided*
Jalapeno and sweet red pepper rings, optional

Beat eggs in a large bowl; add the next eight ingredients and mix well. Stir in 2 cups of cheese. Pour into a greased 13-in. x 9-in. x 2-in. baking dish.

Bake, uncovered, at 325° for 1 hour. Top with remaining cheese. Let stand for 15 minutes before serving. Garnish with peppers if desired. **Yield:** 12-15 servings.

SERVING SUGGESTION

Zippy Corn Bake makes a super supper served with steamed broccoli spears and warm whole-grain rolls.

SPUDS LASAGNA LOAF

I developed this recipe when we had a craving for lasagna but no noodles in the pantry. Potatoes are fabulous in this Italian-style casserole.
—Dixie Terry, Goreville, Illinois

2 large potatoes, peeled and halved widthwise
1 cup (8 ounces) small-curd cottage cheese, drained
1 egg
1 can (8 ounces) tomato sauce
1/4 teaspoon dried basil
1/4 teaspoon dried oregano
1/8 teaspoon salt
Dash garlic powder
1/2 cup shredded mozzarella cheese

Place potatoes in a saucepan and cover with water; bring to a boil. Reduce heat; cover and cook for 15-20 minutes or until tender. Drain. Cool; cut into thin slices. In a bowl, combine cottage cheese and egg; set aside. In another bowl, combine tomato sauce and seasonings.

In a greased 9-in. x 5-in. x 3-in. loaf pan, layer half of the potatoes, half of the cottage cheese mixture and half of the tomato sauce mixture. Repeat layers. Sprinkle with cheese.

Cover and bake at 400° for 30 minutes or until potatoes are tender. Uncover; bake 5-10 minutes longer or until bubbly. Let stand for 5 minutes before serving. **Yield:** 4-6 servings.

RANCH MAC 'N' CHEESE

(Pictured above)

*I came up with the recipe for this creamy and satisfying macaroni and cheese,
which has a special twist. My husband requests it often.*
—Michelle Rotunno, Independence, Missouri

1 package (16 ounces) elbow macaroni
1 cup milk
1/4 cup butter *or* margarine
2 envelopes ranch salad dressing mix
1 teaspoon lemon-pepper seasoning
1 teaspoon garlic herb seasoning
1 teaspoon garlic salt
1 cup cubed Colby cheese
1 cup cubed Monterey Jack cheese
1 cup (8 ounces) sour cream
1/2 cup crushed saltines (about 15
  crackers)
Grated Parmesan cheese

Cook macaroni according to package directions. Meanwhile, in a Dutch oven, combine the next eight ingredients. Cook and stir over medium heat until cheese is melted and mixture begins to thicken.

Reduce heat; stir in the sour cream. Drain macaroni; add the macaroni and cracker crumbs to cheese sauce. Cook until heated through, stirring frequently. Sprinkle with Parmesan cheese. **Yield:** 6-8 servings.

CONFETTI SPAGHETTI PIE

(Pictured above)

*Getting everyone to the dinner table is never a problem when I bake up this great pie.
It's filling, plus it's packed with vitamins from all the veggies.*
—Ruth Lee, Troy, Ontario

1 package (7 ounces) spaghetti
1 medium onion, chopped
2 garlic cloves, minced
2 tablespoons vegetable oil
2 medium tomatoes, chopped
3 tablespoons tomato paste
1/4 cup minced fresh parsley
1/2 teaspoon dried oregano
1/2 to 1 teaspoon salt
1/4 teaspoon pepper
4 eggs, lightly beaten
1/2 cup frozen peas, thawed
1/2 cup frozen cut green beans, thawed
1/2 cup chopped fresh broccoli
1 cup (4 ounces) shredded cheddar
cheese, *divided*
1/4 cup grated Parmesan cheese

Break spaghetti in half; cook according to package directions. Drain and rinse in cold water; set aside. In a skillet, saute onion and garlic in oil until tender. Stir in the tomatoes, tomato paste, parsley, oregano, salt and pepper. Cook until heated through, about 5 minutes.

In a large bowl, toss the spaghetti and eggs. Stir in peas, beans, broccoli, tomato mixture, 1/4 cup cheddar cheese and Parmesan cheese. Transfer to a greased 9-in. springform pan. Place pan on a baking sheet.

Bake, uncovered, at 350° for 25 minutes. Sprinkle with remaining cheddar cheese. Bake 5-10 minutes longer or until a knife inserted near the center comes out clean. Let stand for 10 minutes. Run a knife around edge of pan to loosen; remove sides. Cut into wedges. **Yield:** 6-8 servings.

VEGGIE CHEESE SQUARES

I developed this recipe in my kitchen one busy afternoon when I looked in the fridge and there wasn't much there. With no time to shop, I used what I had. Now this nice and easy dish is a suppertime standby.
—Dixie Terry, Goreville, Illinois

1-1/2 cups fresh broccoli florets
   1 medium sweet red pepper, julienned
   2 garlic cloves, minced
   2 tablespoons olive *or* vegetable oil
   4 eggs
   1 cup milk
   1 cup (4 ounces) shredded cheddar cheese, *divided*
  1/2 teaspoon dried thyme
  1/4 teaspoon salt

In a skillet, saute the broccoli, red pepper and garlic in oil. Spoon into a greased 9-in. square baking dish. In a bowl, combine eggs, milk, 3/4 cup cheese, thyme and salt; mix well. Pour over the broccoli mixture.

Bake, uncovered, at 350° for 25-30 minutes. Sprinkle with the remaining cheese. Bake 5 minutes longer or until the cheese is melted. Let stand for 5 minutes before cutting. **Yield:** 4-6 servings.

BROWN RICE CASSEROLE

As a new bride, I knew how to make scrambled eggs and bran muffins. Unfortunately, you can only live on love for so long. My dear husband held his tongue and ate the many flops that come with being a beginning cook. Many years later, I'm secure in the kitchen, and my family enjoys my cooking. This hearty dish even passes the test for teenage boys.
—Glenda Schwarz, Morden, Manitoba

   2 quarts water
1-1/2 cups uncooked brown rice
   1 cup dry split peas
   1 cup chopped fresh mushrooms
   2 celery ribs, chopped
   2 medium carrots, grated
   1 medium onion, chopped
   2 garlic cloves, minced
   1 tablespoon vegetable oil
   1 can (14-1/2 ounces) diced tomatoes, undrained
  1/2 to 1 teaspoon salt
  1/2 to 1 teaspoon dried thyme
  1/2 to 1 teaspoon dried oregano
  1/2 to 1 teaspoon pepper
   1 cup (4 ounces) shredded cheddar cheese

In a large saucepan, bring water, rice and peas to a boil. Reduce heat; cover and simmer for 20-25 minutes or until tender. Drain and set aside.

In a skillet, saute the mushrooms, celery, carrots, onion and garlic in oil until vegetables are tender. Combine the vegetables, rice mixture, tomatoes and seasonings.

Transfer to a greased 2-1/2-qt. baking dish. Cover and bake at 350° for 30 minutes. Uncover; sprinkle with cheese. Bake 5-10 minutes longer or until the cheese is melted. **Yield:** 9 servings.

SERVING SUGGESTION

For a quick meal, serve Brown Rice Casserole with hot French bread and chilled grapefruit segments sprinkled with brown sugar or cinnamon-sugar.

VEGETABLE NOODLE CASSEROLE

I found the recipe for this casserole, which is my husband Rory's favorite, in an old magazine I bought at a yard sale right after we got married. It has stood the test of time!
—Tara Bricco, Covington, Tennessee

8 ounces wide egg noodles
1 can (10-3/4 ounces) condensed cream of mushroom soup, undiluted
1 cup (8 ounces) sour cream
3/4 cup chopped onion
1 teaspoon salt
1/4 teaspoon pepper
1 package (10 ounces) frozen chopped broccoli, thawed
1 package (8 ounces) frozen cauliflower, thawed and cut into bite-size pieces
1-1/2 cups (6 ounces) shredded Swiss cheese, *divided*

Cook noodles according to package directions. Meanwhile, in a large bowl, combine the soup, sour cream, onion, salt and pepper. Add the broccoli, cauliflower and 1/4 cup of cheese.

Drain noodles; add to soup mixture and stir gently. Pour into a greased 13-in. x 9-in. x 2-in. baking dish. Sprinkle with remaining cheese. Bake, uncovered, at 350° for 30 minutes or until heated through. **Yield:** 6-8 servings.

LASAGNA FLORENTINE

Sliced hard-cooked eggs give a sunny look to this special lasagna from the American Egg Board. The eggs peek through the crumb-and-cheese topping.

1 egg
1 package (10 ounces) frozen chopped spinach, thawed and squeezed dry
1 cup (8 ounces) small-curd cottage cheese
1 can (15 ounces) Italian-style tomato sauce
6 lasagna noodles, cooked and drained
8 hard-cooked eggs, sliced
1 cup (4 ounces) shredded mozzarella cheese
1/4 cup dry bread crumbs
2 tablespoons grated Parmesan cheese
2 tablespoons butter *or* margarine, melted
1 garlic clove, minced

In a bowl, combine the egg, spinach and cottage cheese. In a greased 11-in. x 7-in. x 2-in. baking dish, layer half of the tomato sauce, noodles, spinach mixture, hard-cooked eggs and mozzarella. Repeat layers.

Combine the bread crumbs, Parmesan cheese, butter and garlic; sprinkle over top. Cover and bake at 350° for 35 minutes. Uncover; bake 10 minutes longer or until heated through. Let stand for 10 minutes before serving. **Yield:** 6-8 servings.

PERFECT PARTNERS

For a delicious, easy side dish, toss cooked carrots with orange marmalade.

PEPPY BEAN BAKE

What's great about this casserole is that you just throw it together and pop it in the oven.
While it's baking, I can unwind from work and spend time with my two children.
If company's coming, I just use two cans of everything!
—Paula Roberts, Russellville, Arkansas

1 can (16 ounces) vegetarian baked beans
1 can (16 ounces) kidney beans, rinsed and drained
1 can (15-1/4 ounces) whole kernel corn, drained
1 can (15 ounces) vegetarian chili with beans
1 to 2 jalapeno peppers, seeded and chopped*
1 cup (4 ounces) shredded cheddar cheese
1 cup crushed nacho tortilla chips

In a bowl, combine the baked beans, kidney beans, corn, chili and jalapenos. Transfer to a greased 8-in. square baking dish.

Cover and bake at 350° for 40 minutes. Uncover; sprinkle with cheese and chips. Bake 5-10 minutes longer or until bubbly and cheese is melted. **Yield:** 6 servings.

*Editor's Note: When cutting or seeding hot peppers, use rubber or plastic gloves to protect your hands. Avoid touching your face.

SERVING SUGGESTION

For a simple dish that serves as a salad or dessert, mix canned mandarin oranges and pineapple chunks. Sprinkle with toasted coconut.

CURRIED POTATOES AND BEANS

This recipe came from my grandma's collection. It's a meal in itself with hearty flavor.
—Mrs. Lyle Rees, Darlington, Wisconsin

1 medium onion, chopped
1 tablespoon vegetable oil
1 teaspoon curry powder
1 teaspoon lemon juice
2 hard-cooked eggs
2 cups cubed cooked potatoes
1 can (16 ounces) kidney beans, rinsed and drained
1-1/2 teaspoons salt
1/2 teaspoon pepper
1/2 to 3/4 cup whipping cream

In a skillet, saute onion in oil until tender. Stir in curry powder and lemon juice; cook and stir for 4 minutes. Set egg yolks aside; chop egg whites. In a bowl, combine egg whites, potatoes, kidney beans, salt, pepper and onion mixture. Pour cream over all; gently toss to coat.

Transfer to a greased 1-1/2-qt. baking dish. Bake, uncovered, at 350° for 25-30 minutes or until heated through. Grate egg yolks; sprinkle over the top. **Yield:** 3-4 servings.

GREEN CHILI 'N' RICE CASSEROLE

This recipe is a three-way winner. It's inexpensive, takes only minutes to prepare and tastes great. It's a good way to use up leftover rice.
—Marilyn Scroggs, Lees Summit, Missouri

3 cups cooked long grain rice
1-1/2 cups (6 ounces) shredded cheddar cheese
1-1/2 cups (12 ounces) small-curd cottage cheese
1 can (4 ounces) chopped green chilies, drained
1/3 cup milk
1/3 cup chopped roasted red peppers
1 can (8-3/4 ounces) whole kernel corn, drained
1/4 cup grated Parmesan cheese

In a greased 2-qt. baking dish, combine the first seven ingredients. Sprinkle with Parmesan cheese. Cover and bake at 350° for 30-35 minutes or until heated through. **Yield:** 6-8 servings.

PERFECT PARTNERS

For a fast family meal, serve Green Chili 'n' Rice Casserole with a pound of steamed green beans sprinkled with 2 teaspoons lemon juice and 1/2 teaspoon dried marjoram or tarragon. For dessert, serve instant French vanilla pudding topped with sliced bananas.

MEXICAN TATERS

I created this recipe and tried it out at one of the potlucks held at our church. Everyone loved it! It's grand for a group.
—E. Marilyn Nix, Truth or Consequences, New Mexico

6 cups sliced cooked peeled potatoes
1 large onion, chopped
2 cups salsa
2 tablespoons butter *or* margarine, melted
6 slices Monterey Jack cheese
6 slices cheddar cheese
2 cans (15 ounces *each*) vegetarian chili with beans
1 cup (4 ounces) shredded Monterey Jack cheese
1 cup (4 ounces) shredded cheddar cheese
1 cup crushed tortilla chips

Place potatoes in a greased 13-in. x 9-in. x 2-in. baking dish. Sprinkle with onion. Combine salsa and butter; pour over onion and potatoes. Top with sliced cheeses; spread with chili. Sprinkle shredded cheeses over top. Bake, uncovered, at 350° for 50 minutes. Sprinkle with chips just before serving. **Yield:** 10-12 servings.

PINTO BEANS AND RICE

(Pictured below and on page 202)

*I love to try different foods, and I especially like to see the reaction of
my family when I put new dishes on the dinner table. This was a success. I've since served it at
many potlucks and have been asked for the recipe every time.*
—Linda Romano, Mt. Airy, North Carolina

1 large onion, chopped
2 tablespoons vegetable oil
3/4 cup ketchup
2 to 4 tablespoons brown sugar
1 teaspoon prepared mustard
1 teaspoon liquid smoke, optional
1 teaspoon salt
1/4 teaspoon pepper
3 cups cooked long grain rice
2 cans (15 ounces *each*) pinto beans,
  rinsed and drained

In a large skillet, saute onion in oil until tender. Remove from the heat; stir in ketchup, brown sugar, mustard, liquid smoke if desired, salt and pepper. Stir in rice and beans. Transfer to a greased 1-1/2-qt. baking dish. Bake, uncovered, at 350° for 30-35 minutes or until heated through. **Yield:** 6 servings.

SIDE DISHES

Whether you pick your vegetables from the garden or the grocery store produce aisle, you won't run out of fresh ideas to serve them. This chapter provides 50 family-tested recipes starring vegetables, pasta and rice. Why not try one tonight?

Broccoli Corn Bake (p. 226)
Sweet Potato Souffle (p. 226)
Oven-Roasted Veggies (p. 228)

BROCCOLI CORN BAKE

(Pictured on page 225)

Everyone who eats this dish raves about it. I love it when something so good is so easy to make.
—Breta Soldat, Johnston, Iowa

1-1/2 cups crushed Chicken in a Biskit crackers
3 tablespoons butter *or* margarine, melted
2-1/2 cups frozen broccoli cuts, thawed
1 can (15-1/4 ounces) whole kernel corn, drained
1 can (14-3/4 ounces) cream-style corn

In a bowl, combine cracker crumbs and butter; set aside 1/2 cup for topping. Add vegetables to the remaining crumb mixture; mix well. Transfer to a greased 1-1/2-qt. baking dish. Sprinkle with reserved crumb topping. Bake, uncovered, at 350° for 30-35 minutes or until bubbly and top is golden brown. **Yield:** 6 servings.

SWEET POTATO SOUFFLE

(Pictured on page 225)

It's easy to see why this pretty orange side dish is a seasonal favorite for my family.
—Linda Hoffman, Fort Wayne, Indiana

3 large sweet potatoes (about 3 pounds)
2 tablespoons butter *or* margarine
1 egg, lightly beaten
2 egg whites, lightly beaten
1/4 cup packed brown sugar
1 teaspoon rum extract
1/2 teaspoon salt
1/4 teaspoon ground cinnamon

Arrange sweet potatoes in a microwave-safe dish; prick potatoes several times with a fork. Microwave, uncovered, on high for 18-20 minutes or until tender, turning once. Cool slightly. Cut potatoes in half lengthwise. Scoop out the pulp; discard shell. In a bowl, mash pulp with butter. Stir in the remaining ingredients.

Spoon into a greased 1-1/2-qt. baking dish. Bake, uncovered, at 350° for 40-50 minutes or until heated through. Let stand 10 minutes before serving. **Yield:** 6 servings.

Editor's Note: This recipe was tested in an 850-watt microwave.

PINEAPPLE RICE CASSEROLE

Pineapple and cheese aren't thought of as a perfect pairing, but they are. The taste is the proof.
—Linda Keller, Sylvania, Ohio

1 cup uncooked instant rice
2 tablespoons butter *or* margarine
1 can (8 ounces) crushed pineapple, undrained
2 tablespoons brown sugar
Pinch salt
1/2 cup shredded cheddar cheese

Prepare rice according to package directions. Stir in butter. Add the pineapple, brown sugar and salt; spoon into a greased shallow 1-qt. baking dish. Sprinkle with cheese. Bake, uncovered, at 375° for 15-20 minutes or until heated through and cheese is melted. **Yield:** 4 servings.

FANCY BEAN CASSEROLE

(Pictured below)

My daughter gave me this wonderful recipe, and I've since shared it with many of my friends.
—Venola Sharpe, Campbellsville, Kentucky

3 cups frozen French-style green
    beans
1 can (10-3/4 ounces) condensed
    cream of chicken soup, undiluted
1 can (11 ounces) shoepeg corn,
    drained
1 cup (8 ounces) sour cream
1 can (8 ounces) sliced water
    chestnuts, drained
1/2 cup shredded process cheese
    (Velveeta)
1 medium onion, chopped
3 tablespoons butter *or* margarine
3/4 cup crushed butter-flavored
    crackers (about 18 crackers)
1/4 cup slivered almonds

In a large bowl, combine the first seven ingredients. Transfer to a greased 2-qt. baking dish. In a skillet, melt butter. Add cracker crumbs and almonds; cook and stir until lightly browned. Sprinkle over top.

Bake, uncovered, at 350° for 40-45 minutes or until heated through and topping is golden brown. **Yield:** 6 servings.

OVEN-ROASTED VEGGIES

(Pictured on page 225)

The flavor of rosemary comes through in this colorful, easy way to serve vegetables.
—*June Trom, Blooming Prairie, Minnesota*

10 small unpeeled potatoes
 (about 1-3/4 pounds), quartered
 2 cups whole baby carrots
 1 small onion, cut into wedges
1/4 cup olive *or* vegetable oil
 2 tablespoons lemon juice
 3 garlic cloves, minced
 1 teaspoon dried rosemary, crushed
 1 teaspoon dried oregano
1/2 teaspoon salt
1/2 teaspoon cayenne pepper
 1 medium green pepper, cut into
 1/2-inch strips
 1 medium sweet red pepper, cut into
 1/2-inch strips

Place the potatoes, carrots and onion in an ungreased 13-in. x 9-in. x 2-in. baking dish. In a small bowl, combine the oil, lemon juice, garlic, rosemary, oregano, salt and cayenne. Drizzle over vegetables; toss gently to coat.

Bake, uncovered, at 450° for 30 minutes. Top with pepper strips. Bake 15 minutes longer or until vegetables are tender. **Yield:** 8 servings.

ZUCCHINI DRESSING

Tender green zucchini slices and orange flecks of carrot give this casserole a pretty look.
The stuffing stays nice and moist, while the topping gets crunchy.
—*Bernice Morris, Marshfield, Missouri*

3/4 cup water
1/4 teaspoon salt
 4 medium zucchini, cut into 1/2-inch
 slices
 2 medium carrots, grated
 1 medium onion, chopped
 6 tablespoons butter *or* margarine,
 divided
2-1/4 cups seasoned stuffing croutons,
 divided
 1 can (10-3/4 ounces) condensed
 cream of chicken soup, undiluted
1/2 cup sour cream

In a saucepan, bring water and salt to a boil. Add zucchini. Reduce heat; cover and cook until zucchini is crisp-tender, about 5 minutes. Drain well; set aside.

In another saucepan, saute carrots and onion in 4 tablespoons butter until tender. Remove from the heat; stir in 1-1/2 cups croutons, soup and sour cream. Gently stir in the zucchini.

Pour into a greased shallow 2-qt. baking dish. Melt the remaining butter and toss with remaining croutons; sprinkle over the top. Bake, uncovered, at 350° for 35-40 minutes or until heated through. **Yield:** 6-8 servings.

SERVING SUGGESTION

For a super simple dessert, serve lemon pudding
topped with fresh strawberries or raspberries.

SOUTH COAST HOMINY

(Pictured above)

The first time I tasted this hominy dish, I couldn't eat enough. It's something my stepmother has prepared for a long time. Whenever I fix it for friends or family, there are no leftovers.
—Leslie Hampel, Palmer, Texas

1/2 cup chopped onion
1/2 cup chopped green pepper
  5 tablespoons butter *or* margarine, *divided*
  3 tablespoons all-purpose flour
  1 teaspoon salt
1/2 teaspoon ground mustard
Dash cayenne pepper
1-1/2 cups milk
  1 cup (4 ounces) shredded cheddar cheese
  1 can (15-1/2 ounces) hominy, drained
1/2 cup sliced ripe olives, optional
1/2 cup dry bread crumbs

In a skillet, saute onion and green pepper in 3 tablespoons butter until tender. Add the flour, salt, mustard and cayenne until blended. Gradually add milk. Bring to a boil; cook and stir for 2 minutes or until thickened. Remove from the heat; stir in cheese until melted. Add the hominy and olives if desired.

Pour into a greased 1-1/2-qt. baking dish. Melt remaining butter and toss with bread crumbs; sprinkle over top. Bake, uncovered, at 375° for 30 minutes or until top is golden brown. **Yield:** 6-8 servings.

Vegetable Macaroni

(Pictured below)

This casserole works equally well as a side dish or meatless entree. Even my meat-and-potatoes husband enjoys it, especially with a loaf of crusty French bread.
—Elizabeth Erwin, Syracuse, New York

1 can (10-3/4 ounces) condensed cream of celery soup, undiluted
1 cup (8 ounces) sour cream
1/4 cup milk
1 tablespoon dried minced onion
1/2 teaspoon salt
1/8 teaspoon pepper
2 packages (16 ounces *each*) frozen mixed vegetables, thawed
4 ounces elbow macaroni, cooked and drained
2 cups (8 ounces) shredded cheddar cheese

In a large bowl, combine the soup, sour cream, milk, onion, salt and pepper. Stir in the vegetables, macaroni and cheese. Transfer to a greased 3-qt. baking dish. Cover and bake at 375° for 30-35 minutes or until bubbly. **Yield:** 8 servings.

CHRISTMAS CAULIFLOWER

A Swiss cheese sauce gives this vegetable casserole extra-special taste for any occasion.
My family says Christmas dinner just wouldn't be the same without it.
—Betty Claycomb, Alverton, Pennsylvania

1 large head cauliflower, broken into
   florets
1/4 cup diced green pepper
1 jar (7.3 ounces) sliced mushrooms,
   drained
1/4 cup butter *or* margarine
1/3 cup all-purpose flour
2 cups milk
1 cup (4 ounces) shredded Swiss
   cheese
2 tablespoons diced pimientos
1 teaspoon salt
Paprika, optional

In a large saucepan, cook cauliflower in a small amount of water for 6-7 minutes or until crisp-tender; drain well and set aside.

In a saucepan, saute green pepper and mushrooms in butter for 2 minutes. Add flour; gradually stir in milk. Bring to a boil; cook and stir for 2 minutes or until thickened. Remove from the heat; stir in cheese until melted. Add pimientos and salt.

Place half of the cauliflower in a greased 2-qt. baking dish; top with half of the cheese sauce. Repeat layers. Bake, uncovered, at 325° for 25 minutes or until bubbly. Sprinkle with paprika if desired. **Yield:** 8-10 servings.

HELPFUL HINT

Radishes and sweet red or yellow pepper will
perk up the flavor and color of a mixed green salad.

MUSHROOM STUFFING

I first tried this recipe a few years ago. The hearty corn bread stuffing has plenty of
mushroom and bacon accents. We think it's fabulous with chicken or turkey.
—Kathy Traetow, Waverly, Iowa

4 bacon strips, diced
4 celery ribs, chopped
1 medium onion, chopped
1 pound fresh mushrooms, chopped
1 teaspoon rubbed sage
1/2 teaspoon salt
1/4 teaspoon pepper
1 package (16 ounces) corn bread
   stuffing
1/2 cup chopped celery leaves
2 tablespoons minced fresh parsley
1 cup egg substitute
2-1/2 cups chicken broth
1 tablespoon butter *or* margarine

In a large skillet, cook bacon until crisp; remove with a slotted spoon to paper towels. Drain, reserving 2 tablespoons drippings. Saute celery and onion in the drippings until tender. Add mushrooms, sage, salt and pepper; saute for 5 minutes. Remove from the heat. Stir in stuffing, celery leaves, parsley and bacon; mix well.

Combine egg substitute and broth; add to stuffing mixture and mix well. Spread into a greased 13-in. x 9-in. x 2-in. baking dish (dish will be full). Dot with butter. Cover and bake at 350° for 30 minutes. Uncover; bake 10 minutes longer or until lightly browned. **Yield:** 13 cups (enough to stuff one 16- to 18-pound turkey or three 5- to 7-pound roasting chickens).

CREAMY BROCCOLI CASSEROLE

Mother always made this hot dish for Thanksgiving, Christmas and other special family dinners. When my sisters and I plan a dinner, this dish is still on the menu. I've tried many broccoli casseroles over the years, but none are quite as good as Mom's.
—Beth Osborne Skinner, Bristol, Tennessee

1 package (16 ounces) frozen chopped broccoli
1 can (10-3/4 ounces) condensed cream of mushroom soup, undiluted
1 cup mayonnaise*
1 cup (4 ounces) shredded cheddar cheese
2 eggs, lightly beaten
1 to 2 tablespoons dried minced onion
1/2 cup crushed cheese-flavored snack crackers
1 tablespoon butter *or* margarine, melted

Prepare broccoli according to package directions; drain. In a bowl, combine the soup, mayonnaise, cheese, eggs and onion. Stir in broccoli. Pour into a greased 1-1/2-qt. baking dish. Combine the cracker crumbs and butter; sprinkle over the top.

Bake, uncovered, at 350° for 45-55 minutes or until a knife inserted near the center comes out clean. **Yield:** 6 servings.

*Editor's Note: Reduced-fat or fat-free mayonnaise may not be substituted for regular mayonnaise.

PECAN-TOPPED SWEET POTATOES

My mother-in-law gave me this fantastic recipe, and I like it even more every time I taste it. Vanilla and almond extracts add a new twist to a classic dish.
—Elizabeth Hill, Dalton, Georgia

6 medium sweet potatoes (about 3 pounds)
2/3 cup sugar
1 can (5 ounces) evaporated milk
1/3 cup butter *or* margarine, melted
2 eggs, lightly beaten
1 teaspoon vanilla extract
1/4 teaspoon almond extract
TOPPING:
2 cups crisp rice cereal, crushed
2/3 cup packed brown sugar
3/4 cup chopped pecans
1/4 cup butter *or* margarine, melted

Place sweet potatoes in a large saucepan or Dutch oven; cover with water. Cover and bring to a boil. Reduce heat; cook for 30-45 minutes or until tender. Drain; cool slightly and peel. In a large bowl, mash the potato pulp. Stir in the sugar, milk, butter, eggs and extracts.

Pour into a greased 13-in. x 9-in. x 2-in. baking dish. Combine the topping ingredients until crumbly; sprinkle over the potato mixture. Bake, uncovered, at 375° for 30-35 minutes or until lightly browned. **Yield:** 8-10 servings.

SERVING SUGGESTION

Dress up vanilla ice cream for a colorful dessert. Top each scoop of ice cream with 2 tablespoons seedless raspberry jam and a sprinkling of blueberries.

SCALLOPED TURNIPS

(Pictured above)

My husband and I have five grown children and 13 fun-loving grandchildren.
This is the only kind of cooked turnips any of the kids will eat.
—Mrs. Eldon Larabee, Clearmont, Missouri

3 cups diced peeled turnips
2 cups water
1 teaspoon sugar
2 tablespoons butter *or* margarine
3 tablespoons all-purpose flour
3/4 teaspoon salt
1-1/2 cups milk
1/4 cup crushed cornflakes
2 tablespoons shredded cheddar *or*
    Parmesan cheese
Minced fresh parsley, optional

In a saucepan, bring the turnips, water and sugar to a boil. Reduce heat; cover and simmer for 5-8 minutes or until tender. Drain and set aside. In another saucepan, melt butter; stir in flour and salt until smooth. Gradually add milk. Bring to a boil; cook and stir for 2 minutes or until thickened. Stir in turnips.

Pour into a greased 1-qt. baking dish; sprinkle with cornflake crumbs and cheese. Bake, uncovered, at 350° for 20 minutes or until bubbly. Garnish with parsley if desired. **Yield:** 5 servings.

FLAVORFUL RICE DRESSING

The ingredients for this original recipe are drawn from different types of stuffing I've tried. The combination of bread, rice, spinach and orange is a pleasant surprise.
—Gloria Warczak, Cedarburg, Wisconsin

7 slices day-old bread, torn
1 cup torn corn bread
2/3 cup hot water
1/2 cup thinly sliced celery
1/2 cup chopped onion
1/2 cup sliced fresh mushrooms
1 tablespoon vegetable oil
1 cup firmly packed sliced fresh spinach
1 cup cooked long grain rice
1/2 cup cooked wild rice
1/2 cup orange juice
1 egg, beaten
2 teaspoons rubbed sage
1/2 teaspoon dried thyme
1/2 teaspoon salt
1/4 teaspoon sugar
1/4 teaspoon pepper

In a large bowl, lightly toss bread, corn bread and water. In a skillet, saute celery, onion and mushrooms in oil until tender. Stir into bread mixture. Add the remaining ingredients; mix well. Transfer to a greased 2-qt. baking dish. Cover and bake at 350° for 30 minutes or until a thermometer reads 160°. **Yield:** 8 servings.

PERFECT PARTNERS

When you want something more than a plain green salad, add color and crunch with mandarin orange segments and walnuts.

SCALLOPED ONIONS AND PEAS

With tasty peas and onions smothered in a creamy sauce, this is an irresistible side dish that gets passed around until the bowl is empty. We especially like the crunch of the almonds and the flavor from the Parmesan cheese.
—Denise Goedeken, Platte Center, Nebraska

1/4 cup butter *or* margarine
3 tablespoons all-purpose flour
1/2 teaspoon ground mustard
1/2 teaspoon salt
1-1/2 cups milk
1 teaspoon Worcestershire sauce
3 jars (15 ounces *each*) pearl onions, drained
1 package (10 ounces) frozen peas
1/2 cup sliced almonds
3 tablespoons grated Parmesan cheese
Paprika

In a saucepan over medium heat, melt butter. Stir in the flour, mustard and salt until smooth. Stir in milk and Worcestershire sauce. Bring to a boil; cook and stir for 2 minutes or until thickened. Gently stir in onions, peas and almonds.

Pour into an ungreased 2-qt. baking dish. Sprinkle with Parmesan cheese and paprika. Cover and bake at 350° for 30 minutes or until heated through. **Yield:** 8-10 servings.

CARROT CASSEROLE

(Pictured below)

Each time I make this dish, people rave about how good it is. One friend told me,
"I don't usually eat carrots, but this is delicious!" That made my day.
—Lois Hagen, Stevens Point, Wisconsin

8 cups sliced carrots
2 medium onions, sliced
5 tablespoons butter *or* margarine, *divided*
1 can (10-3/4 ounces) condensed cream of celery soup, undiluted
1/2 teaspoon salt
1/4 teaspoon pepper
1 cup (4 ounces) shredded cheddar cheese
1 cup seasoned croutons

Place carrots in a saucepan and cover with water; bring to a boil. Cook until crisp-tender. Meanwhile, in a skillet, saute onions in 3 tablespoons butter until tender. Stir in the soup, salt, pepper and cheese. Drain carrots; add to the onion mixture.

Pour into a greased 13-in. x 9-in. x 2-in. baking dish. Sprinkle with croutons. Melt remaining butter and drizzle over croutons. Bake, uncovered, at 350° for 20-25 minutes or until heated through. **Yield:** 10-12 servings.

SPINACH MASHED POTATOES

(Pictured above)

A lot of folks say they don't like spinach—until they try this super side dish.
Everyone who has ever tasted it has loved it.
—Karen Wald, Dalton, Ohio

3 pounds potatoes, peeled and
  quartered
1 cup (8 ounces) sour cream
1/2 cup butter *or* margarine
1 teaspoon sugar
1 teaspoon salt
1/2 teaspoon pepper
1/4 to 1/2 teaspoon dill weed
1 package (10 ounces) frozen
  chopped spinach, thawed and
  drained
1/3 cup shredded cheddar cheese

Place the potatoes in a saucepan and cover with water; cover and bring to a boil over medium-high heat. Cook for 15-20 minutes or until very tender. Drain well and place in a mixing bowl; mash. Add the sour cream, butter, sugar, salt, pepper and dill; mix well. Stir in spinach.

Transfer to a greased 2-qt. baking dish. Sprinkle with cheese. Bake, uncovered, at 350° for 30-35 minutes or cheese is melted. **Yield:** 8-10 servings.

SOUR CREAM NOODLES

This fast and flavorful dish is much requested at my house, where it will be a mainstay for years to come. I think noodles and sour cream make the perfect pair.
—Judy Robertson, Russell Springs, Kentucky

1 package (10 ounces) fine egg
   noodles
1-1/4 cups cottage cheese
1-1/4 cups sour cream
1 medium onion, finely chopped
1 tablespoon Worcestershire sauce
1/8 teaspoon garlic salt
2 tablespoons grated Parmesan
   cheese
Paprika, optional

Cook noodles according to package directions; drain and place in a bowl. Add the cottage cheese, sour cream, onion, Worcestershire sauce and garlic salt. Spoon into a greased 2-qt. baking dish. Sprinkle with Parmesan cheese.

Bake, uncovered, at 350° for 35-40 minutes or until top is lightly browned. Sprinkle with paprika if desired. **Yield:** 8 servings.

CRANBERRY WILD RICE PILAF

Dried cranberries, currants and almonds add color and texture to this wonderful side dish.
—Pat Gardetta, Osage Beach, Missouri

3/4 cup uncooked wild rice
3 cups chicken broth
1/2 cup pearl barley
1/4 cup dried cranberries
1/4 cup dried currants
1 tablespoon butter *or* margarine
1/3 cup sliced almonds, toasted

Rinse and drain rice; place in a saucepan. Add broth and bring to a boil. Reduce heat; cover and simmer for 10 minutes. Remove from the heat; stir in the barley, cranberries, currants and butter.

Spoon into a greased 1-1/2-qt. baking dish. Cover and bake at 325° for 55 minutes or until the liquid is absorbed and the rice is tender. Sprinkle with almonds. Fluff with a fork. **Yield:** 6-8 servings.

JALAPENO SALSA POTATOES

This lively dish is a way for my family to eat salsa, which we all enjoy, without tortilla chips.
—Kim Lintner, Milwaukee, Wisconsin

4 large potatoes, peeled and cut
   widthwise into thirds
1 cup salsa
1/3 cup chopped onion
12 slices process American cheese
1 large jalapeno pepper, cut into 12
   rings and seeded*

Place potatoes in a saucepan and cover with water; cover and bring to a boil. Cook until tender, about 20-30 minutes. Drain and place in a greased 11-in. x 7-in. x 2-in. baking dish. Top with salsa, onion, cheese and jalapeno. Bake, uncovered, at 350° for 15-20 minutes or until cheese is melted. **Yield:** 6 servings.

Editor's Note: When cutting or seeding hot peppers, use rubber or plastic gloves to protect your hands. Avoid touching your face.

BROCCOLI RICE BAKE

We start thinking about creamy casseroles like this when the seasons start to change. It's warm and comforting, plus getting it ready for the oven takes only minutes.
—Naomi Cross, Millwood, Kentucky

1 cup chopped celery
1 medium onion, chopped
1/4 cup butter *or* margarine
1 can (10-3/4 ounces) condensed cream of celery soup, undiluted
1 can (10-3/4 ounces) condensed cream of mushroom soup, undiluted
1 cup process cheese sauce
1 cup uncooked quick-cooking rice
1 can (4 ounces) mushroom stems and pieces, drained and chopped
2 packages (10 ounces *each*) frozen broccoli cuts, cooked and drained

In a skillet, saute the celery and onion in butter until tender. In a bowl, combine the soups, cheese sauce, rice and mushrooms. Stir in broccoli and the celery mixture. Transfer to a greased 2-qt. baking dish. Cover and bake at 350° for 35-40 minutes or until bubbly. **Yield:** 6-8 servings.

CROUTON CELERY CASSEROLE

When you tire of carrots, green beans and other vegetables, let celery take the spotlight. Guests have been especially fond of this recipe, which I received from a bridge club friend.
—Elizabeth Parke, Fort Wayne, Indiana

4 cups thinly sliced celery
1 can (10-3/4 ounces) condensed cream of celery *or* chicken soup, undiluted
1 can (8 ounces) sliced water chestnuts, drained and halved
1-1/4 cups seasoned salad croutons, *divided*
1/2 cup plus 2 tablespoons slivered almonds, *divided*
1 tablespoon butter *or* margarine, melted

Place celery in a saucepan and cover with water. Cover and bring to a boil. Uncover; cook for 5-6 minutes or until crisp-tender. Drain and place in a bowl. Add the soup, water chestnuts, 1 cup croutons and 1/2 cup almonds. Transfer to a greased 1-1/2-qt. baking dish.

Crush remaining croutons; toss with butter and remaining almonds. Sprinkle over the top. Bake, uncovered, at 350° for 20-25 minutes or until heated through and top is golden brown. **Yield:** 6-8 servings.

SERVING SUGGESTION

For a quick dessert, slice apples and pears. Drizzle with caramel topping, maple syrup or vanilla yogurt.

TOMATO MOZZARELLA BAKE

(Pictured above and on page 224)

You don't often think of casseroles to serve in summertime,
but this one is scrumptious with fresh-from-the-garden tomatoes.
—Elaine Seip, Medicine Hat, Alberta

3 tablespoons butter *or* margarine, softened, *divided*
8 slices French bread (1 inch thick)
2/3 cup chopped green pepper
1/3 cup chopped onion
2 garlic cloves, minced
4 eggs
4 bacon strips, cooked and crumbled
2 teaspoons sugar
1 teaspoon salt
1 teaspoon dried oregano
1/2 teaspoon pepper
2 medium tomatoes
1 cup (4 ounces) shredded mozzarella cheese

Spread 2 tablespoons butter over both sides of bread. Place on a baking sheet; bake at 400° for about 3 minutes on each side or until lightly toasted. Cut into 1-in. cubes. Reduce heat to 350°.

In a skillet, saute green pepper, onion and garlic in remaining butter until tender. In a large bowl, lightly beat the eggs. Stir in bread cubes, vegetable mixture, bacon, sugar, salt, oregano and pepper. Transfer to a greased 11-in. x 7-in. x 2-in. baking dish.

Cut each tomato into four thick slices; arrange over the top. Sprinkle with cheese. Bake, uncovered, at 350° for 30-35 minutes or until a knife inserted near the center comes out clean. **Yield:** 6-8 servings.

CREAMY PEA CASSEROLE

My sister-in-law shared this time-tested recipe with me a few years back.
It's a welcome addition to church or family dinners.
—Mary Pauline Maynor, Franklinton, Louisiana

1 medium onion, chopped
3 celery ribs, finely chopped
1/2 medium sweet red pepper, chopped
6 tablespoons butter *or* margarine
1 can (10-3/4 ounces) condensed
  cream of mushroom soup,
  undiluted
1 tablespoon milk
2 cups frozen peas, thawed
1 can (8 ounces) sliced water
  chestnuts, drained
1/2 to 3/4 cup crushed butter-flavored
  crackers (about 12 crackers)

In a skillet, saute the onion, celery and red pepper in butter for 8-10 minutes or until tender. Stir in soup and milk; heat through. Stir in peas and water chestnuts. Transfer to a greased 1-1/2-qt. baking dish. Sprinkle with the cracker crumbs. Bake, uncovered, at 350° for 25-30 minutes or until bubbly. **Yield:** 6 servings.

PLEASING CHEESE POTATOES

My family can't get enough of this melt-in-your-mouth casserole, which won
a third-place prize in a contest sponsored by our local newspaper.
—Rena Crane, Kenosha, Wisconsin

1 package (32 ounces) frozen Tater
  Tots
3 eggs, lightly beaten
2 cans (10-3/4 ounces *each*)
  condensed cream of potato soup,
  undiluted
1 cup (8 ounces) sour cream
1/4 cup chopped green pepper
1/4 cup chopped onion
4 cups (16 ounces) shredded cheddar
  cheese

Arrange Tater Tots in a greased 13-in. x 9-in. x 2-in. baking dish. In a bowl, combine the eggs, soup, sour cream, green pepper and onion until blended. Stir in the cheese. Pour over Tater Tots. Bake, uncovered, at 350° for 50-55 minutes or until bubbly and golden brown. Let stand for 10 minutes before serving. **Yield:** 8-10 servings.

CREAMED SPINACH

This delicious recipe is a life-saver during the holidays, when time is short.
With only three ingredients, it's also easy to double.
—Sherri Hoover, Perth Road, Ontario

2 packages (10 ounces *each*) frozen
  chopped spinach, thawed and well
  drained
2 cups (16 ounces) sour cream
1 envelope onion soup mix

In a bowl, combine all ingredients. Spoon into a greased 1-qt. baking dish. Cover and bake at 350° for 25-30 minutes or until heated through. **Yield:** 4 servings.

Baked Ratatouille

*This recipe is heavenly when made with homegrown vegetables. It's so good,
I sometimes make the casserole all for myself, then eat it for lunch a few days in a row.*
—*Catherine Lee, San Jose, California*

4 bacon strips, cut into 2-inch pieces
1 cup sliced onion
1 can (14-1/2 ounces) diced tomatoes, undrained
1/3 cup tomato paste
1/4 cup olive *or* vegetable oil
1 large garlic clove, minced
1 teaspoon salt
1 teaspoon Italian seasoning
1 large eggplant (about 1-1/4 pounds), peeled and cubed
4 medium zucchini, sliced
1 large green pepper, cut into strips
8 to 12 ounces sliced Monterey Jack cheese

In a large skillet, cook the bacon and onion over medium heat until bacon is crisp; drain. Stir in the tomatoes, tomato paste, oil, garlic, salt and Italian seasoning.

Spread half into a greased 13-in. x 9-in. x 2-in. baking dish. Layer with half of the eggplant, zucchini, green pepper and cheese. Repeat layers. Bake, uncovered, at 375° for 50-55 minutes or until hot and bubbly. **Yield:** 8 servings.

Spiced Apple-Carrot Casserole

*Fresh carrots and crisp apples combine for wonderful flavor in this unusual casserole
with sugar-and-spice goodness. What a nice addition to a special meal!*
—*Barbara Waltz, Cinnaminson, New Jersey*

2 cups sliced carrots
1 tablespoon brown sugar
1/4 teaspoon ground ginger
1/8 teaspoon ground nutmeg
3 medium apples, peeled and thinly sliced
1 tablespoon butter *or* margarine

Place 1 in. of water in a saucepan; add carrots. Bring to a boil. Reduce heat; cover and simmer for 7-9 minutes or until crisp-tender. Drain. In a small bowl, combine the brown sugar, ginger and nutmeg.

In a greased 1-1/2-qt. baking dish, layer half of the apples and carrots. Sprinkle with half of the brown sugar mixture. Repeat layers. Dot with butter. Cover and bake at 350° for 35-40 minutes or until apples are crisp-tender and carrots are tender. **Yield:** 6-8 servings.

SERVING SUGGESTION

*Add pizzazz to plain chocolate pudding by stirring in 1 tablespoon
instant coffee granules with the milk. Top with a dollop of whipped cream
and a maraschino cherry for pretty presentation.*

BISCUIT-TOPPED TOMATO CASSEROLE

(Pictured at right)

This is one of my favorite ways to prepare fresh tomatoes from our garden.
Since it's just my husband and me, I sometimes halve the tomato mixture, then
make the rest of the topping into garlic-cheese drop biscuits to eat with other meals.
—Jayme Buzard, Wichita, Kansas

2 tablespoons cornstarch
1 tablespoon sugar
2 tablespoons cold water
8 medium tomatoes, seeded and chopped
1 medium green pepper, chopped
1 teaspoon salt
1/8 teaspoon pepper
TOPPING:
1 cup all-purpose flour
2 teaspoons baking powder
1 teaspoon garlic powder
1/4 teaspoon baking soda
1/4 teaspoon chicken bouillon granules
1/4 cup cold butter *or* margarine
1/2 cup shredded cheddar cheese
1/2 cup plus 1 tablespoon buttermilk

In a large saucepan, combine cornstarch and sugar. Stir in water until smooth. Stir in tomatoes. Bring to a boil; cook and stir for 2 minutes or until thickened. Remove from the heat. Stir in the green pepper, salt and pepper; keep warm.

In a bowl, combine the first five topping ingredients. Cut in butter until mixture resembles coarse crumbs. Stir in cheese and buttermilk just until moistened.

Transfer tomato mixture to a greased 11-in. x 7-in. x 2-in. baking dish. Drop topping into eight mounds onto hot tomato mixture. Bake, uncovered, at 400° for 20-25 minutes or until a toothpick inserted in biscuits comes out clean. **Yield:** 6 servings.

ZUCCHINI CORN MEDLEY

(Pictured at right)

One day when I was a girl, a neighbor brought over a dish similar to this one. I hadn't had it
in 20 years but kept thinking about the fabulous flavor combination, do I decided to re-create it.
I don't know if it's the same, but my family likes it today as much as I did back then.
—Marian Quaid-Maltagliati, Nipomo, California

2 medium zucchini, cut into 1/2-inch slices
1/4 cup water
1 can (15-1/2 ounces) hominy, drained
1 can (15-1/4 ounces) whole kernel corn, drained
1 jalapeno pepper, seeded and chopped*
1/2 teaspoon salt
1 cup (4 ounces) shredded pepper Jack cheese

In a 1-1/2-qt. microwave-safe dish, combine the zucchini and water. Cover and microwave on high for 2 minutes; drain. Stir in the hominy, corn, jalapeno and salt. Cover and microwave on high for 3-4 minutes. Sprinkle with cheese. Cook, uncovered, on high for 1-2 minutes until cheese is melted and vegetables are tender. Let stand for 2 minutes before serving. **Yield:** 6-8 servings.

*Editor's Note: When cutting or seeding hot peppers, use rubber or plastic gloves to protect your hands. Avoid touching your face. This recipe was tested in an 850-watt microwave.

BACON RANCH POTATOES

When I prepare mashed potatoes, I often make extras, just so we can have this casserole the next day.
—Kathryn Hostetler, West Farmington, Ohio

6 cups mashed potatoes (prepared
  with milk and butter)
1 cup cottage cheese
1/2 cup milk
1 medium onion, finely chopped
2 tablespoons ranch salad dressing
  mix
1 pound sliced bacon, cooked and
  crumbled
2 cups (8 ounces) shredded Monterey
  Jack cheese
1 cup crushed butter-flavored
  crackers (about 25 crackers)
1/4 cup butter *or* margarine, melted

In a bowl, combine the potatoes, cottage cheese, milk, onion and dressing mix. Spread in a greased 3-qt. baking dish. Top with bacon and cheese. Combine cracker crumbs and butter; sprinkle over top. Bake, uncovered, at 350° for 35-40 minutes or until bubbly. **Yield:** 8-10 servings.

SCALLOPED PINEAPPLE

This comforting side dish is a special treat for holidays, especially Christmas. It's golden and delicious.
—Janet Pensabene, Annandale, Virginia

1 cup butter *or* margarine, softened
1-1/2 cups sugar
3 eggs
4 cups firmly packed cubed bread
  (crusts removed)
1 can (20 ounces) pineapple chunks,
  drained

In a mixing bowl, cream butter and sugar. Add eggs, one at a time, beating well after each addition. Stir in the bread cubes and pineapple. Spoon into a greased 2-qt. baking dish. Bake, uncovered, at 375° for 40-45 minutes or until golden. **Yield:** 8-10 servings.

MUSHROOM BARLEY BAKE

I serve this with baked chicken, particularly when we want a change from rice dishes.
—Carol Funk, Richard, Saskatchewan

1 large onion, chopped
1 cup sliced fresh mushrooms
2 tablespoons butter *or* margarine
3 cups water
1 tablespoon chicken bouillon
  granules
1/4 teaspoon salt
1/8 teaspoon pepper
1 cup pearl barley
1 tablespoon minced fresh parsley

In a saucepan, saute onion and mushrooms in butter until tender. Add water, bouillon, salt and pepper; mix well. Bring to a boil. Add barley and parsley. Pour into a greased 2-qt. baking dish. Cover and bake at 350° for 80-90 minutes or until the barley is tender. **Yield:** 6 servings.

SWEET ONION CASSEROLE

(Pictured below)

This easy casserole is incredibly tasty. My family asks for it with steak or chicken.
—Bobbie McMahan, Anderson, South Carolina

**5 large sweet onions, halved and
    sliced**
1/2 cup butter *or* margarine
**1/2 cup crushed butter-flavored
    crackers (about 12 crackers)**
1/2 cup grated Parmesan cheese

In a large skillet, saute onions in butter until tender. Transfer half to a greased 2-qt. baking dish; sprinkle with half of the cracker crumbs and cheese. Repeat layers. Bake, uncovered, at 350° for 25-30 minutes or until golden brown and bubbly. **Yield:** 8-10 servings.

CORNY BACON CASSEROLE

(Pictured below)

Corn is my three boys' favorite vegetable, so we eat a lot of it.
This recipe has been a favorite for years. My husband, Bob, and the boys really enjoy it.
—Marcia Hostetter, Canton, New York

6 bacon strips, diced
1 medium onion, chopped
2 tablespoons all-purpose flour
2 garlic cloves, minced
1/2 teaspoon salt
1/2 teaspoon pepper
1 cup (8 ounces) sour cream
3-1/2 cups fresh *or* frozen corn
1 tablespoon chopped fresh parsley
1 tablespoon chopped fresh chives

In a large skillet, cook bacon until crisp; remove to paper towels. Drain, reserving 2 tablespoons drippings. Saute onion in drippings until tender. Add flour, garlic, salt and pepper. Cook and stir until bubbly; cook and stir 1 minute more. Remove from the heat; stir in the sour cream until smooth. Add corn, parsley and half of the bacon; mix well.

Pour into a greased 1-qt. baking dish. Sprinkle with remaining bacon. Bake, uncovered, at 350° for 20-25 minutes or until heated through. Sprinkle with chives. **Yield:** 6-8 servings.

CREAMY ASPARAGUS AND GREEN BEANS

Unlike most kids, my son doesn't consider asparagus "yucky". He loves it...especially in this dish. Whenever I serve this creamy combination, there's never any left.
—Teresa Kachermeyer, Frederick, Maryland

1 can (10-3/4 ounces) condensed creamy chicken mushroom soup, undiluted
1/2 cup milk
1 package (10 ounces) frozen cut green beans, thawed and drained
1 package (8 ounces) frozen asparagus cuts and tips, thawed and drained
1 can (4 ounces) mushroom stems and pieces, drained
2 cups cubed day-old bread
2 tablespoons sliced almonds
2 tablespoons butter *or* margarine, melted

In a large bowl, combine the soup and milk until blended. Add the beans, asparagus and mushrooms; mix well. Pour into a greased 8-in. square baking dish. Cover and bake at 350° for 20 minutes. Toss bread cubes, almonds and butter; sprinkle over the top. Bake, uncovered, 15-20 minutes longer or until bubbly. **Yield:** 6-8 servings.

TIMELY TIP

You can enjoy fresh-tasting corn on the cob even when the calendar says it's winter. In August, freeze fresh ears with the husks on in plastic freezer bags. Serve them in December or January for a taste of summer.

SWEET-AND-SOUR BAKED BEANS

This recipe has proven to be a great standby for parties, barbecues and potlucks. I especially like it because I can keep all the ingredients on hand for last-minute preparation.
—Barbara Nielsen, Chula Vista, California

1 pound sliced bacon, diced
4 large onions, sliced
1 cup packed brown sugar
1/2 cup cider vinegar
1-1/2 teaspoons ground mustard
2 cans (16 ounces *each*) New England-style baked beans, undrained
2 cans (15 ounces *each*) butter beans, rinsed and drained
1 can (16 ounces) kidney beans, rinsed and drained
1 can (15-1/4 ounces) lima beans, rinsed and drained

In a skillet, cook bacon until crisp; remove to paper towels. Drain, reserving 2 tablespoons drippings. Add onions, brown sugar, vinegar and mustard to drippings; cook for 10 minutes, stirring frequently.

Pour into a large bowl; stir in beans and bacon. Transfer to an ungreased 3-qt. baking dish. Bake, uncovered, at 350° for 1-1/2 hours or until bubbly. **Yield:** 18-20 servings.

SECRET BRUSSELS SPROUTS

My husband and I have always loved brussels sprouts, but our kids wouldn't touch them until I made this recipe. Tomato juice and cheese give this vegetable a place on the family table.
—Diane Hixon, Niceville, Florida

1 small onion, sliced
2 tablespoons butter *or* margarine
2 tablespoons all-purpose flour
1 cup tomato juice
1 teaspoon sugar
1/2 teaspoon salt
1/8 teaspoon pepper
2 packages (10 ounces *each*) frozen brussels sprouts *or* 1-1/4 pounds fresh brussels sprouts, cooked and drained
1/4 cup shredded cheddar cheese

In a skillet, saute onion in butter until tender. Remove and set aside. Stir flour into the drippings until blended. Add tomato juice. Bring to a boil; cook and stir for 2 minutes or until thickened. Stir in the sugar, salt, pepper and onion.

Place the brussels sprouts in a greased 1-qt. baking dish; top with the onion mixture. Sprinkle with the cheese. Bake, uncovered, at 350° for 15 minutes or until heated through. **Yield:** 6 servings.

BUTTERNUT SQUASH CASSEROLE

This casserole is versatile! It can be served hot today and cold tomorrow, as a main dish for meatless meals or as a side dish for a dinner party. Any way you serve it, it's scrumptious.
—Patricia Sheffer, Seneca, Pennsylvania

5 cups shredded peeled butternut squash
Juice and grated peel of 1 lemon
1 cup raisins
1/3 cup chopped dried apricots
1 medium tart apple, cubed
2 cups ricotta *or* small-curd cottage cheese
1 egg, lightly beaten
3 tablespoons plain yogurt, sour cream *or* buttermilk
1 teaspoon ground cinnamon
1/8 teaspoon ground nutmeg
1/2 cup chopped walnuts

In a large bowl, toss the squash with lemon juice and peel. Place half in a greased 11-in. x 7-in. x 2-in. baking dish. Combine raisins, apricots and apple; sprinkle over squash.

In a small bowl, combine cheese, egg, yogurt, cinnamon and nutmeg; spread over fruit mixture. Top with remaining squash. Sprinkle with nuts. Cover and bake at 375° for 35-40 minutes or until squash is tender. **Yield:** 10-12 servings.

SERVING SUGGESTION

A simple BLT salad is packed with flavor. Just toss iceberg lettuce with crumbled cooked bacon and chopped tomato. Top with the creamy dressing of your choice.

ONION POTATO PIE

(Pictured above)

*I found a basic potato pie recipe and added the sweet onions, for which our area is famous.
I've used this recipe as a side dish for a main meal and as a brunch entree.*
—Gwyn Frasco, Walla Walla, Washington

8 cups frozen shredded hash brown
  potatoes, thawed
6 tablespoons butter *or* margarine,
  divided
3/4 teaspoon salt, *divided*
1 large sweet onion, diced
1/4 cup chopped sweet red pepper
1 cup (4 ounces) shredded cheddar
  cheese
3 eggs, lightly beaten
1/3 cup milk

Gently squeeze potatoes to remove excess water. Melt 5 tablespoons butter; add to potatoes along with 1/2 teaspoon salt. Press onto the bottom and up the sides of a greased 9-in. pie plate to form a crust. Bake at 425° for 25-30 minutes or until edges are browned. Cool to room temperature.

In a saucepan, saute the onion and red pepper in remaining butter until tender. Spoon into the crust; sprinkle with cheese. Combine the eggs, milk and remaining salt; pour over onion mixture. Bake at 350° for 20-25 minutes or until a knife inserted near the center comes out clean. Let stand for 5 minutes before serving. **Yield:** 6-8 servings.

GRANDMOTHER'S CORN PUDDING

(Pictured above)

Corn pudding is a popular side dish on Maryland's Eastern Shore. My grandmother always served this pudding for holidays and family reunions. Today, my family can't wait for special occasions, so I whip up this comforting dish at least once or twice a month to keep them happy!
—Susan Brown Langenstein, Salisbury, Maryland

4 eggs
1 cup milk
1 can (14-3/4 ounces) cream-style corn
1/2 cup sugar
5 slices day-old bread, crusts removed
1 tablespoon butter *or* margarine, softened

In a bowl, beat eggs and milk. Add corn and sugar; mix well. Cut bread into 1/2-in. cubes; place in a greased 9-in. square baking dish. Pour egg mixture over bread. Dot with butter. Bake, uncovered, at 350° for 50-60 minutes or until a knife inserted near the center comes out clean. **Yield:** 9 servings.

SCALLOPED CABBAGE

If I find a recipe that I think my family will like, I test it out. I found this one while traveling some years ago. My family loved it and it has become one of our favorites.
—Barbara Calhoun, Marquette Heights, Illinois

5 to 6 cups shredded cabbage
2 medium onions, finely chopped
1 medium green pepper, finely chopped
1/4 cup butter *or* margarine
2 cups (8 ounces) shredded sharp cheddar cheese
2 cups coarsely crushed sour cream and chive croutons, *divided*
1 cup milk *or* half-and-half cream

In a large saucepan, cook cabbage in boiling water for 4-5 minutes or until almost tender; drain. In a small saucepan, saute onions and green pepper in butter until tender. Add to the cabbage. Stir in cheese and 1-1/2 cups of croutons.

Transfer to a greased 13-in. x 9-in. x 2-in. baking dish. Pour milk over the top; do not stir. Sprinkle with remaining croutons. Bake, uncovered, at 350° for 20-25 minutes or until bubbly. **Yield:** 6-8 servings.

TOMATO ZUCCHINI CASSEROLE

This recipe is always a hit. In fact, I usually have to double it, and still there are no leftovers. The crumb topping is flavored with bits of onion.
—Alison Relkov, Cochrane, Alberta

1 cup (4 ounces) shredded cheddar cheese
1/3 cup shredded mozzarella cheese
1 teaspoon minced fresh basil
   or 1/2 teaspoon dried basil
1 teaspoon minced fresh oregano
   or 1/2 teaspoon dried oregano
1 garlic clove, minced
1/2 teaspoon salt
1/4 teaspoon pepper
5 small zucchini, thinly sliced
1/4 cup butter *or* margarine, *divided*
2 medium tomatoes, thinly sliced
2 tablespoons finely chopped onion
1/2 cup dry bread crumbs

In a bowl, combine the first seven ingredients; set aside. In a large skillet, saute zucchini in 1 tablespoon of butter until crisp-tender, about 5 minutes; drain. Arrange the zucchini in a greased 8-in. square baking dish; sprinkle with half of the cheese mixture. Top with tomatoes and remaining cheese mixture.

In a saucepan, saute onion in remaining butter until tender; add bread crumbs and toss to combine. Sprinkle over top. Bake, uncovered, at 375° for 20-25 minutes or until vegetables are tender. **Yield:** 6 servings.

SERVING SUGGESTION

Add a sweet sensation to a spinach salad by tossing in cubed canned pears and chopped pecans.

ALMOND POTATO PUFF

(Pictured below)

Our garden produces an abundance of potatoes, so we eat them often. This recipe is a refreshing change from fried or mashed potatoes. My children love the almond topping.
—Carol Ann Hass, Des Moines, Iowa

1-1/2 pounds potatoes, peeled and quartered
1 small onion, chopped
2 tablespoons butter *or* **margarine**
2 eggs
3/4 cup whipping cream, warmed
1/2 cup ground almonds
1/2 teaspoon salt
Dash ground nutmeg
1/2 cup shredded cheddar cheese
1/4 cup slivered almonds

Place potatoes in a saucepan and cover with water; cover and bring to a boil. Cook until tender, about 15 minutes; drain and place in a mixing bowl.

In a skillet, saute onion in butter until tender; add to the potatoes. On low speed, beat in eggs, one at a time, until smooth. Beat in cream (mixture will be thin). Add the ground almonds, salt and nutmeg.

Spoon into a greased 1-1/2-qt. baking dish. Sprinkle with the cheese and slivered almonds. Bake, uncovered, at 400° for 20 minutes or until a thermometer reads 160°. **Yield:** 6 servings.

MUSHROOM CASSEROLE

When I make this buttery-tasting casserole, my family fights over every last bite.
The Swiss cheese provides a different, mild flavor when it melts.
—Susan Vetter, Cape Coral, Florida

1 package (16 ounces) wide egg
   noodles
2 pounds fresh mushrooms, sliced
1/2 cup butter *or* margarine, *divided*
1-1/2 teaspoons salt
3/4 teaspoon pepper
4 cups (16 ounces) shredded Swiss
   cheese

Cook noodles according to package directions; drain. In a large skillet, saute mushrooms in 1/4 cup butter for 10-15 minutes or until tender.

Place a third of the noodles in a greased 13-in. x 9-in. x 2-in. baking dish; sprinkle with 1/2 teaspoon salt and 1/4 teaspoon pepper. Top with 1-1/3 cups cheese and a third of the mushrooms. Repeat layers twice. Dot with remaining butter.

Bake, uncovered, at 350° for 25-30 minutes or until bubbly and cheese is melted. **Yield:** 8-10 servings.

ONION RICE CASSEROLE

Stuttgart, Arkansas is the rice capital of America—and I've been there many times.
It's a good thing my family enjoys rice as much as I do!
—Dorothy Smith, El Dorado, Arkansas

1-1/3 cups uncooked long grain rice
1 can (10-1/2 ounces) condensed beef
   consomme
1 can (10-1/2 ounces) condensed
   French onion soup, undiluted
3 tablespoons butter *or* margarine

Combine all ingredients in a 1-1/2-qt. microwave-safe dish. Cover and microwave on high for 5 minutes. Microwave at 50% power for 15 minutes. Let stand for 5 minutes before serving. Fluff with a fork. **Yield:** 6-8 servings.

Editor's Note: This recipe was tested in an 850-watt microwave.

SCALLOPED SWEET POTATOES

This comforting blend of sweet potatoes, apples and pecans has a small yield, so you won't end up
with a pan of leftovers. Now that our three boys are grown, I cook for just my husband and me.
—Marjorie Wilkerson, Dighton, Kansas

1 large sweet potato, peeled and
   sliced
1 large tart apple, peeled and sliced
1/3 cup dry bread crumbs
1/3 cup light corn syrup
1/8 teaspoon salt
1 tablespoon butter *or* margarine
1 tablespoon chopped pecans

In a greased 1-qt. baking dish, layer half of the sweet potato slices, apple slices and bread crumbs. Repeat layers. Pour corn syrup over top; sprinkle with salt. Dot with butter; sprinkle with pecans. Cover and bake at 400° for 35 minutes or until sweet potato and apple are tender. **Yield:** 2 servings.

MACARONI AU GRATIN

Everyone likes this easy, tasty side dish. When I take it to parties, I'm always asked for the recipe, and I carry home an empty container.
—Jeannine Hopp, Menomonee Falls, Wisconsin

1 package (7 ounces) elbow macaroni
1/4 cup butter *or* margarine
1/4 cup all-purpose flour
2 cups milk
8 ounces process cheese (Velveeta), cubed
1 tablespoon chopped onion
1/2 teaspoon Worcestershire sauce
1/2 teaspoon salt
1/4 teaspoon pepper
1/4 teaspoon ground mustard
2 tablespoons seasoned bread crumbs

Cook macaroni according to package directions; drain. Place in a greased 2-qt. baking dish; set aside.

In a saucepan, melt butter over medium heat. Stir in the flour until smooth. Gradually add the milk. Bring to a boil; cook and stir for 2 minutes or until thickened. Reduce heat; stir in the cheese, onion, Worcestershire sauce, salt, pepper and mustard until the cheese is melted.

Pour over macaroni and mix well. Sprinkle with the bread crumbs. Bake, uncovered, at 375° for 30 minutes or until heated through. **Yield:** 6 servings.

MICROWAVE SCALLOPED CORN

This recipe earns big points for flavor and ease of preparation. It's the only corn scallop recipe I use anymore.
—Sue Gronholz, Columbus, Wisconsin

2 eggs
1 can (14-3/4 ounces) cream-style corn
2/3 cup milk
1/2 cup crushed saltines (about 15 crackers)
2 tablespoons butter *or* margarine, melted
1 tablespoon sugar
1/4 teaspoon salt
Pepper to taste
Paprika

In a bowl, beat eggs. Stir in the corn, milk, cracker crumbs, butter, sugar, salt and pepper; mix well. Pour into a greased 1-qt. microwave-safe dish.

Cover and microwave at 70% power for 6-7 minutes or until a knife inserted near the center comes out clean. Let stand for 5 minutes before serving. Sprinkle with paprika. **Yield:** 4 servings.

Editor's Note: This recipe was tested in an 850-watt microwave.

SERVING SUGGESTION

For a fun and fast sundae, break a large chocolate chip cookie in half. Crumble half over a scoop of vanilla ice cream. Drizzle with chocolate syrup. Place the other cookie half on top for garnish.

HAZELNUT BROCCOLI BAKE

(Pictured below)

Oregon's fertile Willamette Valley produces a lot of hazelnuts, and this is one of my favorite dishes that calls for them. I love to experiment with recipes. This is one of my success stories.
—Florence Snyder, Hillsboro, Oregon

8 cups chopped fresh broccoli *or* 2 packages (10 ounces *each*) chopped frozen broccoli
5 tablespoons butter *or* margarine, *divided*
3 tablespoons all-purpose flour
1-1/2 cups milk
2 teaspoons chicken bouillon granules
1 cup seasoned stuffing mix
1/4 cup water
2/3 cup chopped hazelnuts, toasted

Cook the broccoli until crisp-tender. Meanwhile, in a saucepan over medium heat, melt 3 tablespoons butter. Stir in flour until smooth. Gradually add milk and bouillon. Bring to a boil; cook and stir for 2 minutes or until thickened. Drain broccoli; stir into sauce.

Transfer to a greased 9-in. square baking dish. In a bowl, combine the stuffing mix, water and nuts. Melt the remaining butter; pour over stuffing mixture and toss. Spoon over the broccoli. Bake, uncovered, at 350° for 25-30 minutes or until heated through. **Yield:** 6 servings.

BREAKFAST & BRUNCH

Breakfast is the most important meal of the day... and it could be the most delicious, too, with the 41 recipes in this chapter. From delicate quiches to hearty casseroles, there's something for everyone. The mouth-watering aromas will wake up any sleepyhead!

PEAR OVEN OMELET (P. 264)

MAPLE FRENCH TOAST CASSEROLE (P. 258)
ASPARAGUS STRATA (P. 258)

MAPLE FRENCH TOAST CASSEROLE

(Pictured on page 257)

*When I first served this to family visiting from California, they all wanted the recipe.
I'd never had so many compliments on my cooking before! The recipe was
originally from my grandmother, given to me on my wedding day.
—Melissa Faye Paxton, Clifton Forge, Virginia*

7 cups cubed French bread
1/2 cup golden raisins
1 package (3 ounces) cream cheese,
   softened
1 cup warm whipping cream
   (70° to 80°)
1/4 cup maple syrup
6 eggs
1/2 teaspoon vanilla extract
1/4 teaspoon ground cinnamon
1/8 teaspoon salt
Additional maple syrup

Place bread in a greased 2-qt. baking dish; press down gently. Sprinkle with raisins. In a small mixing bowl, beat the cream cheese until fluffy. Gradually beat in whipping cream and syrup; mix well. Whisk together the eggs, vanilla, cinnamon and salt; add to cream cheese mixture.

Pour evenly over the bread; lightly press bread into egg mixture with a spatula. Cover; refrigerate for 8 hours or overnight.

Remove from the refrigerator 30 minutes before baking. Cover and bake at 375° for 25 minutes. Uncover; bake 20-25 minutes longer or until center is set and the top is golden brown. Serve with syrup. **Yield:** 6 servings.

ASPARAGUS STRATA

(Pictured on page 257)

*The original recipe for this wonderful egg dish called for sausage, but fresh asparagus
is tasty—and healthier, too! I serve this easy, elegant dish with a salad and mini pecan rolls.
—Amy Grover, Salem, Massachusetts*

4 cups water
1 pound fresh asparagus, trimmed
   and cut into 1/2-inch pieces
2 cups milk
6 bread slices, crusts removed and
   cubed
6 eggs, lightly beaten
1 cup (4 ounces) shredded cheddar
   cheese
1 teaspoon salt

In a large saucepan, bring water to a boil. Add asparagus; boil, uncovered, for 3 minutes. Drain and immediately place asparagus in ice water. Drain and pat dry.

In a bowl, combine the asparagus, milk, bread cubes, eggs, cheese and salt. Transfer to a greased 2-qt. baking dish. Cover and refrigerate for 5 hours or overnight.

Remove from the refrigerator 30 minutes before baking. Bake, uncovered, at 350° for 45-55 minutes or until bubbly and asparagus is tender. **Yield:** 6 servings.

APPLE PAN GOODY

(Pictured below)

We enjoy this tasty breakfast almost weekly. It's a recipe I found years ago and adapted to my family's taste. The servings are generous and satisfy everyone—even voracious teenagers.
—Jeanne Bredemeyer, Orient, New York

4 to 5 medium tart apples, peeled
    and sliced
3/4 cup dried cranberries
6 tablespoons brown sugar
1 teaspoon ground cinnamon,
    divided
3 tablespoons butter *or* margarine
6 eggs
1-1/2 cups orange juice
1-1/2 cups all-purpose flour
3/4 teaspoon salt
2 tablespoons sugar
Maple syrup, optional

In a large skillet, saute apples, cranberries, brown sugar and 3/4 teaspoon cinnamon in butter until apples begin to soften, about 6 minutes. Transfer to a greased 13-in. x 9-in. x 2-in. baking dish.

In a blender, combine the eggs, orange juice, flour and salt; cover and process until smooth. Pour over apple mixture. Sprinkle with sugar and remaining cinnamon. Bake, uncovered, at 425° for 20-25 minutes or until a knife inserted near the center comes out clean. Serve with syrup if desired. **Yield:** 8 servings.

BREAKFAST SUPREME

Friends shared this recipe with me many years ago, when we spent the night at their home.
One taste and you'll see why it has "supreme" in its name. It's that good!
—Laurie Harms, Grinnell, Iowa

1 pound bulk pork sausage
1 pound ground beef
1 small onion, chopped
3/4 cup sliced fresh mushrooms
1/2 cup chopped green pepper
1 to 1-1/2 teaspoons salt
1/4 to 1/2 teaspoon pepper
2 tablespoons butter *or* margarine, melted
2 cups (8 ounces) shredded cheddar cheese, *divided*
12 eggs
2/3 cup whipping cream

In a large skillet, cook the sausage, beef, onion, mushrooms and green pepper over medium heat until meat is no longer pink; drain. Stir in salt and pepper; set aside.

Pour butter into an ungreased 13-in. x 9-in. x 2-in. baking dish. Sprinkle with 1 cup cheese. Beat eggs; pour over cheese. Top with sausage mixture. Pour the cream over sausage mixture. Sprinkle with remaining cheese. Cover and refrigerate for 8 hours or overnight.

Remove from the refrigerator 30 minutes before baking. Bake, uncovered, at 325° for 35-40 minutes or until set. Let stand for 10 minutes before cutting. **Yield:** 12 servings.

PERFECT PARTNERS

A spinach salad is transformed into a pretty brunch dish by adding fresh raspberries, sliced almonds and raspberry vinaigrette dressing.

HAM 'N' EGG TORTILLA BAKE

This recipe came about one day when I needed to make my husband's lunch and we were out of bread. This is now one of his favorites. It's also a great brunch casserole.
—Lauren Budweg, Oberlin, Ohio

1 cup sliced fresh mushrooms
1 medium onion, chopped
1/2 cup chopped green pepper
1/4 cup butter *or* margarine
6 eggs
1/4 cup milk
1/4 teaspoon pepper
1 cup cubed fully cooked ham
1 can (10-3/4 ounces) condensed cream of mushroom soup, undiluted
10 flour tortillas (8 inches)
1-1/2 cups (6 ounces) shredded cheddar cheese

In a large skillet, saute the mushrooms, onion and green pepper in butter until tender. Meanwhile, in a bowl, whisk together the eggs, milk and pepper; add the ham. Pour into the skillet. Cook and stir over medium heat until eggs are completely set.

In a greased 13-in. x 9-in. x 2-in. baking dish, spread half of the soup. Place 3 tablespoons egg mixture down the center of each tortilla; sprinkle each with 1 tablespoon cheese. Roll up and place seam side down over soup.

Spread remaining soup over tortillas. Sprinkle with remaining cheese. Bake, uncovered, at 350° for 20-25 minutes or until heated through. **Yield:** 5 servings.

FARMER'S STRATA

(Pictured above)

You can assemble this casserole ahead and bake it just before leaving for an after-church potluck.
People go back for seconds because it includes tasty ingredients like bacon, cheese and potatoes.
—Pat Kuether, Westminster, Colorado

1 pound sliced bacon, cut into
   1/2-inch pieces
2 cups chopped fully cooked ham
1 small onion, chopped
10 slices bread, cubed
1 cup cubed cooked potatoes
3 cups (12 ounces) shredded cheddar
   cheese
8 eggs
3 cups milk
1 tablespoon Worcestershire sauce
1 teaspoon ground mustard
Pinch salt and pepper

In a large skillet, cook bacon over medium heat until crisp. Remove to paper towels. Add ham and onion to drippings. Cook and stir until onion is tender; drain. In a greased 13-in. x 9-in. x 2-in. baking dish, layer half of the bread cubes, potatoes and cheese. Top with ham mixture and bacon.

Layer with remaining bread, potatoes and cheese. In a bowl, beat the eggs, milk, Worcestershire sauce, mustard, salt and pepper. Pour over cheese. Cover and refrigerate overnight.

Remove from the refrigerator 30 minutes before baking. Bake, uncovered, at 325° for 65-70 minutes or until a knife inserted near the center comes out clean. Let stand for 10 minutes before serving. **Yield:** 12-16 servings.

SCRAMBLED EGG CASSEROLE

(Pictured below)

The aroma of ham and green onions sauteeing creates a sneak preview of this delicious casserole.
—Mary Anne McWhirter, Pearland, Texas

1/2 cup butter *or* margarine, *divided*
  2 tablespoons all-purpose flour
1/2 teaspoon salt
1/8 teaspoon pepper
  2 cups milk
  1 cup (4 ounces) shredded process
    cheese (Velveeta)
  1 cup cubed fully cooked ham
1/4 cup sliced green onions
 12 eggs, beaten
  1 jar (4-1/2 ounces) sliced
    mushrooms, drained
1-1/2 cups soft bread crumbs
Additional sliced green onions, optional

In a saucepan, melt 2 tablespoons butter. Add the flour, salt and pepper until smooth. Gradually stir in the milk. Bring to a boil; cook and stir for 2 minutes or until thickened. Remove from the heat. Stir in cheese.

In a large skillet, saute ham and onions in 3 tablespoons butter until onions are tender. Add eggs; cook and stir until eggs are set. Add mushrooms and cheese sauce; mix well. Pour into a greased 11-in. x 7-in. x 2-in. baking dish. Melt remaining butter; toss with bread crumbs. Sprinkle over top. Cover and refrigerate for 2-3 hours or overnight.

Remove from the refrigerator 30 minutes before baking. Bake, uncovered, at 350° for 25-30 minutes or until golden brown. Sprinkle with onions if desired. Let stand 5-10 minutes before serving. **Yield:** 6-8 servings.

POTATO HAM BAKE

I love to experiment with new recipes. When I found this recipe, I played with it a bit. I always get compliments when I put it on the table.
—Cheryl Runia, Lebanon, Oregon

2 cups (8 ounces) shredded
   cheddar cheese
2 cups (8 ounces) shredded
   mozzarella cheese
1 can (4 ounces) mushroom stems
   and pieces, drained
1 medium onion, chopped
1/3 cup *each* chopped sweet red and
   green pepper
3 tablespoons butter *or* margarine
3 cups cubed cooked potatoes
2 cups cubed fully cooked ham
1/2 cup all-purpose flour
2 tablespoons minced fresh parsley
1 teaspoon salt
1/2 teaspoon pepper
8 eggs, lightly beaten
1-3/4 cups milk

Combine the cheeses; sprinkle half into a greased 13-in. x 9-in. x 2-in. baking dish. In a skillet, saute the mushrooms, onion and peppers in butter until crisp-tender. Sprinkle over the cheese. Add the potatoes and ham. Sprinkle with remaining cheese. In a bowl, combine the flour, parsley, salt and pepper. Add the eggs and milk; mix until smooth. Pour over the top.

Bake, uncovered, at 350° for 35-45 minutes or until a knife inserted near the center comes out clean. Let stand for 10 minutes before serving. **Yield:** 8-12 servings.

SOUTH-OF-THE-BORDER QUICHE

This dish is deliciously different from a traditional quiche with a pastry crust. The corn bread base gives a nice country-style texture, while green chilies add a subtle zest.
—Marjorie Hennig, Seymour, Indiana

1 package (8-1/2 ounces) corn
   bread/muffin mix
2 tablespoons butter *or* margarine,
   melted
1 tablespoon water
13 eggs
1 cup (4 ounces) shredded Monterey
   Jack cheese, *divided*
1 pound bulk pork sausage, cooked
   and drained
1 cup milk
1 can (14-3/4 ounces) cream-style
   corn
2 cans (4 ounces *each*) chopped green
   chilies
2 tablespoons finely chopped onion
1 cup salsa

In a bowl, combine the muffin mix, butter, water and 1 egg; stir just until moistened. Spread in a greased 13-in. x 9-in. x 2-in. baking dish. Sprinkle with 1/2 cup cheese. In a large bowl, beat the remaining eggs. Add the sausage, milk, corn, chilies and onion; pour over batter.

Bake, uncovered, at 350° for 60-70 minutes or until a knife inserted near the center comes out clean. Top with salsa and sprinkle with the remaining cheese. Bake 10 minutes longer or until cheese is melted. Let stand for 5 minutes before cutting. **Yield:** 12-14 servings.

PEAR OVEN OMELET

(Pictured above and on page 256)

An abundant crop of pears was the inspiration for this recipe. What a great way to start the day! My husband and children request this omelet frequently.
—Sandra Lackie, Creemore, Ontario

2 tablespoons butter *or* margarine
1/4 teaspoon ground cinnamon
1/8 teaspoon ground ginger
3 tablespoons sugar, *divided*
3 medium ripe pears, peeled and thinly sliced
2 tablespoons all-purpose flour
4 eggs, *separated*
1/2 teaspoon vanilla extract

In an ovenproof 10-in. skillet, melt butter over medium heat. Stir in cinnamon, ginger and 1 tablespoon of sugar. Cook for 1 minute or until the sugar is dissolved. Reduce heat; add the pears. Cook for 5 minutes or until softened, stirring occasionally. Remove from the heat; arrange the pears evenly in the skillet.

In a bowl, whisk the flour, 1 tablespoon sugar, egg yolks and vanilla until smooth. In a small mixing bowl, beat the egg whites with remaining sugar until stiff peaks form. Gently fold into the egg yolk mixture just until blended. Spread over the pears. Bake, uncovered, at 400° for 10 minutes or until puffed and golden brown. **Yield:** 4 servings.

DOUBLE-CHEESE HAM SOUFFLE

I've made this for holiday breakfasts and shower brunches. It's a big hit. It's also a welcome change at covered-dish dinners at church. There's never another one like it there.
—Anita Gattis, Hawkinsville, Georgia

16 slices day-old bread, crusts removed and cubed
1 pound cubed fully cooked ham
3 cups (12 ounces) shredded cheddar cheese
1 cup (4 ounces) shredded Swiss cheese
6 eggs
3 cups milk
1/2 teaspoon onion powder
1/2 teaspoon ground mustard
1/8 teaspoon pepper
Dash to 1/8 teaspoon cayenne pepper
1-1/2 cups finely crushed cornflakes
3 tablespoons butter *or* margarine, melted

Place half of the bread cubes in a greased 13-in. x 9-in. x 2-in. baking dish. Top with ham, cheeses and remaining bread cubes. In a bowl, whisk together the eggs, milk and seasonings; pour over the top. Cover and refrigerate for 8 hours or overnight.

Remove from the refrigerator 30 minutes before baking. Combine the cornflakes and butter; sprinkle over casserole. Bake, uncovered, at 375° for 40-45 minutes or until a knife inserted near the center comes out clean. Let stand for 10 minutes before serving. **Yield:** 8-10 servings.

GRITS 'N' SAUSAGE CASSEROLE

You could call this the "So Good Casserole", because that's what people say when they try it. It's a Southern specialty.
—Marie Poppenhager, Old Town, Florida

3 cups water
1 cup quick-cooking grits
3/4 teaspoon salt, *divided*
2 pounds bulk pork sausage, cooked and drained
2 cups (8 ounces) shredded cheddar cheese, *divided*
3 eggs
1-1/2 cups milk
2 tablespoons butter *or* margarine, melted
Pepper to taste

In a saucepan, bring water to a boil. Slowly whisk in the grits and 1/2 teaspoon salt. Reduce heat; cover and simmer for 5 minutes, stirring occasionally.

In a large bowl, combine grits, sausage and 1-1/2 cups cheese. Beat the eggs and milk; stir into grits mixture. Add the butter, pepper and remaining salt.

Transfer to a greased 13-in. x 9-in. x 2-in. baking dish. Bake, uncovered, at 350° for 1 hour or until a knife inserted near the center comes out clean. Sprinkle with remaining cheese; bake 15 minutes longer or until cheese is melted. Let stand for 5 minutes before cutting. **Yield:** 10-12 servings.

Editor's Note: This casserole can be covered and refrigerated overnight. Remove from the refrigerator 30 minutes before baking. Bake as directed.

CRUSTLESS CHEESE QUICHE

I've served this yummy, golden quiche for breakfast, brunch and even dinner.
—Deanna Sheridan, Greentown, Indiana

3 eggs
1-1/2 cups milk
1/2 cup biscuit/baking mix
1/2 cup butter *or* margarine, melted
1/8 teaspoon pepper
6 bacon strips, cooked and crumbled
1 cup (4 ounces) shredded cheddar cheese

In a mixing bowl, combine the first five ingredients. Beat on low speed for 3 minutes or until blended. Transfer to a greased 9-in. pie plate. Sprinkle with bacon and cheese; lightly press down into batter. Bake, uncovered, at 350° for 45 minutes or until a knife inserted near the center comes out clean. Let stand for 10 minutes before serving. **Yield:** 6 servings.

SUNSHINE BAKED EGGS

My son-in-law loves to cook, and he experimented with my standby recipe for eggs by adding cottage cheese and crushed pineapple. It's so delicious, we make these eggs all the time!
—Jane Zielinski, Rotterdam Junction, New York

1 pound sliced bacon, diced
14 eggs
1-1/3 cups small-curd cottage cheese
1 can (8 ounces) crushed pineapple, drained
1 teaspoon vanilla extract
Minced fresh parsley, optional

In a large skillet, cook bacon over medium heat until crisp. Remove to paper towels. Drain, reserving 2 tablespoons drippings.

In a large bowl, lightly beat eggs; add bacon and drippings, cottage cheese, pineapple and vanilla. Pour into a greased 11-in. x 7-in. x 2-in. baking dish. Bake, uncovered, at 350° for 40-45 minutes or until a knife inserted near the center comes out clean. Let stand for 5 minutes before serving. Garnish with parsley if desired. **Yield:** 8 servings.

BACON 'N' EGG BAKE

Our two daughters live about 3 hours away. Whenever I ask what they would like me to make that's special when they visit, they mention this casserole.
—Greta Larter, Windermere, British Columbia

6 tablespoons butter *or* margarine
6 tablespoons all-purpose flour
2 cups milk
1 cup process cheese sauce
1 cup (8 ounces) sour cream
12 hard-cooked eggs, sliced
1 pound sliced bacon, cooked and crumbled
Toasted English muffins, optional

In a large saucepan, melt the butter; stir in flour until smooth. Gradually add the milk. Bring to a boil; cook and stir for 2 minutes or until thickened. Remove from the heat; stir in the cheese sauce and sour cream.

Pour half into a greased 11-in. x 7-in. x 2-in. baking dish. Top with half of the eggs and bacon; repeat layers. Cover and bake at 350° for 25 minutes or until heated through. Serve with English muffins if desired. **Yield:** 6-8 servings.

HEARTY EGG CASSEROLE

(Pictured above)

*Here in cattle country, our days always seem to be busy. This dish is true
to its name—it's filling and keeps us going all morning. We also
like to serve it to breakfast guests to give them a taste of true country cooking.*
—*Mike Yaeger, Brookings, South Dakota*

1 pound bulk pork sausage
1 medium onion, chopped
1-1/2 cups (6 ounces) shredded cheddar
  cheese, *divided*
1 package (10 ounces) frozen
  chopped spinach, thawed and
  squeezed dry
1 jar (4-1/2 ounces) sliced
  mushrooms, drained
12 eggs
2 cups whipping cream
1/4 teaspoon ground nutmeg

In a skillet, cook sausage and onion over medium heat until meat is no longer pink; drain. Remove from the heat; stir in 1 cup cheese, spinach and mushrooms. Transfer to a greased 13-in. x 9-in. x 2-in. baking dish.

In a bowl, beat eggs. Add cream and nutmeg; mix well. Pour over sausage mixture. Bake, uncovered, at 350° for 35-40 minutes or until a knife inserted near the center comes out clean. Sprinkle with remaining cheese. Let stand for 5 minutes before cutting. **Yield:** 12 servings.

EGGSQUISITE BREAKFAST CASSEROLE

I developed this recipe over 20 years ago. The rich, warm sauce tastes especially good on cold winter mornings. I hope your family enjoys it as much as mine!
—Bee Fischer, Jefferson, Wisconsin

1 pound sliced bacon, diced
2 packages (4-1/2 ounces *each*) sliced dried beef, cut into thin strips
1 jar (4-1/2 ounces) sliced mushrooms, drained
1/2 cup all-purpose flour
1/8 teaspoon pepper
4 cups milk
16 eggs
1 cup evaporated milk
1/4 teaspoon salt
1/4 cup butter *or* margarine
Minced fresh parsley, optional

In a large skillet, cook bacon over medium heat until crisp. Remove to paper towels; drain, reserving 1/4 cup drippings. Add the beef, mushrooms, flour and pepper to the drippings; cook until thoroughly combined. Gradually add milk. Bring to a boil; cook and stir for 2 minutes or until thickened. Stir in bacon; set aside.

In a large bowl, beat the eggs, evaporated milk and salt. In another skillet, melt butter over medium heat. Add egg mixture; cook and stir until eggs are completely set. Spoon half into a greased 13-in. x 9-in. x 2-in. baking dish; pour half of the sauce over eggs. Top with remaining eggs and sauce.

Cover and bake at 300° for 45-50 minutes or until heated through. Let stand for 5 minutes before serving. Garnish with parsley if desired. **Yield:** 12-16 servings.

BREAKFAST KUGEL

Noodle dishes are high on my family's list of favorites. In fact, they could eat lasagna any time of the day. This is like breakfast lasagna with cheese, apples and raisins.
—Carol Miller, Northumberland, New York

3 cups (24 ounces) small-curd cottage cheese
1 teaspoon vanilla extract
1/4 teaspoon salt
5 medium tart apples, peeled and thinly sliced
1 teaspoon ground cinnamon
2 cups applesauce
2 cups raisins
1 package (16 ounces) lasagna noodles, cooked and drained
1 cup (4 ounces) shredded cheddar cheese

In a blender, combine the cottage cheese, vanilla and salt; cover and process until smooth. Toss apples with cinnamon.

Combine applesauce and raisins; spread 3/4 cup into a greased 13-in. x 9-in. x 2-in. baking dish. Top with a fourth of the noodles, and a third of the applesauce mixture, cottage cheese mixture and apples. Repeat layers twice. Top with remaining noodles; sprinkle with cheddar cheese.

Cover and bake at 350° for 60-70 minutes or until apples are tender. Let stand for 15 minutes before cutting. **Yield:** 12 servings.

BAKED HAM 'N' CHEDDAR SANDWICHES

(Pictured above)

I've been baking these classic sandwiches for breakfast for just over 30 years.
My family really likes them, so I make this often.
—Rita Bertino, Vineland, New Jersey

3 tablespoons butter *or* margarine, softened
8 slices day-old Italian bread (3/4 inch thick)
8 slices American *or* cheddar cheese
8 thin slices deli ham
1 tablespoon grated Parmesan cheese
2 eggs
2 cups milk
1 teaspoon seasoned salt
1/2 teaspoon pepper
1/4 teaspoon ground mustard

Spread butter on one side of each slice of bread. Place four slices butter side down in a greased 13-in. x 9-in. x 2-in. baking dish. Top with American cheese, ham and Parmesan. Top with remaining bread, butter side up. In a bowl, whisk the eggs, milk and seasonings. Pour over bread; turn each sandwich. Bake, uncovered, at 350° for 35 minutes or until golden brown. **Yield: 4 servings.**

BACON MUSHROOM BAKE

I'm the mother of two teenagers, co-owner of a plumbing business with my husband and I work part-time, so a tried-and-true recipe like this is treasured. I always make it for our family's Christmas brunch.
—Tammi Evans, Battle Creek, Michigan

18 eggs
1-1/2 cups half-and-half cream, *divided*
1 can (10-3/4 ounces) condensed cream of chicken soup, undiluted
1/2 pound fresh mushrooms, sliced
2 tablespoons butter *or* margarine
1 pound sliced bacon, cooked and crumbled
2 cups (8 ounces) shredded cheddar cheese

In a mixing bowl, beat the eggs with 1 cup cream. Pour into a lightly greased large skillet. Cook and stir over medium heat until eggs are set. Combine the soup and remaining cream; set aside.

In another skillet, saute mushrooms in butter until tender. In an ungreased 13-in. x 9-in. x 2-in. baking dish, layer the eggs, bacon, mushrooms and cheese. Pour soup mixture over top. Bake, uncovered, at 350° for 40 minutes or until heated through. Let stand for 5 minutes before serving. **Yield:** 10-12 servings.

SERVING SUGGESTION

For a simple fruit salad that adds color to the breakfast table, combine fresh raspberries, sliced bananas and canned peaches.

INDIVIDUAL BRUNCH CASSEROLES

I created this recipe one Sunday morning when I needed to use up some potatoes. Our two daughters especially look forward to sitting down to these individual casseroles.
—Peggy Meador, Kell, Illinois

3 cups shredded uncooked potatoes
3/4 cup diced onion
1/2 cup diced celery
1/2 cup diced green pepper
2 to 4 tablespoons vegetable oil
4 eggs
1/2 teaspoon salt
1/4 teaspoon pepper
1 cup (4 ounces) shredded cheddar cheese
1/2 pound sliced bacon, cooked and crumbled
1 can (4 ounces) mushroom stems and pieces, drained

In a large skillet, saute the potatoes, onion, celery and green pepper in 2 tablespoons oil until vegetables are tender, adding additional oil if necessary. Remove from the heat.

In a large bowl, beat eggs, salt and pepper. Add cheese, bacon and mushrooms; mix well. Stir in potato mixture. Pour into four greased individual baking dishes. Bake, uncovered, at 350° for 25-35 minutes or until a knife inserted near the center comes out clean. Let stand for 5 minutes before serving. **Yield:** 4 servings.

ASPARAGUS HAM QUICHE

(Pictured below)

*This fantastic dish is easy to make, has a nice blend of flavors and looks inviting. I served it
at a baby shower brunch. The recipe can be cut in half when you're entertaining a smaller crowd.*
—Joyce Leach, Armstrong, Iowa

2 packages (10 ounces *each*) frozen
  cut asparagus, thawed
1 pound fully cooked ham, chopped
2 cups (8 ounces) shredded Swiss
  cheese
1 medium onion, chopped
6 eggs
2 cups milk
1-1/2 cups biscuit/baking mix
2 tablespoons dried vegetable flakes
1/4 teaspoon pepper

In two greased 9-in. pie plates, layer the asparagus, ham, cheese and onion. In a bowl,
beat eggs. Add remaining ingredients and
mix well. Pour half over asparagus mixture
in each pie plate. Bake at 375° for 30 minutes or until a knife inserted near the center comes out clean. **Yield:** 2 quiches (6 servings each).

SHEPHERD'S INN BREAKFAST PIE

(Pictured below)

Running a bed-and-breakfast keeps us busy. Once in a while I get creative and try to improve on an already good dish. That's how I came up with this one. It's a favorite among our guests.
—Ellen Berdan, Salkum, Washington

1-1/2 pounds bulk pork sausage
   4 cups frozen Tater Tots
   1 cup (4 ounces) shredded cheddar cheese
   4 eggs
1/2 cup milk
   1 tablespoon minced green onion
1/8 teaspoon pepper
Dash garlic powder
Minced chives
   2 tomatoes, sliced and quartered

In a skillet, cook the sausage over medium heat until no longer pink; drain. Spread in an ungreased 11-in. x 7-in. x 2-in. baking dish. Top with Tater Tots; sprinkle with cheese. In a mixing bowl, beat the eggs, milk, onion, pepper and garlic powder just until blended. Pour over cheese.

Cover and bake at 350° for 30 minutes. Uncover; bake 20-25 minutes longer. Sprinkle with chives. Garnish with tomato. **Yield:** 6 servings.

GOLDEN EGG BAKE

As a camp cook, I make breakfast for groups ranging in size from 25 to 350.
This egg bake is a must for Sunday brunch because everybody loves it.
—Judy Martin, Onamia, Minnesota

2-3/4 cups cubed fully cooked ham
1-3/4 cups shredded cheddar cheese
    5 teaspoons dried minced onion
    6 eggs, beaten
2-2/3 cups milk
1-1/3 cups biscuit/baking mix
    1/4 teaspoon salt
    1/4 teaspoon pepper
    1/4 to 1/2 teaspoon ground mustard

Place the ham, cheese and onion in a greased 13-in. x 9-in. x 2-in. baking dish. In a bowl, combine the remaining ingredients; mix well. Pour over ham mixture.

Bake, uncovered, at 325° for 50-60 minutes or until a knife inserted near the center comes out clean. Let stand for 5-10 minutes before serving. **Yield:** 12 servings.

CHILI 'N' CHEESE GRITS

Although I live in a big city, I'm really a country cook. Most of our friends laugh
about eating grits, but there's never any leftovers from this recipe.
—Rosemary West, Las Vegas, Nevada

2 cups water
2 cups milk
1 cup grits
2 egg yolks
1 cup (4 ounces) shredded cheddar
  cheese, *divided*
1/4 cup butter *or* margarine, cubed
1 can (4 ounces) chopped green
  chilies, drained
1 teaspoon salt

In a large saucepan, bring water and milk to a boil. Add grits; cook and stir over medium heat for 5 minutes or thickened. In a small bowl, beat egg yolks. Stir a small amount of hot grits into yolks; mix well. Return all to the pan, stirring constantly.

Add 3/4 cup cheese, butter, chilies and salt. Pour into a greased 1-1/2-qt. baking dish. Sprinkle with remaining cheese. Bake, uncovered, at 350° for 30-35 minutes or until golden brown. **Yield:** 6-8 servings.

SAUSAGE QUICHE SQUARES

With three kinds of cheese, this quiche is rich and creamy. Sausage adds a hint of spiciness.
—Bernaldine Moesta, Valparaiso, Indiana

5 eggs
1/2 pound bulk pork sausage, cooked
  and drained
1 cup small-curd cottage cheese
1 cup (4 ounces) shredded cheddar
  cheese
1 cup (4 ounces) shredded Swiss
  cheese
1/4 cup all-purpose flour
1/2 teaspoon baking powder

In a mixing bowl, beat the eggs. Add the remaining ingredients; mix until blended. Pour into a greased 9-in. square baking dish. Bake, uncovered, at 350° for 35-40 minutes or until a knife inserted near the center comes out clean. Let stand for 5 minutes before serving. **Yield:** 6 servings.

BAKED BREAKFAST BURRITOS

(Pictured above)

Every week, I try a minimum of three new recipes. This one sounded different, so I made it.
When I served it to my grown children, not a morsel was left!
—Carol Towey, Pasadena, California

6 to 8 bacon strips, diced
8 fresh mushrooms, sliced
6 green onions, sliced
1/3 cup chopped green pepper
1 garlic clove, minced
8 eggs
1/4 cup sour cream
3/4 cup shredded cheddar *or* Monterey
    Jack cheese, *divided*
3 tablespoons enchilada *or* taco sauce
1 tablespoon butter *or* margarine
4 large flour tortillas (9 inches)
Sour cream and additional enchilada *or*
  taco sauce, optional

In a large skillet, cook bacon over medium heat until crisp; remove to paper towels. Drain, reserving 1 tablespoon of drippings. Saute the mushrooms, onions, green pepper and garlic in drippings until tender; keep warm.

In a bowl, beat eggs and sour cream. Stir in 1/4 cup cheese and enchilada sauce. In another skillet, melt butter; add egg mixture. Cook over medium heat, stirring occasionally, until eggs are completely set.

Remove from the heat. Add bacon and mushroom mixture. Spoon down center of tortillas; roll up. Place seam side down in a greased 11-in. x 7-in. x 2-in. baking dish. Sprinkle with remaining cheese.

Bake, uncovered, at 350° for 5 minutes or until the cheese is melted. Serve with sour cream and additional enchilada sauce if desired. **Yield:** 4 servings.

HARD-COOKED EGG CASSEROLE

My husband's mother was a wonderful cook from Wisconsin. This was a favorite of her children back then, and my kids loved it when they were growing up, too.
—Lois Horn, Beaufort, South Carolina

4-1/2 teaspoons all-purpose flour
2 cups milk
1 can (10-3/4 ounces) condensed cream of mushroom soup, undiluted
1/2 pound fresh mushrooms, sliced
1/4 cup butter *or* margarine, *divided*
1 cup dry bread crumbs
1-1/2 pounds cubed fully cooked ham
4 hard-cooked eggs, chopped

In a saucepan, combine flour and milk until smooth; stir in mushroom soup. Bring to a boil; cook and stir for 2 minutes or until thickened. In a skillet, saute mushrooms in 2 tablespoons butter until tender. Add to the sauce. In the same skillet, brown bread crumbs in the remaining butter.

In a greased 2-qt. baking dish, layer half of the ham, eggs and buttered bread crumbs. Pour half of the mushroom sauce evenly over the top. Layer with remaining ham, eggs, sauce and bread crumbs. Cover and bake at 375° for 40-45 minutes or until heated through. **Yield:** 6 servings.

SAUSAGE HOMINY BAKE

This casserole spotlights hominy, which is a basic ingredient in Southern cooking. It's especially nice to serve on cold winter days for a hearty brunch or supper.
—Mary Ellen Andrews, Newville, Alabama

1 pound bulk hot pork sausage
6 hard-cooked eggs, sliced
2 cans (15-1/2 ounces *each*) hominy, drained
1 can (10-3/4 ounces) condensed cream of mushroom soup, undiluted
1 cup (8 ounces) sour cream
1/4 teaspoon Worcestershire sauce
1 cup (4 ounces) shredded cheddar cheese
1 cup soft bread crumbs
3 tablespoons butter *or* margarine, melted

In a large skillet, cook sausage over medium heat until no longer pink; drain. Spoon into an ungreased 2-1/2-qt. baking dish. Layer with eggs and hominy. Combine the soup, sour cream and Worcestershire sauce; spread over hominy.

Sprinkle with cheese. Combine bread crumbs and butter; sprinkle over top. Bake, uncovered, at 325° for 30-35 minutes or until bubbly and golden brown. **Yield:** 6-8 servings.

TIMELY TIP

To peel hard-cooked eggs with ease, gently roll the egg between your palm and the countertop to create numerous hairline cracks in the shell. Starting at the large end, peel the egg under cold running water.

ITALIAN SAUSAGE BISCUIT BAKE

(Pictured at right)

This recipe is a keeper because all the components of a great breakfast go into one dish, making the morning less hectic for the cook. My family says it reminds them of their favorite fast-food sandwich—only better, of course!
—Amanda Denton, Barre, Vermont

1-1/4 pounds bulk Italian sausage
   2 tubes (12 ounces *each*) refrigerated buttermilk biscuits, *divided*
1-1/3 cups chopped sweet red peppers
   8 eggs
  3/4 cup milk
  1/2 cup minced fresh parsley
1-1/2 cups (6 ounces) shredded Monterey Jack cheese
   1 tablespoon butter *or* margarine, melted
   2 teaspoons dried oregano

In a large skillet, cook sausage over medium heat until no longer pink; drain. Arrange 10 biscuits in a greased 13-in. x 9-in. x 2-in. baking dish. Sprinkle the sausage and red peppers over the top. In a bowl, combine the eggs, milk and parsley. Pour over sausage. Sprinkle with cheese.

Bake, uncovered, at 350° for 20 minutes. Top with remaining biscuits. Brush biscuits with butter and sprinkle with oregano. Bake 15-20 minutes longer or until biscuits are golden brown. Let stand for 5 minutes before serving. **Yield:** 10 servings.

HELPFUL HINT
Here's how to tell if an egg is fresh: Dissolve 2 tablespoons of salt in 2 cups of cool water. Add the egg. If it sinks, it's fresh. If it floats, discard it.

CANADIAN BACON WITH EGGS

This dish is perfect to serve guests because the eggs and Canadian bacon bake at the same time. Maple syrup adds an element of surprise.
—Lorna Herndon, Elyria, Ohio

   2 tablespoons butter *or* margarine
 12 eggs
1/2 cup sour cream
1/2 cup milk
  1 teaspoon salt
  2 tablespoons sliced green onions
3/4 pound Canadian bacon, cut into 12 slices
1/4 cup maple syrup

Melt butter in an 11-in. x 7-in. x 2-in. baking dish in a 325° oven; tilt to coat bottom and sides. In a bowl, beat the eggs, sour cream, milk and salt. Stir in onions. Pour into prepared baking dish. Bake, uncovered, for 30 minutes or just until eggs are completely set.

Meanwhile, place bacon in an 8-in. square baking dish. Pour syrup over top. Cover and bake for 15 minutes or until heated through. Cut egg dish into squares; serve with Canadian bacon. **Yield:** 6 servings.

ITALIAN SAUSAGE BISCUIT BAKE

Curried Rice Ham Rolls

(Pictured above)

My mother gave me this recipe, which had been handed down to her. She prepared these hearty ham rolls for church luncheons, and they were a huge success every time.
—Pamela Witte, Hastings, Nebraska

1 medium onion, chopped
2 tablespoons butter *or* margarine
4 cups cooked brown *or* long grain rice
1 tablespoon dried parsley flakes
1 teaspoon salt
1/2 teaspoon curry powder
12 slices deli ham (1/8 inch thick)
4 hard-cooked eggs, sliced
CURRY SAUCE:
1/4 cup butter *or* margarine
2 tablespoons cornstarch
1/4 teaspoon curry powder
1/4 teaspoon salt
2 cups milk, *divided*

In a skillet, saute onion in butter until tender, about 3 minutes. In a large bowl, combine the rice, parsley, salt, curry powder and onion; mix well. Spoon about 1/3 cup down the center of each ham slice; roll up. Secure with toothpicks if desired. Place seam side down in a greased 13-in. x 9-in. x 2-in. baking dish. Arrange eggs on top.

For the sauce, melt butter in a saucepan. Combine the cornstarch, curry powder, salt and 1/3 cup milk; mix well. Gradually stir into butter; add remaining milk. Bring to a boil; cook and stir for 2 minutes or until thickened. Pour over ham rolls. Cover and bake at 375° for 25 minutes. Uncover; bake 10 minutes longer or until heated through. **Yield:** 6 servings.

RANCH-STYLE QUICHE

*Ranch salad dressing mix gives this quiche a slight tang. I make it
every year on Christmas morning for my husband and me.*
—Denise Anderson, Seattle, Washington

1 cup (4 ounces) shredded Swiss
  cheese
1 pastry shell (9 inches), baked and
  cooled
3 eggs
1-1/4 cups whipping cream
1 envelope ranch salad dressing mix
4 bacon strips, cooked and crumbled

Sprinkle cheese into pastry shell. In a bowl, whisk eggs until foamy. Add the remaining ingredients. Pour over cheese. Bake, uncovered, at 400° for 15 minutes. Reduce heat to 350°. Cover edges with foil; bake 15-20 minutes longer or until a knife inserted near the center comes out clean. **Yield:** 6-8 servings.

ALMOND CHEESE CASSEROLE

*My aunt, Jacquie Moore, used to make this wonderful breakfast dish when
I lived on her ranch during my summer vacations from school.*
—Margaret Neff, Eagle, Colorado

10 slices day-old bread, crusts
  removed and cubed (about 4 cups)
2 cups (8 ounces) shredded
  cheddar cheese
2-2/3 cups milk
4 eggs, lightly beaten
1 teaspoon salt
1/8 to 1/4 teaspoon almond extract
1/4 cup butter *or* margarine, melted
1/2 cup slivered almonds

In a greased 2-qt. baking dish, layer a fourth of the bread and cheese. Repeat three times. In a bowl, whisk together milk, eggs, salt and extract; pour over top. Cover; refrigerate for 8 hours or overnight.

Remove from the refrigerator 30 minutes before baking. Drizzle with butter and sprinkle with almonds. Bake, uncovered, at 350° for 40-45 minutes or until firm and golden brown. **Yield:** 6-8 servings.

FRENCH TOAST LASAGNA

*Convenience is a part of the recipe when you start with packaged frozen
French toast. You can make your own if you prefer. It's fabulous either way.*
—Kathy Kittell, Lenexa, Kansas

1 cup (8 ounces) sour cream
1/3 cup packed brown sugar
2 packages (12-1/2 ounces *each*)
  frozen French toast
1/2 pound thin sliced deli ham
2 cups (8 ounces) shredded three-
  cheese blend, *divided*
1 can (21 ounces) apple pie filling
1 cup granola with raisins

In a small bowl, combine sour cream and brown sugar; refrigerate until serving. In a greased 13-in. x 9-in. x 2-in. baking dish, layer six slices French toast, ham, 1-1/2 cups cheese and remaining French toast. Spread with pie filling and sprinkle with granola. Bake, uncovered, at 350° for 25 minutes. Top with remaining cheese. Bake 5 minutes longer or until cheese is melted. Serve with sour cream mixture. **Yield:** 4-6 servings.

LATTICE SAUSAGE PIE

(Pictured below)

I often serve this hearty egg dish to family and friends for special occasions.
They just rave over the flavor. Crescent rolls make a tasty, easy crust.
—Jennifer Polk, Lincoln, Nebraska

   2 tubes (8 ounces *each*) refrigerated
      crescent rolls
  12 ounces pork sausage links, cooked
      and cut into 1/2-inch pieces
   1 medium onion, chopped
   1 tablespoon butter *or* margarine
   1 jar (4-1/2 ounces) sliced
      mushrooms, drained
   2 packages (3 ounces *each*) cream
      cheese, cut into 1/4-inch cubes
   4 ounces process cheese (Velveeta),
      cut into 1/4-inch cubes
   2 tablespoons chopped pimientos
   6 eggs
 2/3 cup half-and-half cream
   1 tablespoon dried parsley flakes
 1/2 teaspoon salt
 1/2 teaspoon pepper
 1/2 teaspoon garlic powder
Paprika

Unroll one tube of crescent roll dough; press onto the bottom and up the sides of a greased 11-in. x 7-in. x 2-in. baking dish to form a crust. Seal seams and perforations. Sprinkle sausage over crust.

In a skillet, saute the onion in butter until tender; add the mushrooms. Spoon over sausage. Top with cheeses and pimientos. In a bowl, beat the eggs, cream, parsley, salt, pepper and garlic powder; pour over all.

Unroll remaining dough; seal seams and perforations. Cut into 1/2-in. lengthwise strips. Use strips to form a lattice crust on top. Sprinkle with paprika.

Bake at 350° for 50-55 minutes or until a knife inserted near the center comes out clean; cover loosely with foil if browning too quickly. Let stand for 10-15 minutes before cutting. **Yield:** 8-10 servings.

GREEN CHILI QUICHE SQUARES

Chilies add spark to this cheesy quiche. You can vary the flavor based on the kind of croutons you buy. I like to serve fresh fruit on the side.
—Connie Willson, Huntington Beach, California

3 cups seasoned salad croutons
1 can (4 ounces) chopped green chilies
4 cups (16 ounces) shredded cheddar cheese
6 eggs
3 cups milk
2 teaspoons ground mustard
1 teaspoon salt
1/4 teaspoon garlic powder

Arrange croutons in a greased 13-in. x 9-in. x 2-in. baking dish. Sprinkle with chilies and cheese. In a bowl, beat the eggs, milk, mustard, salt and garlic powder. Pour over cheese. Cover and refrigerate for 8 hours or overnight.

Remove from the refrigerator 30 minutes before baking. Bake, uncovered, at 350° for 40-45 minutes or until a knife inserted near the center comes out clean. Let stand for 10 minutes before cutting. **Yield:** 10-12 servings.

SERVING SUGGESTION

Mix up a fruit salad of sliced apples, pears and bananas. Drizzle with caramel ice cream topping or sweetened whipping cream.

SAVORY SALAMI STRATA

The mild Italian flavor makes this dish a great choice for a brunch. I served it at my daughter's First Communion celebration. The wonderful aroma greeted guests as they came in the house.
—Peggy Nelson, Webster, Minnesota

Butter *or* margarine, softened
16 slices bread, crusts removed
1 cup diced fresh tomato
1/4 cup diced green pepper
8 slices salami *or* pepperoni
2 cups (8 ounces) shredded mozzarella cheese
6 eggs
3 cups milk
1 teaspoon dried basil
1/2 teaspoon salt
1/2 teaspoon Italian seasoning

Butter one side of each slice of bread. Place eight slices buttered side up in a greased 13-in. x 9-in. x 2-in. baking dish. Set aside 1 tablespoon each of the tomato and green pepper. Layer salami, cheese, remaining tomato and green pepper over bread. Top with remaining bread.

In a bowl, beat the eggs, milk, basil, salt and Italian seasoning. Pour over bread. Sprinkle with reserved tomatoes and green pepper. Cover and refrigerate for at least 4 hours.

Remove from the refrigerator 30 minutes before baking. Bake, uncovered, at 325° for 55 minutes or until golden brown. **Yield:** 8 servings.

SOUTHWESTERN EGG BAKE

My sister, Bari, gave me this recipe after I tried it at her daughter's graduation party.
Good thing she made plenty—she had to keep refilling the dish!
—Terry Bray, Haines City, Florida

5 green onions, thinly sliced
1 tablespoon butter *or* margarine
8 eggs
1 cup milk
1 can (4 ounces) chopped green
  chilies
1/4 teaspoon salt
1/4 teaspoon pepper
1/4 teaspoon ground cumin
2-1/2 cups (10 ounces) shredded
  Monterey Jack cheese
6 bacon strips, cooked and crumbled

In a skillet, saute the onions in butter until tender; set aside. In a bowl, combine the eggs, milk, chilies, salt, pepper and cumin. Stir in cheese, bacon and reserved onions.

Transfer to a greased 2-qt. baking dish. Bake, uncovered, at 350° for 35-40 minutes or until a knife inserted near the center comes out clean. Let stand for 10 minutes before serving. **Yield:** 6-8 servings.

SERVING SUGGESTION

To complement Southwestern Egg Bake, serve warm
blueberry or lemon poppy seed muffins and sliced fresh fruit.

OVERNIGHT SAUSAGE STRATA

This dish is convenient since you prepare it the night before baking. I always serve this when we have
overnight guests because there's no morning prep time. I get to visit while it's in the oven.
—Elizabeth Link, Charlotte, North Carolina

7 cups cubed day-old bread
1/4 cup butter *or* margarine, melted
8 eggs, lightly beaten
2-1/2 cups milk
1 teaspoon Dijon mustard
1/2 teaspoon Italian seasoning
1/4 teaspoon pepper
1 pound bulk pork sausage, cooked
  and drained
1-1/2 cups (6 ounces) shredded cheddar
  cheese

Place bread cubes in a greased 13-in. x 9-in. x 2-in. baking dish. Drizzle with butter. In a large bowl, combine the eggs, milk, mustard, Italian seasoning and pepper; mix well. Pour over bread. Crumble sausage over top; sprinkle with cheese. Cover and refrigerate for 8 hours or overnight.

Remove from the refrigerator 30 minutes before baking. Bake, uncovered, at 325° for 45-55 minutes or until a knife inserted near the center comes out clean. Let stand for 10 minutes before serving. **Yield:** 8-10 servings.

BAKED EGGS 'N' HAM FOR ONE

(Pictured below)

I give this single-serving dish Southwestern flair and zip by using cheese flavored with jalapeno peppers, but regular cheddar cheese also produces tasty results.
—Carolyn Crump, Center, Texas

1/4 **cup seasoned stuffing croutons**
2 **tablespoons chopped fully cooked ham**
1 **tablespoon butter** *or* **margarine, melted**
2 **eggs**
1 **tablespoon shredded cheddar cheese**

In a greased shallow 2-cup baking dish, toss the croutons, ham and butter. Break the eggs carefully on top. Sprinkle with cheese. Bake, uncovered, at 350° for 15-18 minutes or until the eggs are completely set. **Yield:** 1 serving.

WORLD FAVORITES

Bring international flavors to
your table with this chapter.
You'll find 35 family-favorite
casseroles with influences
from Greece, Mexico, Italy,
China and Lithuania—among
others. So why not take a "trip"
to another region? All you
have to pack is your appetite!

EASY TACO
CASSEROLE (P. 295)

PEPPERONI RIGATONI (P. 286)
BEAN 'N' CHEESE BURRITOS (P. 286)

PEPPERONI RIGATONI

(Pictured on page 285)

My friend and I worked out this recipe as a main dish for the cafeteria at work. It's also become a favorite among teenagers at our church, who make a beeline for it at potlucks.
—Becky Fisk, Ashland City, Tennessee

1 package (16 ounces) rigatoni *or* large tube pasta
1 jar (28 ounces) spaghetti sauce
1 package (3-1/2 ounces) sliced pepperoni, halved
2 cups (8 ounces) shredded Monterey Jack cheese

Cook pasta according to package directions; drain. Add spaghetti sauce and toss to coat. Place half in a greased shallow 3-qt. microwave-safe dish. Top with half of the pepperoni and cheese. Repeat layers.

Cover and microwave on high for 7-9 minutes or until heated through and the cheese is melted. Let stand for 5 minutes before serving. **Yield:** 6-8 servings.

Editor's Note: This recipe was tested in an 850-watt microwave.

SERVING SUGGESTION

A traditional salad of mixed greens, tomato wedges and sliced mushrooms would pair nicely with Pepperoni Rigatoni.

BEAN 'N' CHEESE BURRITOS

(Pictured on page 285)

This is a recipe from my mom that I adapted. She made it with tortillas, but we both agree it's easier and quicker using frozen burritos. I make it about once each month.
—Karen Middleton, Elyria, Ohio

8 frozen bean and cheese burritos (about 5 ounces *each*), thawed
1 can (10-3/4 ounces) condensed cream of chicken soup, undiluted
1 can (10 ounces) enchilada sauce
1/2 cup milk
2 cups (8 ounces) shredded Mexican cheese blend *or* cheddar cheese, *divided*
1 can (4 ounces) chopped green chilies
1 cup sliced ripe olives
1/2 cup sliced green onions
6 cups shredded lettuce
Salsa and sour cream, optional

Arrange burritos in a greased 13-in. x 9-in. x 2-in. baking dish. In a bowl, whisk the soup, sauce and milk until blended; stir in 1 cup of cheese and the chilies. Pour over burritos. Sprinkle with olives, onions and remaining cheese.

Bake, uncovered, at 350° for 30-35 minutes or until bubbly and lightly browned. Serve on a bed of lettuce with salsa and sour cream if desired. **Yield:** 6-8 servings.

GREEK PASTA BAKE

(Pictured below)

My mom taught me to cook, and I love trying and creating new recipes. I developed this one on a cold and snowy afternoon many years ago. Tangy lemon and herbs are complemented by the subtle sweetness of cinnamon.
—Carol Stevens, Basye, Virginia

1/2 pound ground beef
1/2 pound ground lamb
  1 large onion, chopped
  4 garlic cloves, minced
  3 teaspoons dried oregano
  1 teaspoon dried basil
1/2 teaspoon salt
1/4 teaspoon pepper
1/4 teaspoon dried thyme
  1 can (15 ounces) tomato sauce
  1 can (14-1/2 ounces) diced tomatoes, undrained
  1 tablespoon lemon juice
  1 teaspoon sugar
1/4 teaspoon ground cinnamon
  2 cups uncooked large tube pasta
  4 ounces feta cheese, crumbled

In a large skillet or Dutch oven, cook beef and lamb over medium heat until no longer pink; drain. Stir in onion, garlic, oregano, basil, salt, pepper and thyme; mix well. Add the tomato sauce, tomatoes and lemon juice. Bring to a boil. Reduce heat; simmer, uncovered, for 20 minutes, stirring occasionally. Stir in the sugar and cinnamon. Simmer, uncovered, 15 minutes longer.

Meanwhile, cook the pasta according to package directions; drain. Stir into meat mixture. Transfer to a greased 2-qt. baking dish. Sprinkle with feta cheese. Cover and bake at 325° for 45 minutes. Uncover; bake 15 minutes longer or until heated through. **Yield:** 6 servings.

ASIAN BEEF NOODLES

(Pictured above)

We've raised beef the majority of our lives, so I like to try new recipes that feature it.
This recipe is different and absolutely delicious.
—Margery Bryan, Royal City, Washington

1 package (3 ounces) beef-flavored ramen noodles
1 pound boneless beef sirloin steak (3/4 inch thick)
1 jalapeno pepper, seeded and finely chopped*
1 tablespoon vegetable oil
2 tablespoons water
1 tablespoon steak sauce
1 medium carrot, shredded
2 tablespoons sliced green onion
1/4 cup peanut halves

Set aside seasoning packet from noodles. Prepare noodles according to package directions; drain and set aside. Cut steak into 3-in. x 1/2-in. strips. In a large skillet, stir-fry the beef and jalapeno in oil for 1-2 minutes or until meat is no longer pink. Remove and keep warm.

In the same skillet, combine noodles, water, steak sauce, carrot, onion and contents of seasoning packet. Cook and stir until heated through. Return beef to the pan. Sprinkle with peanuts. Serve immediately. **Yield:** 4 servings.

*Editor's Note: When cutting or seeding hot peppers, use rubber or plastic gloves to protect your hands. Avoid touching your face.

CHEESY CHICKEN MANICOTTI

Our youngest daughter tweaked this recipe to our tastes. To stuff the shells, we cut off the end of a disposable cake-decorating bag and slipped the filling inside. It worked like a charm. No mess!
—Gale Sparling, Pembroke, Ontario

8 manicotti shells
1 can (10-3/4 ounces) condensed tomato soup, undiluted
1/2 cup half-and-half cream
1/2 cup sour cream
1/2 cup water
2 tablespoons mayonnaise*
1 to 2 tablespoons grated Parmesan cheese
FILLING:
1 egg
3 cups (12 ounces) shredded mozzarella cheese, *divided*
2 cups cubed cooked chicken
1/2 cup small-curd cottage cheese
1 to 2 tablespoons grated Parmesan cheese
1/8 teaspoon pepper
1 tablespoon minced chives, optional

Cook manicotti according to package directions. Meanwhile, in a bowl, combine the soup, cream, sour cream, water, mayonnaise and Parmesan cheese. Spread about 3/4 cup into a greased 11-in. x 7-in. x 2-in. baking dish. In another bowl, combine the egg, 1 cup of mozzarella cheese, chicken, cottage cheese, Parmesan cheese and pepper.

Drain manicotti shells; stuff each with about 1/3 cup of chicken mixture. Arrange over sauce. Pour remaining sauce over the shells. Top with the remaining mozzarella cheese. Sprinkle with chives if desired. Bake, uncovered, at 350° for 40-45 minutes or until heated through and bubbly. **Yield:** 4 servings.

*Editor's Note: Reduced-fat or fat-free mayonnaise may not be substituted for regular mayonnaise.

LITHUANIAN POTATO DISH

I received this recipe from my Lithuanian mother-in-law 43 years ago. This dish is as important to my family during the holidays as the Christmas tree.
—June Gerdzunas, Mokena, Illinois

1/2 pound sliced bacon, diced
1 large onion, chopped
1/2 cup butter *or* margarine
1/4 cup all-purpose flour
1/2 to 1 teaspoon salt
1/4 teaspoon pepper
2 eggs, beaten
1 can (5 ounces) evaporated milk
1/2 cup milk
2-1/2 pounds potatoes, peeled and shredded
Sour cream, optional

In a large skillet, cook bacon and onion; drain. Add butter and stir until melted. Remove from the heat. In a large bowl, whisk the flour, salt, pepper, eggs, evaporated milk and milk until smooth. Stir in the potatoes and bacon mixture.

Transfer to a greased 11-in. x 7-in. x 2-in. baking dish. Bake, uncovered at 350° for 60-65 minutes or until golden. Serve with sour cream if desired. **Yield:** 8-10 servings.

SOUTHWESTERN LASAGNA

(Pictured below)

I first tasted this lasagna at a church potluck more than 20 years ago. I asked for the recipe and have made it many times since. It's one of our favorites.
—Norma Hoffmaster, Long Beach, California

1-1/2 pounds ground beef
   1 medium onion, chopped
   1 can (15 ounces) enchilada sauce
   1 can (14-1/2 ounces) diced tomatoes, undrained
   1 can (2-1/4 ounces) sliced ripe olives, drained
   1 teaspoon salt
1/4 teaspoon garlic powder
1/4 teaspoon pepper
   1 egg
   1 cup small-curd cottage cheese
1/2 pound Monterey Jack cheese, thinly sliced
   8 corn tortillas (8 inches), halved
1/2 cup shredded cheddar cheese

In a large skillet, cook the beef and onion over medium heat until meat is no longer pink; drain. Stir in the enchilada sauce, tomatoes, olives, salt, garlic powder and pepper; bring to a boil. Reduce heat; simmer, uncovered, for 20 minutes.

In a small bowl, combine egg and cottage cheese. Spread a third of the meat sauce in a greased 13-in. x 9-in. x 2-in. baking dish. Top with half of the Monterey Jack cheese, cottage cheese mixture and tortillas. Repeat layers. Top with remaining meat sauce. Sprinkle with cheddar cheese.

Cover and bake at 350° for 20 minutes. Uncover; bake 10 minutes longer or until cheese is melted. Let stand for 15 minutes before cutting. **Yield:** 6-8 servings.

MEXICAN CASSEROLE

My husband and I both work full-time, so we have little time to cook. This dish is quick and delicious. We freeze leftovers as individual servings for lunch.
—Jean Isken, Sussex, Wisconsin

1 pound ground turkey
1 medium onion, chopped
1 can (14-1/2 ounces) diced tomatoes, undrained
1 envelope taco seasoning
7 flour tortillas (10 inches)
2 eggs
1-1/3 cups small-curd cottage cheese
1-1/2 cups (6 ounces) shredded cheddar cheese, *divided*
Chopped fresh tomatoes, shredded lettuce and sour cream, optional

In a large skillet, cook turkey and onion over medium heat until meat is no longer pink; drain. Add tomatoes and taco seasoning; cook and stir until thickened, about 5 minutes.

Layer four tortillas, overlapping slightly, on the bottom and up the sides of a greased 13-in. x 9-in. x 2-in. baking dish. Top with meat mixture and remaining tortillas. Combine the eggs, cottage cheese and 3/4 cup cheddar cheese; pour over tortillas.

Cover and bake at 350° for 45-55 minutes or until a knife inserted near the center comes out clean. Sprinkle with remaining cheese. Serve with tomatoes, lettuce and sour cream if desired. **Yield:** 8 servings.

MOM'S CHINESE DISH

When I was looking for a different pork dish, I remembered this family favorite had been accidentally filed away. Now it's back on our menus...much to my family's delight.
—Patricia Harroun, Las Vegas, Nevada

4 bacon strips, diced
1-1/2 pounds pork tenderloin
1 garlic clove, minced
3/4 cup water, *divided*
3 tablespoons soy sauce
1/4 teaspoon ground ginger
1/4 teaspoon pepper
1 large green *or* sweet red pepper, julienned
1 medium onion, julienned
3 celery ribs, thinly sliced
2 tablespoons cornstarch
1 can (8 ounces) sliced water chestnuts, drained
1 can (8 ounces) sliced bamboo shoots, drained
Hot cooked rice *or* chow mein noodles

In a large skillet, cook bacon until crisp; remove to paper towels. Cut pork into 3-in. x 1/2-in. strips. Stir-fry pork and garlic in the drippings for 2-3 minutes. Stir in 1/2 cup water, soy sauce, ginger and pepper. Reduce heat; cover and simmer for 3 minutes. Add green pepper, onion and celery; stir-fry for 3 minutes or until crisp-tender.

Combine cornstarch and remaining water until smooth; add to skillet. Bring to a boil; cook and stir for 2 minutes or until thickened. Stir in the water chestnuts, bamboo shoots and bacon; heat through. Serve over rice or chow mein noodles. **Yield:** 6 servings.

CHICKEN TORTILLA CASSEROLE

(Pictured at right)

I started making this delicious dish about 15 years ago, after my husband and I were married.
—Pamela Hoekstra, Hudsonville, Michigan

1/2 cup chicken broth
1/2 cup chopped onion
1/4 cup chopped celery
  3 cups cubed cooked chicken
 10 flour tortillas (6 inches), torn into
      bite-size pieces
  1 can (10-3/4 ounces) condensed
      cream of chicken soup, undiluted
  1 can (4 ounces) chopped green
      chilies
3/4 cup shredded cheddar cheese,
      divided
3/4 cup shredded Monterey Jack
      cheese, *divided*
1/2 teaspoon white pepper
  1 cup salsa

In a saucepan, bring the broth, onion and celery to a boil. Reduce heat; cover and simmer for 5-7 minutes or until vegetables are tender. Place in a large bowl; add chicken, tortillas, soup, chilies, 1/2 cup cheddar cheese, 1/2 cup Monterey Jack cheese and pepper.

Transfer to a greased 11-in. x 7-in. x 2-in. baking dish. Top with salsa and remaining cheeses. Bake, uncovered, at 350° for 30-35 minutes or until heated through. **Yield:** 4-6 servings.

SPANISH CHICKEN

(Pictured at right)

I'm always on the lookout for good, fast recipes. This one is easy to cook and serve.
I've found that even children like eating chicken this way.
—Mrs. Robert Trygg, Duluth, Minnesota

  4 boneless skinless chicken breast
      halves
  2 tablespoons vegetable oil
  1 medium onion, chopped
1/4 cup chopped green pepper
  1 garlic clove, minced
  1 can (14-1/2 ounces) diced tomatoes,
      undrained
  1 cup water
3/4 cup uncooked long grain rice
  2 teaspoons chicken bouillon
      granules
  1 to 3 teaspoons chili powder
1/8 teaspoon ground cinnamon
1/8 teaspoon ground cumin
1/8 teaspoon pepper
1/2 cup picante sauce
1/2 cup shredded cheddar cheese
  1 can (2-1/4 ounces) sliced ripe olives,
      drained

In a large skillet, brown chicken in oil for 2-3 minutes on each side. Remove and keep warm. In the same skillet, saute the onion, green pepper and garlic until tender. Stir in the tomatoes, water, rice, bouillon and seasonings. Bring to a boil. Pour into a greased 11-in. x 7-in. x 2-in. baking dish; top with chicken.

Cover and bake at 350° for 35-40 minutes or until rice is tender. Uncover; spoon picante sauce over chicken and sprinkle with cheese. Bake 5 minutes longer or until cheese is melted. Garnish with olives. **Yield:** 4 servings.

CHICKEN TORTILLA CASSEROLE
SPANISH CHICKEN

REFRIED BEANS AND RICE

*My children and grandchildren ask for this casserole all the time. I invented the recipe
out of necessity one day using just what I had on hand.*
—Wanda Jacobs, Willard, Missouri

1 pound ground beef
1 small onion, chopped
1/2 cup chopped green pepper
1 envelope taco seasoning
3/4 cup water
1 can (16 ounces) kidney beans,
   rinsed and drained
1 can (14-1/2 ounces) stewed
   tomatoes
1 can (8 ounces) tomato sauce
1 cup uncooked instant rice
1 can (16 ounces) refried beans
Shredded cheddar cheese and chopped
  green onions, optional

In a large skillet, cook the beef, onion and green pepper over medium heat until meat is no longer pink; drain. Add taco seasoning and water. Simmer, uncovered, for 10 minutes. Add the kidney beans, tomatoes and tomato sauce.

Bring to a boil. Reduce heat; add rice. Cover and let stand for 5 minutes or until rice is tender. Drop rounded spoonfuls of refried beans over rice; heat through. Garnish with cheese and onions if desired. **Yield:** 8 servings.

PERFECT PARTNERS

*For a tasty salad, pair fresh spinach and crumbled cooked bacon.
Add crunch with sliced almonds, sesame seeds or water chestnuts.*

CORNED BEEF CASSEROLE

*This recipe has been a favorite in our family for more than 50 years.
My kids still request it when they come to visit, and it was one of the first recipes
they called long distance to ask for after they got married.*
—Jeri Butters, Englewood, Florida

1 medium onion, chopped
2 tablespoons butter *or* margarine
2 tablespoons all-purpose flour
1-1/2 teaspoons salt
1 teaspoon Worcestershire sauce
1/4 teaspoon pepper
2-1/2 cups milk
3 medium potatoes, cooked and
   cubed
1 can (15-1/4 ounces) whole kernel
   corn, drained
1 can (12 ounces) corned beef
1 tube (12 ounces) refrigerated
   buttermilk biscuits

In a large saucepan, cook onion in butter over medium heat until tender; remove from the heat. Stir in the flour, salt, Worcestershire sauce and pepper until blended. Gradually add the milk. Bring to a boil; cook and stir for 2 minutes or until thickened and bubbly. Stir in the potatoes, corn and corned beef.

Transfer to a greased 13-in. x 9-in. x 2-in. baking dish. Bake, uncovered, at 400° for 30 minutes or until bubbly. Top with biscuits. Bake 10-15 minutes longer or until biscuits are golden brown. **Yield:** 8-10 servings.

EASY TACO CASSEROLE

(Pictured above and on page 284)

Your family will enjoy this mildly spicy, quick-and-easy meal with Southwestern flair.
—Flo Burtnett, Gage, Oklahoma

1 pound ground beef
1 cup salsa
1/2 cup mayonnaise *or* salad dressing*
2 teaspoons chili powder
2 cups crushed tortilla chips
1 cup (4 ounces) shredded Colby cheese
1 cup (4 ounces) shredded Monterey Jack cheese
1 medium tomato, chopped
2 cups shredded lettuce

In a large skillet, cook beef over medium heat until no longer pink; drain. Stir in the salsa, mayonnaise and chili powder. In an ungreased 2-qt. baking dish, layer half of the meat mixture, chips and cheeses. Repeat layers. Bake, uncovered, at 350° for 20-25 minutes or until heated through. Just before serving, top with tomato and lettuce. **Yield:** 4 servings.

*Editor's Note: Reduced-fat or fat-free mayonnaise or salad dressing may not be substituted for regular mayonnaise or salad dressing.

ITALIAN CASSEROLE

(Pictured above)

I come from a huge family, and it seems there is always a potluck occasion. Graduation parties are the perfect place for me to bring this hearty main dish. It's easy to make and serve.
—Rita Goshaw, South Milwaukee, Wisconsin

1-1/2 pounds bulk Italian sausage
1-1/2 pounds ground beef
   1 large onion, chopped
   1 medium green pepper, chopped
   2 cans (15 ounces *each*) tomato sauce
   2 cans (6 ounces *each*) tomato paste
1/2 cup water
   1 teaspoon dried basil
   1 teaspoon dried oregano
   1 teaspoon salt
   1 teaspoon pepper
1/8 teaspoon garlic powder
   2 cans (8-3/4 ounces *each*) whole kernel corn, drained
   2 cans (2-1/4 ounces *each*) sliced ripe olives, drained
   1 package (16 ounces) wide egg noodles, cooked and drained
   8 ounces cheddar cheese, cut into strips

In a Dutch oven, cook sausage, beef, onion and green pepper over medium heat until meat is no longer pink; drain. Add tomato sauce and paste, water and seasonings; bring to a boil. Reduce heat; cover and simmer for 15 minutes. Stir in the corn and olives. Cover and simmer for 5 minutes. Stir in noodles.

Pour into two greased 3-qt. baking dishes. Top with cheese. Cover and bake at 350° for 25-30 minutes or until heated through. **Yield:** 16-20 servings.

HEARTY HOMINY

My daughter always asks me to make this dish at Thanksgiving and Christmas.
The recipe came from my sister-in-law.
—Marilyn King, Fredonia, Kansas

2 cans (15-1/2 ounces *each*) hominy, drained
1 can (15 ounces) chili without beans
1 medium onion, chopped
1 cup corn chips, coarsely crushed
1 cup (4 ounces) shredded cheddar cheese, *divided*

In a bowl, combine the hominy, chili, onion, corn chips and 1/2 cup cheese. Transfer to a greased 2-qt. baking dish. Top with remaining cheese. Bake, uncovered, at 350° for 30-35 minutes or until heated through. **Yield:** 6-8 servings.

CHICKEN ENCHILADAS

These are great for a family dinner or party. I've also cut the baked enchiladas into
three sections and served them as appetizers with chips and salsa.
—Elaine Anderson, Aliquippa, Pennsylvania

1 envelope enchilada sauce mix
2 cups cubed cooked chicken
2 cups (8 ounces) shredded Monterey Jack cheese, *divided*
1/3 cup sliced ripe olives
1-1/3 cups chopped fresh tomatoes, *divided*
1/4 cup chopped green pepper
2 tablespoons chopped green onion
10 flour tortillas (6 inches)
2 cups shredded lettuce

Prepare enchilada sauce according to package directions. In a bowl, combine 1/2 cup prepared sauce, chicken, 1 cup of cheese, olives, 1/3 cup of tomatoes, green pepper and onion.

Place a rounded 1/4 cupful of chicken mixture down the center of each tortilla. Roll up and place seam side down in a greased 13-in. x 9-in. x 2-in. baking dish. Pour remaining enchilada sauce over top.

Cover and bake at 350° for 30 minutes. Uncover; sprinkle with remaining cheese. Bake 5-10 minutes longer or until cheese is melted. Top with lettuce and remaining tomatoes. **Yield:** 5 servings.

BEEFY BEANS 'N' RICE

This easy skillet dish has a nice barbecue flavor that goes over well in winter.
—Rebecca Roberts, Odessa, Texas

1 pound ground beef
1 medium onion, chopped
2 cups cooked rice
1 can (15 ounces) ranch-style *or* chili beans
6 ounces process cheese (Velveeta), cubed
3 tablespoons water

In a large skillet, cook beef and onion over medium heat until meat is no longer pink; drain. Stir in the rice, beans, cheese and water. Cook and stir over medium-low heat until cheese is melted. **Yield:** 4 servings.

SPEEDY TACO FEAST

My two teenagers enjoy the taco taste of this hearty main dish, and I appreciate the fact that there's no mess. We like to eat it on cool fall days or snowy winter nights.
—Janice Steimer, Rochester, New York.

2 pounds ground beef
2 envelopes taco seasoning
1-1/2 cups water
1 jar (16 ounces) salsa
1 can (8-3/4 ounces) whole kernel corn, drained
2 cups (8 ounces) shredded taco *or* Mexican cheese blend
2 packages (8-1/2 ounces *each*) corn bread/muffin mix
Sour cream, optional

In a large skillet, cook beef over medium heat until no longer pink; drain. Add the taco seasoning, water, salsa and corn; cook and stir until heated through, about 15 minutes. Transfer to a greased 13-in. x 9-in. x 2-in. baking dish. Sprinkle with cheese.

Prepare corn bread mix according to package directions. Spoon batter evenly over cheese. Bake, uncovered, at 350° for 40-45 minutes or until a toothpick inserted near the center of corn bread comes out clean. Serve with sour cream if desired. **Yield:** 8 servings.

GROUND BEEF NOODLE CASSEROLE

My mother shared this recipe with me soon after I was married. Most everything I know about cooking, I learned from her. This recipe has always been a family favorite, and it's a time-saver as well because it uses spaghetti sauce and gravy mix.
—Christina Takacs, West Springfield, Massachusetts

1 envelope brown gravy mix
1 cup cold water
1 pound ground beef
1 small onion, diced
3 garlic cloves, minced
1 jar (14 ounces) spaghetti sauce
1/2 cup half-and-half cream
1-1/2 teaspoons Italian seasoning
1/2 teaspoon dried rosemary, crushed
Salt and pepper to taste
8 ounces wide egg noodles, cooked and drained
2/3 cup grated Parmesan cheese, *divided*

In a small bowl, combine gravy mix and water until smooth; set aside. In a large skillet, cook the beef, onion and garlic over medium heat until meat is no longer pink; drain. Add spaghetti sauce, cream, seasonings and gravy; bring to a boil. Reduce heat; cover and simmer for 15 minutes.

Add the noodles and 1/3 cup of Parmesan cheese; mix well. Transfer to a greased 3-qt. baking dish; sprinkle with remaining Parmesan. Cover and bake at 350° for 30 minutes or until heated through. **Yield:** 6 servings.

PERFECT PARTNERS

Need a simple side dish? Give broccoli a color and flavor pick-me-up by sprinkling 2 teaspoons of grated orange or lemon peel over 1 pound of steamed florets.

MEXICAN SKILLET SUPPER

(Pictured below)

A co-worker gave me this recipe. I added a few things for extra zip, and it always turns out well.
—Kathy Willis, Pryor, Oklahoma

1 pound ground beef
2 celery ribs, chopped
1 small green pepper, chopped
1/4 cup chopped onion
1 package (8.6 ounces) beef taco pasta dinner mix*
1 teaspoon chili powder
3-2/3 cups hot water
2 cups (8 ounces) shredded cheddar cheese
1 can (14-1/2 ounces) stewed tomatoes, cut up
1 can (2-1/4 ounces) sliced ripe olives, drained
Sour cream, optional

In a large skillet, cook beef, celery, green pepper and onion over medium heat until meat is no longer pink and vegetables are tender; drain. Set aside topping packet from the dinner mix for another use. Stir the contents of dinner mix seasoning packet, chili powder and water into beef mixture.

Bring to a boil. Stir in noodles from dinner mix. Reduce heat; cover and simmer for 12-15 minutes or until noodles are tender. Stir in the cheese, tomatoes and olives; heat through. Serve with sour cream if desired. **Yield:** 6-8 servings.

*Editor's Note: This recipe was tested with Hamburger Helper dinner mix.

ORIENTAL BEEF NOODLE TOSS

(Pictured at right)

I received this recipe from a friend who is a nurse, Marge Mizzen. We always share new recipes, especially for easy meals like this, because our schedules keep us both quite busy.
—Sue Livangood, Waukesha, Wisconsin

1 pound ground beef
2 packages (3 ounces *each*) Oriental-flavored ramen noodles
1 package (16 ounces) frozen Oriental vegetable blend
2 cups water
4 to 5 tablespoons soy sauce
1/4 teaspoon ground ginger
3 tablespoons thinly sliced green onions

In a large skillet, cook beef over medium heat until no longer pink; drain. Stir in contents of one noodle seasoning packet; set aside and keep warm.

Break the noodles; place in a large saucepan. Add the contents of second seasoning packet, vegetables, water, soy sauce and ginger. Bring to a boil. Reduce heat; cover and simmer for 6-10 minutes or until vegetables and noodles are tender. Stir in the beef and onions. **Yield:** 4-6 servings.

SERVING SUGGESTION

A hearty casserole like Lasagna Roll-Ups needs only simple side dishes, such as garlic bread or breadsticks, crisp apple wedges or greens with sliced tomatoes.

LASAGNA ROLL-UPS

(Pictured at right)

This is far better tasting than any store-bought lasagna. Ham and spinach combine for fabulous flavor.
—Delia Kennedy, Deer Park, Washington

1 package (10 ounces) frozen spinach, thawed and squeezed dry
1 egg, beaten
1-3/4 cups ricotta cheese
4 tablespoons grated Parmesan cheese, *divided*
1/2 teaspoon salt
1/4 teaspoon pepper
1/8 teaspoon ground nutmeg
8 thin slices deli ham, halved lengthwise
8 lasagna noodles, cooked and drained
1 jar (14 ounces) spaghetti sauce

In a bowl, combine the spinach, egg, ricotta cheese, 2 tablespoons Parmesan cheese, salt, pepper and nutmeg. Place two pieces of ham on each noodle. Spread with 1/3 cup spinach mixture. Roll up and place seam side down in a greased 13-in. x 9-in. x 2-in. baking dish. Top with spaghetti sauce.

Cover and bake at 350° for 40-45 minutes or until heated through. Uncover; sprinkle with remaining Parmesan. Let stand for 15 minutes before cutting. **Yield:** 4 servings.

Oriental Beef Noodle Toss
Lasagna Roll-Ups

PORK CHOPS OLÉ

(Pictured below)

This recipe is a fun and simple way to give pork chops south-of-the-border flair.
The flavorful seasoning, rice and melted cheddar cheese make this dish a crowd-pleaser.
—Laura Turner, Channelview, Texas

6 bone-in loin pork chops (1/2 inch thick)
2 tablespoons vegetable oil
Seasoned salt and pepper to taste
3/4 cup uncooked long grain rice
1-1/2 cups water
1 can (8 ounces) tomato sauce
2 tablespoons taco seasoning
1 medium green pepper, chopped
1/2 cup shredded cheddar cheese

In a large skillet, brown pork chops on both sides in oil; sprinkle with seasoned salt and pepper. In a greased 13-in. x 9-in. x 2-in. baking dish, combine rice, water, tomato sauce and taco seasoning; mix well. Arrange chops over rice; top with green pepper.

Cover and bake at 350° for 1-1/2 hours or until meat juices run clear. Uncover; sprinkle with cheese. Bake 5 minutes longer or until cheese is melted. **Yield:** 4-6 servings.

CHEESY CHILI RELLENOS

I got this meatless main dish recipe in South Dakota. It also makes a good side dish. I live on a cattle ranch and cook three meals a day, so I'm always interested in finding different recipes.
—Mary Morrow, Jordan Valley, Oregon

3 cans (4 ounces *each*) whole green chilies, drained*
1-1/2 cups (6 ounces) shredded Monterey Jack cheese
1-1/2 cups (6 ounces) shredded cheddar cheese
1/3 cup all-purpose flour
1 cup half-and-half cream
2 eggs, beaten
1 can (8 ounces) tomato sauce

Split chilies open lengthwise. Rinse out seeds and place chilies on paper towels to drain. Combine cheeses; set aside 1/2 cup for topping. In a bowl, combine the flour, cream and eggs until smooth.

In a greased deep 1-1/2-qt. baking dish, layer half of cheese, chilies and egg mixture. Repeat layers. Pour tomato sauce over the top; sprinkle with reserved cheese. Bake, uncovered, at 350° for 50-55 minutes or until knife inserted near the center comes out clean. Let stand for 5 minutes before serving. **Yield:** 6-8 servings.

*Editor's Note: When cutting or seeding hot peppers, use rubber or plastic gloves to protect your hands. Avoid touching your face.

SERVING SUGGESTION

Add walnuts, shredded carrots and croutons to a bag of mixed greens, and you have a crunchy salad to serve alongside Cheesy Chili Rellenos.

PORK LO MEIN

My husband teases me about using him as the guinea pig in the kitchen. But he's always an eager participant whenever I present attractive, tasty meals like this at dinnertime.
—Billie Bethel, Waynesville, North Carolina

1 pound ground pork
2 medium carrots, thinly sliced
1 large onion, chopped
1 garlic clove, minced
2 packages (3 ounces *each*) Oriental- *or* chicken-flavored ramen noodles
1-1/2 cups water
1 cup frozen peas
6 cups shredded romaine

In a large skillet coated with nonstick cooking spray, cook pork, carrots, onion and garlic over medium heat until the meat is no longer pink; drain. Break noodles into skillet; stir in contents of seasoning packets. Add water and peas; mix well.

Bring to a boil. Reduce heat; simmer, uncovered, for 6-8 minutes or until noodles and vegetables are tender, stirring often. Add romaine; heat and stir until wilted. **Yield:** 4 servings.

TORTILLA BEEF CASSEROLE

When I first started making this casserole, I wrapped up the tortillas like enchiladas, but this way is much easier and just as good. I've also made it with ground turkey instead of beef.
—Janice Wedemeyer, Holland, Michigan

2 pounds ground beef
1 can (26 ounces) condensed chicken
  with rice soup, undiluted
1 jar (16 ounces) picante sauce
6 flour tortillas (9 inches)
2 cups (8 ounces) shredded
  Colby/Monterey Jack cheese
2 cups (8 ounces) shredded Mexican
  cheese blend *or* cheddar cheese
Sour cream, tomatoes, chopped lettuce,
  ripe olives, onions *and/or* additional
  picante sauce, optional

In a Dutch oven, cook the beef over medium heat until no longer pink; drain. Drain broth from soup, reserving rice mixture (discard broth or refrigerate for another use). Stir rice mixture and picante sauce into beef. Bring to a boil. Reduce heat; simmer, uncovered, for 5 minutes.

Place four tortillas on the bottom and up the sides of a greased 13-in. x 9-in. x 2-in. baking dish. Spread with half of the beef mixture. Combine cheeses; sprinkle half over beef. Top with remaining tortillas, beef mixture and cheese.

Bake, uncovered, at 350° for 25-30 minutes or until heated through and cheese is melted. Let stand for 10 minutes before serving. Serve with sour cream, tomatoes, lettuce, olives, onions and/or picante sauce if desired. **Yield:** 8-10 servings.

CHOW MEIN CHICKEN

I sometimes make this recipe with leftover chicken and rice. My children keep me running most of the day, so a quick casserole for dinner helps smooth out bumps in our schedule.
—Beth Pallwitz, Tacoma, Washington

1 cup cubed cooked chicken
1/4 cup chopped celery
1/4 cup chopped onion
2 teaspoons vegetable oil
2 tablespoons soy sauce
1 to 1-1/4 teaspoons ground ginger
1 can (10-3/4 ounces) condensed
  cream of chicken soup, undiluted
2 cups cooked rice
1/2 cup chow mein noodles

In a large skillet, saute chicken, celery and onion in oil until chicken is no longer pink and vegetables are tender. Add soy sauce and ginger; cook and stir for 1-2 minutes. Add soup; cook and stir until bubbly. Stir in rice.

Transfer to a greased 1-qt. baking dish. Cover and bake at 350° for 25 minutes or until heated through. Uncover; sprinkle with noodles. Bake 5-10 minutes longer or until noodles are crisp. **Yield:** 3-4 servings.

FOLD-OVER TORTILLA BAKE

(Pictured above)

Here's something different from tacos—and it's special enough for dinner guests.
—Deborah Smith, DeWitt, Nebraska

1 pound ground beef
1 large onion, chopped
2 cans (14-1/2 ounces *each*) stewed tomatoes
1 cup enchilada sauce
1 to 2 teaspoons ground cumin
1/2 teaspoon salt
1/4 teaspoon pepper
12 flour *or* corn tortillas (6 inches)
2 packages (3 ounces *each*) cream cheese, softened
1 can (4 ounces) chopped green chilies, drained
1 cup (4 ounces) shredded Monterey Jack cheese

In a large skillet, cook beef and onion over medium heat until the meat is no longer pink; drain well. Stir in tomatoes, enchilada sauce, cumin, salt and pepper. Bring to a boil. Reduce heat; cover and simmer for 5 minutes. Pour half into a greased 13-in. x 9-in. x 2-in. baking dish; set aside.

Stack the tortillas and wrap in foil; warm at 350° for 8-10 minutes. Spread warm tortillas with cream cheese and top with chilies; fold in half.

Arrange folded tortillas over meat sauce; pour remaining sauce over top. Cover and bake at 350° for 15 minutes. Uncover; sprinkle with cheese. Bake 5 minutes longer or until cheese is melted. **Yield:** 6 servings.

RAVIOLI LASAGNA

(Pictured above)

*When you taste this casserole, you'll think it came from a complicated, from-scratch recipe.
Really, though, it starts with frozen ravioli and has only three other ingredients.*
—Patricia Smith, Asheboro, North Carolina

1 pound ground beef
1 jar (28 ounces) spaghetti sauce
1 package (25 ounces) frozen sausage
or **cheese ravioli**
1-1/2 cups (6 ounces) shredded
mozzarella cheese

In a large skillet, cook beef over medium heat until no longer pink; drain. In a greased 2-1/2-qt. baking dish, layer a third of the spaghetti sauce, half of the ravioli and beef and 1/2 cup cheese; repeat layers. Top with remaining sauce and cheese. Cover and bake at 400° for 40-45 minutes or until heated through. **Yield:** 6-8 servings.

NACHO CHICKEN BAKE

You can add zip to this cheesy chicken casserole by using picante sauce that suits your taste.
It's great with hot sauce but also good when toned down to mild.
—Martha Williams, Loving, New Mexico

8 cups nacho cheese tortilla chips
2 cans (10-3/4 ounces *each*)
    condensed cream of chicken soup,
    undiluted
1 can (10 ounces) chunk white
    chicken, drained
1 cup picante sauce
1 cup (4 ounces) shredded cheddar
    cheese
1 medium onion, chopped
1 can (4 ounces) chopped green
    chilies
Additional shredded cheddar cheese,
    optional
Shredded lettuce and chopped fresh
    tomatoes

Arrange chips in a greased 13-in. x 9-in. x 2-in. baking dish. In a bowl, combine the soup, chicken, picante sauce, cheese, onion and chilies; pour over chips. Sprinkle with additional cheese if desired. Bake, uncovered, at 325° for 40-45 minutes or until bubbly. Serve with lettuce and tomatoes. **Yield:** 8-10 servings.

TAMALE CASSEROLE

This is an easy after-work dish that's so tasty. It starts with tamales from a jar.
—Regina Albright, Southaven, Mississippi

1 jar (13-1/2 ounces) tamales
1 can (15 ounces) chili with beans
1 medium onion, chopped
2 cups corn chips, coarsely crushed,
    divided
1 cup (4 ounces) shredded cheddar
    cheese
1 to 2 ounces sliced cheddar cheese

Cut tamales into 3/4-in. slices. Place in a greased shallow 1-qt. baking dish. Top with half of the chili and onion. Sprinkle with 1/3 cup corn chips and shredded cheese. Top with remaining chili and onion.

Cover and bake at 350° for 30 minutes. Uncover; sprinkle with the remaining corn chips. Arrange cheese slices over top. Bake 5-10 minutes longer or until chips are crisp and cheese is melted. **Yield:** 3-4 servings.

> ## SERVING SUGGESTION
> *Dress up a simple dessert by serving it in a parfait glass.*
> *Cubed cantaloupe or honeydew become special when*
> *drizzled with lemon yogurt or splashed with ginger ale.*

CURRIED CHICKEN AND RICE

A curry sauce makes this version of chicken and rice stand out from all the others.
Your guests will think you spent hours in the kitchen preparing this impressive dish!
—Tammi Lewis, Bellevue, Ohio

1 cup chicken broth
1 teaspoon curry powder
1/2 teaspoon paprika
1 package (6 ounces) long grain and
  wild rice mix
1/2 pound fresh mushrooms, sliced
10 ounces fresh pearl onions, cooked
1/2 medium green pepper, julienned
1 broiler/fryer chicken (3-1/2 to 4
  pounds), cut up
CURRY SAUCE:
1 carton (8 ounces) plain yogurt
1/2 cup ricotta cheese
1/3 cup chutney
1 tablespoon all-purpose flour
2 teaspoons curry powder
2 tablespoons slivered almonds

In an ungreased 13-in. x 9-in. x 2-in. baking dish, combine broth, curry powder, paprika and contents of rice seasoning mix. Top with the rice, mushrooms, onions and green pepper. Arrange chicken pieces over top. Cover and bake at 425° for 50 minutes.

Meanwhile, in a blender or food processor, combine yogurt, ricotta, chutney, flour and curry powder; cover and process until smooth. Pour over chicken. Sprinkle with almonds. Increase temperature to 475°. Bake, uncovered, for 5-10 minutes or until bubbly and golden brown. **Yield:** 4-6 servings.

EAST INDIAN VEGETABLE CASSEROLE

My husband requests this a lot because he likes ethnic food. My son loves the raisins and peanuts.
To save time, I chop up the vegetables the night before.
—Cheryl Gross, Elgin, Illinois

1 medium green pepper, chopped
3/4 cup chopped onion
2 tablespoons butter *or* margarine
1 cup uncooked long grain rice
3/4 cup thinly sliced carrots
3/4 cup thinly sliced celery
1/2 to 3/4 teaspoon hot pepper sauce
1/2 teaspoon ground cardamom
1/2 teaspoon ground nutmeg
2 cups beef broth
3/4 cup raisins
1/2 cup chopped dry roasted peanuts

Place the green pepper, onion and butter in a 2-qt. microwave-safe bowl. Cover and microwave on high for 4 minutes, stirring once. Stir in rice, carrots, celery, hot pepper sauce, cardamom and nutmeg; set aside.

Place broth in a 2-qt. microwave-safe bowl. Cover and microwave on high for 4-5 minutes or until boiling. Add raisins; let stand for 1 minute. Stir into rice mixture.

Cover and microwave on high for 15-18 minutes or until rice is tender, stirring twice. Sprinkle with peanuts. Let stand for 3 minutes before serving. **Yield:** 4-6 servings.

Editor's Note: This recipe was tested in an 850-watt microwave.

SAUSAGE CHEESE SHELLS

(Pictured below)

When I was living in California, I tasted this rich cheesy pasta dish at a neighborhood Italian restaurant. I got the recipe and made a few changes to it in my own kitchen.
—Lori Mecca, Grants Pass, Oregon

1 pound bulk Italian sausage
1 large onion, chopped
1 package (10 ounces) frozen chopped spinach, thawed and well drained
1 package (8 ounces) cream cheese, softened
1 egg, beaten
2 cups (8 ounces) shredded mozzarella cheese, *divided*
2 cups (8 ounces) shredded cheddar cheese
1 cup small-curd cottage cheese
1/4 cup grated Parmesan cheese
1/4 teaspoon salt
1/4 teaspoon pepper
1/8 teaspoon ground cinnamon, optional
20 jumbo pasta shells, cooked and drained

SAUCE:
1 can (29 ounces) tomato sauce
1 tablespoon dried minced onion

1-1/2 teaspoons dried basil
1-1/2 teaspoons dried parsley flakes
2 garlic cloves, minced
1 teaspoon sugar
1 teaspoon dried oregano
1/2 teaspoon salt
1/4 teaspoon pepper

In a large skillet, cook sausage and onion over medium heat until meat is no longer pink; drain. Transfer to a large bowl. Stir in spinach, cream cheese, egg and 1 cup mozzarella. Add cheddar cheese, cottage cheese, Parmesan cheese, salt, pepper and cinnamon if desired; mix well.

Stuff shells and arrange in a greased 13-in. x 9-in. x 2-in. baking dish. Combine sauce ingredients; mix well. Spoon over the shells. Cover and bake at 350° for 40 minutes. Uncover; sprinkle with the remaining mozzarella. Bake 5 minutes longer or until cheese is melted. **Yield:** 8-10 servings.

This handy index lists every recipe by category, major ingredient and/or cooking method, so you can easily locate recipes to suit your needs.

SPINACH (continued)
Hearty Egg Casserole, 267
Herbed Vegetable Squares, 206
Lasagna Florentine, 220
Lasagna Roll-Ups, 300
Pizza Pasta Pie, 207
Potato Lasagna, 92
Sausage Cheese Shells, 309
Sausage Spinach Pockets, 190
Spinach Beef Pie, 178
Spinach Linguine with Ham, 79
Spinach Mashed Potatoes, 236
Spinach Ravioli Bake, 144
Three-Cheese Chicken, 26

SQUASH (also see Zucchini)
Butternut Squash Casserole, 248
Pantry Pork Dish, 77
Turkey Squash Casserole, 38
Winter Squash Quiche, 212

STEWS
Baked Beef Stew, 47
Beef and Biscuit Stew, 60
Oven Stew and Biscuits, 63
Turkey Biscuit Stew, 136

STOVETOP/SKILLET DISHES
Asian Beef Noodles, 288
Beef and Rice for Two, 56
Beef 'n' Tomato Mac, 129
Beefy Beans 'n' Rice, 297
Beefy Pasta and Rice, 123
Bratwurst Potato Skillet, 80
Country Goulash Skillet, 62
Creamy Bean Goulash, 133
Farmhouse Pork and Apple Pie, 181
Fettuccine Alfredo, 126
Ground Beef Stroganoff, 129
Hobo Hash, 142
Hot Dogs 'n' Rice, 83
Italian Noodles, 135
Italian Sausage Fried Rice, 78
Kielbasa Casserole for Two, 88
Mexican Skillet Supper, 299
Mom's Chinese Dish, 291
Pork Lo Mein, 303
Ranch Mac 'n' Cheese, 217
Refried Beans and Rice, 294
Sausage Skillet Supper, 136
Shrimp Chicken Skillet, 107
Skillet Casserole, 59
Smoky Potato Skillet, 130
Spicy Chicken Corn Skillet, 40
Stick-to-Your-Ribs Supper, 82
Stovetop Ham and Penne, 81
Stovetop Hamburger Casserole, 127
Zesty Pork and Pasta, 145

STRATA
Asparagus Strata, 258
Farmer's Strata, 261
Overnight Sausage Strata, 282
Savory Salami Strata, 281
Veggie-Packed Strata, 204

STUFFING & STUFFING MIX
Farmhouse Chicken, 16
Chicken 'n' Stuffing, 18

Chicken Stuffing Bake, 34
Crunchy Chicken Casserole, 124
Fiesta Chicken 'n' Stuffing, 177
Mushroom Stuffing, 231
Pork Chops with Apple Stuffing, 93
Stuffing-Topped Chicken and Broccoli, 32

SWEET POTATOES
Apple Ham Bake, 76
Pecan-Topped Sweet Potatoes, 232
Scalloped Sweet Potatoes, 253
Smoked Pork Chops with Sweet
  Potatoes, 98
Sweet Potato Souffle, 226

TOMATOES
Bacon Tomato Casserole, 84
Baked Ratatouille, 241
Beef 'n' Tomato Mac, 129
Beefy Eggplant Parmigiana, 45
Biscuit-Topped Tomato Casserole, 242
Chili Casserole, 99
Country Goulash Skillet, 62
Deep-Dish Beef Bake, 159
Dinner in a Dish, 55
Four-Cheese Bow Ties, 164
Garden Medley Casserole, 160
Hamburger Hot Dish, 46
Harvest Chicken and Vegetables, 22
Hot Dogs 'n' Rice, 83
Italian Sausage Fried Rice, 78
Pork Spanish Rice, 94
Savory Tomato Pie, 193
Summer Veggie Pie, 194
Tomato Garlic Chicken, 12
Tomato Mozzarella Bake, 239
Tomato Zucchini Casserole, 251

TORTILLAS
Baked Breakfast Burritos, 274
Chicken Enchiladas, 297
Chicken Tortilla Casserole, 292
Fold-Over Tortilla Bake, 305
Ham 'n' Egg Tortilla Bake, 260
Layered Tortilla Pie, 139
Mexican Casserole, 291
Southwestern Lasagna, 290
Tortilla Beef Casserole 304
Tortilla Torte, 213

TUNA (also see Fish & Seafood; Shrimp)
Broccoli Tuna Bake, 104
Broccoli Tuna Squares, 116
Cheesy Tuna Lasagna, 115
Crunchy Tuna Surprise, 135
Microwave Tuna 'n' Chips, 146
Tuna Crunch Casserole, 148
Tuna in the Straw Casserole, 108
Tuna Noodle Hot Dish, 106
Tuna Spaghetti Pie, 184

TURNIPS
Scalloped Turnips, 233

TURKEY
Almond Turkey Casserole, 25
Mexican Casserole, 291
Popover with Hot Turkey Salad, 200
Turkey Asparagus Casserole, 122

Turkey Bean Bake, 39
Turkey Biscuit Stew, 136
Turkey Broccoli Bake, 197
Turkey Manicotti, 27
Turkey Noodle Casserole, 15
Turkey Potato Supper, 23
Turkey Potpie, 189
Turkey Rice Casserole, 162
Turkey Sausage and Noodles, 17
Turkey Squash Casserole, 38

VEGETABLES (also see specific kinds)
Main Dishes
  Baked Beef Stew, 47
  Beef and Biscuit Stew, 60
  Beefy Eggplant Parmigiana, 45
  Brown Rice Casserole, 219
  Cheddar Chicken Spirals, 137
  Chicken Lasagna, 18
  Colorful Chicken Casserole, 20
  Confetti Spaghetti Pie, 218
  Cordon Bleu Casserole, 13
  Creamy Chicken Curry, 27
  Crunchy Chicken Casserole, 124
  East Indian Vegetable Casserole, 308
  Garden Medley Casserole, 160
  Golden Chicken 'n' Taters, 22
  Harvest Chicken and Vegetables, 22
  Microwave Corn Bread Casserole, 87
  Oriental Beef Noodle Toss, 300
  Party Beef Casserole, 51
  Potato Vegetable Quiche, 182
  Tuna in the Straw Casserole, 108
  Turkey Biscuit Stew, 136
  Turkey Noodle Casserole, 15
  Vegetable Noodle Casserole, 220
  Vegetarian Quiche, 209
  Veggie Cheese Squares, 219
  Veggie Noodle Casserole, 171
  Veggie Noodle Ham Casserole, 89
  Veggie-Packed Strata, 204
  Wild Wild Rice, 24
Meat Pies
  Beef Potpie with Biscuits, 44
  Chicken Potpie, 197
  Easy Potpie, 126
  Lattice Chicken Potpie, 12
  Savory Chicken Pie, 179
  Turkey Potpie, 189
  Vegetable Beef Pie, 196
Side Dishes
  Vegetable Macaroni, 230

ZUCCHINI
Baked Ratatouille, 241
Fryer Chicken with Veggies, 29
Garden Lasagna, 215
Garden Medley Casserole, 160
Herbed Vegetable Squares, 206
Summer Veggie Pie, 194
Tomato Zucchini Casserole, 251
Vegetarian Quiche, 209
Veggie-Packed Strata, 204
Zippy Beef Bake, 60
Zucchini Beef Bake, 52
Zucchini Corn Medley, 242
Zucchini Dressing, 228
Zucchini Pie, 194
Zucchini Sausage Squares, 93

Refer to this index for a complete alphabetical listing of all the recipes in this book.

Use this index as a guide to the many helpful hints,
timely tips and serving suggestions throughout the book.